CHARLES REES
MISSION ACCOMPLISHED

authorHOUSE

AuthorHouse™ UK
1663 Liberty Drive
Bloomington, IN 47403 USA
www.authorhouse.co.uk
Phone: UK TFN: 0800 0148641 (Toll Free inside the UK)
  UK Local: 02036 956322 (+44 20 3695 6322 from outside the UK)

© 2021 Charles Rees. All rights reserved.

No part of this book may be reproduced, stored in a retrieval system, or transmitted by any means without the written permission of the author.

Published by AuthorHouse 03/17/2021

ISBN: 978-1-6655-8733-4 (sc)
ISBN: 978-1-6655-8732-7 (e)

Print information available on the last page.

Any people depicted in stock imagery provided by Getty Images are models, and such images are being used for illustrative purposes only.
Certain stock imagery © Getty Images.

This book is printed on acid-free paper.

Because of the dynamic nature of the Internet, any web addresses or links contained in this book may have changed since publication and may no longer be valid. The views expressed in this work are solely those of the author and do not necessarily reflect the views of the publisher, and the publisher hereby disclaims any responsibility for them.

CONTENTS

BOOK 1 – I WAS NOT A GOOD MEDICAL STUDENT

Introduction xi

PART ONE
PRE-CLINICAL

Four Young Men and a Body! 1
I was not a good medical student 10

PART TWO
CLINICAL

Crossing the Road 33
3rd MB 44
4th MB 49
The final year 59

BOOK 2 – BLUNT BUT GOOD

Leeds 69
Chapel Allerton 76
Maternity 80
Poole 89
General Practice 104
Making a difference 110

BOOK 3 – LIFE AND DECLINE OF THE FAMILY DOCTOR

Introduction 121

A Family Doctor 125
How did it all start?...131
Why Clayford? 133
First day...137
Worst moment...140
Mental illness 142
Epidemics..144
Strange infections..150
Funny moments..152
Wimborne Road..155
Lake Wobegon?...159
Minor illness 160
On-call 163
Home deliveries..170
Medieval Medicine..174
Dark and tender secrets 176
PTSD...179
Most difficult time 182
Asylum Duff 184
Creatures great and small 185
The Patients 187
Old Sam – Young Sam 188
Parkes 190
The Reverend 191
The Raven 194
A bull in a field and crossdressing..196
Gone Fishin 198
Learning Quickly 199
Idle men 201
...and frustrated women 204
No blue light... 206
Aladdin's cave...207

Training	209
Computer	214
From opportunistic to population and the rise of the worried well	216
Equipment	220
Progress	223
Cometh a white knight	227
Slowly de-skilled	229
Varicose veins	232
Family diaspora	234
Changing working practices	235
Co-morbidity	237
2004	240
Final observations	241
Looking back	243
Finally – the flip side	247

I WAS NOT A GOOD MEDICAL STUDENT

MISSION ACCOMPLISHED BOOK 1
BY DR CHARLES REES

INTRODUCTION

When I eventually gave up all clinical work in 2017 I began to reflect how it all started.

When I was ten, the family moved to Southport in Lancashire from Bournemouth. My mother, who was said to have developed asthma when she was nineteen, became ill during the second winter there, presumably with a chest infection. We all took turns to be with her; there was no television then, we just had to sit by an electric fire to keep her company. Eventually, she grew worse and was admitted to a hospital. I went to stay with a saint of a lady, Mrs Murgatroyd. She was totally selfless and lived for her family, friends and anyone in need. She was an extraordinary woman. She had two sons but had had a third child, a daughter, who was born severely handicapped. She was told to take the baby girl home and turn her every two hours and she would live for a fortnight. Mrs Murgatroyd took her baby home and turned her every two hours for eighteen months before she died. Mrs Murgatroyd would bring me bars of white chocolate and assorted books. One book I loved was a series about a doctor who went to Tanganyika, as it then was. I believe they came from the Jungle Doctor series by Paul White. Occasionally, as the weeks passed, I was able to visit my mother from the garden of the hospital. Children were dirty things and not to be allowed in as they might bring infection. I stood in the garden and talked to her as she leant out of the window. The visits became fewer, and when the phone rang, Mrs Murgatroyd would answer it after closing the door. One Monday evening, my father arrived and told me that my sisters and I were going to the hospital, as Mummy was going to die. We trailed in to see her in an oxygen tent. She did not see us. The next morning, my father arrived and said she had died at 4 am that Tuesday morning. She was 47.

The years that followed were difficult for the family as my sisters left home and my father remarried. His new wife had been a nurse in the Queen Alexandra's Royal Army Nursing Corps and had received the Burma Star during World War Two. You had to be within a certain distance of enemy lines for two years to get it so not for the faint hearted. According to her mother, she had never had any childhood infections or any of the infectious diseases she nursed, which was just about everything except Typhus. She was a frequent smoker but gave my father at least fifteen years of a quality life after his stroke. I always say it's the smoking that got her because she died when she was 97 in comparison to her mother who did not smoke and died at 101.

However, the point is that, by the time I was fifteen, I had decided I did not like illness in general and death in particular. I was determined I would do something about it - I would become a doctor. And whatever one might think about that sort of vocational slush, it made me a doctor at twenty-three and gave me forty-eight years of fascinating work. One of my daughters had obtained a degree in Maths and had a good career in London. But she had decided it was not going to fulfil her and she changed course, gave it all up and was lucky enough to get into Hull and York Medical School. She found she had qualified on exactly the same day of the week and date of the year that my mother had died and which had made me resolute in my career. Coincidence? Probably. Spooky? Definitely.

PART ONE
PRE-CLINICAL

CHAPTER 1
FOUR YOUNG MEN AND A BODY!

The old Medical School Leeds

O<small>N MY FIRST DAY</small> 1968 at the Medical School at Leeds University we registered in the morning and so our first medical experience was in the afternoon. We trailed into the anatomy lecture theatre. It was the classical lecture theatre like the one Rembrandt painted in *The Dissection*. Although the old Medical School has been largely gutted the building itself has been preserved and the lecture theatre is the only part of the inside still as it was. The body language of the students said it all as the swots filed into the front row and those like myself ascended to the top and rearmost row. The speaker was Archie Durward, the Professor of Anatomy, of New Zealand origin and a legend. He was the senior member of the triumvirate who were to be our masters for the next two years. The other two were the Professors of Physiology and Biochemistry. This was the standard, traditional teaching of medicine. There would be two years of pre-clinical teaching, and then the dreaded examination of 2^{nd}MB. If that hurdle was passed there would be three more years of clinical work. We started with the reading of a register in which all eighty of us declared ourselves to be present. After an introduction in which the professor said he would be starting with the anatomy of sex he asked us if we knew the difference between male and female. At least five hands went up much to my surprise! Without telling us he just said, "thank God, this morning I asked the dentists and none of them knew!" One of the front row who became a great friend, was an active learner, by which I mean he never stopped asking questions. Unfortunately, he had a stutter which became worse the more intense he got. Archie was well into the anatomy of ejaculation and was explaining the system of closing of the bladder sphincter and the opening of the seminal vesicle sphincter. Bill kept interrupting with one question after another about this crucial piece of sexual clockwork. The professor, sensing that there may be something more to Bill's questions than the anatomy of the sexual organs, gently approached him and put a hand on his shoulder, "my boy, just have faith in your sphincters!" Bill is still working in Western Australia.

MISSION ACCOMPLISHED

The author with Bill, "have faith in your sphincters!"

The professor then walked out of the theatre and although I don't remember instruction or command we all followed him like sheep, into a large room. There in front of us on stainless steel tables lay twenty-four naked corpses. I had never seen a dead body before naked or clothed. But there they were, mostly male but some female. We were shown to our tables. I was standing next to Howard and opposite John and Dave. We dissected that corpse for the next two years. It reeked of formalin. As the weeks and months went by our white coats smelt of formalin, our clothes smelt of formalin, our hands smelt of formalin. Eventually, we smelt of formalin! For the next few weeks I was woken with nightmares of dead bodies. I have no idea if my colleagues had the same experience but I do know that one of our number took one look at the bodies and was never seen again. Each morning and afternoon the register was read out and the absence of an acknowledgement to this name bore witness to the horror of that moment.

Our dissection began with the arm and continued until most of the deceased had found its way into the stainless-steel bucket which each table possessed.

The Medical School was ancient and the anatomy department its foundation. Years later working in Dorset I worked with a semi-retired doctor who qualified at Leeds thirty years before I did. According to him the anatomy porter would receive a call from St James' Hospital on the other side of Leeds to say that a body was ready for the department. He would travel across, pick up the body wrapped in its shroud and take it back on the tram. (It was said that a journey on those vibrating trams was the simplest way of reducing an incarcerated inguinal hernia!) On his return he would visit a pub, the Tunbridge outside the Medical School, sadly demolished in my first term, lean the body outside while he downed a pint, and then take the corpse the last 50 yards to the back of the anatomy department. On the left as you went in was a stone coffin kept full of brine and into this the body would be dumped as its first step to preservation. Indeed, all the time I was there the stone coffin resided.

At the end of two weeks we were interrogated with the dreaded 'viva.' The test 'viva voce' was given by our tutors or the anatomy demonstrators. The anatomy demonstrators were young doctors who had committed themselves to surgery. To do this in those days they had to pass the primary examination to the Royal College of Surgeons, an examination with a 95% failure rate. This made them somewhat bitter and frustrated and it was we, the poor first year students, who were the release valve for their frustration. There was little we could do except either get angry or get good. The ladies could turn on the waterworks but frankly the demonstrators were all male and milked their dominance. Also, annoyingly, all the ladies were good! This experience, doleful in my case, was repeated every two weeks. There is no escape in a viva. You can't glare at an exam paper and slink away home. The torturer is there in front of you noting every weakness. The mark was then put on a card which we kept, as an unforgettable record of triumph or failure. If a student had particularly bad marks the record would be there for the next examiner who would therefore give a particularly severe test thus resulting in another low mark.

The student, before learning anatomy had to learn a new language of 'anterior, distal, caudal' etc whilst being able to see the subject three dimensionally. Medical exams were, for those who were not in the distinction class, a matter of pass or fail. At the end of the first term I had just failed. I was determined to do better next time and put my whole effort into the subject. At the second term exam I just passed. I had not passed with flying colours as I had hoped and expected. Just passed. It occurred to me that I could 'just pass' again with less effort. I would become a 'just enough' sort of student. It is a fine line and a bit of an art form but it can work. In later years after qualification I had to pay for any and all exams I took. I never failed those!

An added trauma to the first day occurred at the end. The eagle-eyed professor had noted me on the back row despite trying to look invisible. He approached me to my horror. He had noted that I was wearing a round neck sweater under a jacket. He asked me pointedly if I intended to become a professional person. Why was I not wearing a collar and tie? From then on I always wore a collar and tie however mucky the Leeds air made it. I eventually realised that when people see a doctor they want to have confidence in that person and the best way for that to happen is to be clean, tidy and frankly ordinary. They don't want to be looking at tattoos or piercings. It's about them, not you. I was not the only one who came to Archie's notice. The said Bill was called one day to Archie's room. He remembers the dirty carpet on front of his desk that he made you stand on whilst he told you off. Bill had forgotten to shave for a couple of days after some good drinking sessions - "Beresford you are a dirty continental bastard".

Thus it was that we four dissected our corpse. As I write I can say that we all qualified, are still in good health and still meet from time to time. To say we are friends would not be the correct terminology. Yes we are friends but the bonds forged over that corpse go deeper than casual friendship. For two years we chatted and gossiped and suffered and learnt. We have a deep experience in common.

A near death experience!

Physiology was an altogether different experience from anatomy. It was dynamic and definitely more dangerous. As one approached the Medical School one could hear the sound of dogs barking on the roof. Sooner or later these dogs would appear in one demonstration or other by the physiologists for our education. Mercifully they were deeply unconscious and never again awoken. Luckily the physiologists who put the dogs to sleep after the experiment, realised that the experiments they were going to perform on us, must result in the survival of the student, but I used to wonder how they felt about it.

The experiments occurred on Wednesday mornings going into the afternoon. One of the more innocent experiments involved giving a student alcohol and testing reflexes. One of our number was six foot and five inches and came from Guyana. He was big in all departments allegedly but was also very laid back and slow. Interestingly the effect of alcohol in his case was to speed him up but in all others had the predicted effect. It slowed us down. But no-one asked if we might be driving or more likely, riding a bike let alone any other risky pursuit. Our welfare was not their business!

One of the most dangerous experiments was set for us with no warning or explanation. It was the contention of the physiologists that breathlessness was caused, not by lack of oxygen, but by rising carbon dioxide levels in the blood. Therefore, if you could reduce the oxygen levels without raising the carbon dioxide the person (student, patient, guinea pig, victim) would not become breathless as they became depleted of oxygen. We never asked what he or she would become! Thus, it was that we were placed in groups of four. As I remember it my group consisted of John, Howard, Dave (not Dissection Dave) and myself, and Dave actually volunteered to be the subject, to give it a euphemism. Dave was rigged up with a system to re-breathe his own air which was passed over caustic soda to remove the carbon dioxide. He was asked to sign his name and the experiment started. A minute later he was asked to sign his name which he did. After two minutes he was asked again and did so perhaps not quite as clearly. After three minutes he was asked to write his name and his hand, after attempting a scrawl, slid off the paper. At this point a physiology demonstrator appeared suddenly and disconnected Dave who mercifully began to breath properly. Later when he had recovered his wits he confessed that apart from his initial signing he remembered nothing, nothing at all. He had been quietly becoming hypoxic, (prior to becoming brain dead!) No warning was given to us. No explanation given beforehand. No consent was asked for, let alone given and no medical history taken. Now, after reflection, I wonder by what right they thought they could do those things to us. At the time we accepted it as normal! When Dave qualified he fled to Tel Aviv and became a surgeon. I often wonder if it was to escape his experiences at our medical school.

One experiment used an antihistamine to suppress a histamine response. Histamine triggers acid production in the stomach so an antihistamine should produce less stomach acid. A tube was passed into the stomach of the volunteer (again, not me) to measure this. I imagine that the antihistamine used would be chlorpheniramine (Piriton) being common at the time and cheap. However, it has serious sedating issues. The experiment was duly performed in the morning and we left on time. That Wednesday some of us were playing football for the Medical School against Manchester University Medical School, which was not far by coach. When the game started, one of our number, Monks, had not come out of the changing room but when he did after just one minute the score was already 1-1. Clearly something was amiss and indeed it was. It so happened that although the team was taken from the whole medical school, because of clinical duties the team was chosen from the first two pre-clinical years and all the back four were in our year. It became apparent that not only had they taken part in the experiment but they had all had the chlorpheniramine. They were all over the place. But we had a decent team and a sharp attack. Eventually we lost the game 6-4. We might even have won if our defence had not been sedated!

Antidiuretic hormone was the subject of another experiment. A litre and a half of water had to be drunk and urine output measured over the next few hours. The subjects, (and no, I never volunteered) were injected with antidiuretic hormone to compare. Those without the injection passed their water quickly and those with the injection an hour or two later.

At the time I was staying in a hall of residence which was comfortable and had its own bar. At mid evening I drifted in to get some company where I was met by one of our number who looked particularly miserable. I asked him what was up. "Well," he said, "I drank the water as directed but since then nothing has happened. I got home and had a couple of cups of tea to see if that would move it but no go. Then I came down to the bar and I have had three pints so far." In other words he had imbibed at least seven pints of fluid without a renal response. I couldn't help feeling that drinking all that beer on top of the rest was not the best course of action. But as they say, we were where we were! He then admitted that he was last in the queue for the hormone and they had run out and had to get a fresh batch. It was clear that he had been given the wrong dose. Exactly how much too much remained to be seen. His parting shot which sounded like a massive understatement was that he would make a complaint if nothing happened. The next morning I went down to breakfast to be met by a doleful sight. It was my friend from the night before, red eyed and exhausted. "It wore off at 3am and I haven't stopped since!"

Alas he never got past the second year or the dreaded 2nd MB. He was in fact already an optician and simply returned to his previous profession. I imagine the 2nd MB course was traumatic enough as it was for us all. But having tasted medicine I wonder if he ever knew what else he missed. Not for him, the night work, the weekends, Christmas or Easter on call or the joys of the phone coming through to the house. Not for him a call in the middle of the night after a day's work with another day's work to follow. Just a civilised job protecting people's sight during civilised hours. Poor thing!

Teaching in those days seemed to feel it obligatory that we had maximum experience of whatever it was we were learning. Anatomy meant dissection of a corpse and it didn't end there. Neuroanatomy meant slicing a brain with an impressive thing like a bread knife. We all had our half skeletons and Howard took his to neuroanatomy and on leaving noticed it to be a bit heavy. On inspection he found that someone had put a whole brain inside it! This would have, if discovered, been a dismissal offence. Physiology meant being exposed to all manner of threats and challenges to our person. A few years later the anaesthesiologists, instead of simply warning us of the explosive nature of anaesthetic gases wanted us to experience it as though we were at Universal Studios Florida. We were duly marched out in groups of five or six to the rubble north of the Medical School which had once been streets that housed thousands of people but was due for redevelopment. The anaesthetist inflated a balloon with various gases and oxygen to which was connected an electric wire. He instructed us to get down behind a wall and then without any verbal foreplay let off the loudest explosion I have ever heard, and yes, I have been to Universal Studios Florida and been blown up three times. The neighbourhood shook! The modern student gets most of their experiences online. I have no doubt they learnt as much but trust me, our learning experiences were unforgettable!

Biochemistry

If anatomy had proved difficult and physiology a challenge, biochemistry was a mystery. It was bedevilled by the Henderson/Hasselbach equation, Krebs cycle and benzene rings. They were nothing compared to the rings going round my head. Very few of us admitted to enjoying biochemistry but Dave, (that is Dissection Dave and not Near Death Experience Dave) really did. He ended up teaching it and I think still does. It was strange because he had a clear idea of what he wanted from medicine. We often chatted round our corpse as to why we were there and what we wanted. Most of us had some higher purpose but Dave was clear. "I want to drive around in a big car wearing a big coat and feel important." You had to admire his mission statement! In the end he fell in love with biochemistry as well as his slender attractive wife. Just as he still loves biochemistry his wife remains slim and attractive and he still loves her! As a digression, the fourth member of our dissection table was John who later observed that anaesthetists did not need gases to send people to sleep. He of course became an anaesthetist and was finally head of anaesthetics at Leeds General Infirmary!

The Professor of Biochemistry was a strange chap. I believe he probably knew a lot about biochemistry but he did not know a lot about dressing. He could never get the right jacket button in the right jacket buttonhole and the rest of his attire was equally chaotic. He was the junior of the three pre-clinical professors and therefore liked to throw his weight around by failing us. He would sit behind his desk dressed like Charlie Chaplin, sucking on a cherry pipe and then spitting on the floor to his left. The carpet was thick with gooey spital which undoubtedly took our minds off Krebs cycle.

CHAPTER 2

I WAS NOT A GOOD MEDICAL STUDENT

S ADLY, I WAS NOT A good medical student. The problem was I was eighteen and had discovered women and drink. I look back and think I was too young. But then I think not. Mature students are very special people because they are probably successful in another role. Why would they give it up for ritual humiliation, hard work, sleeplessness and little thanks. Years later I went to a talk by one of my colleagues, by then a consultant in dermatology. He likened us to Nelson, the statue thereof at Trafalgar Square. You might be up there and think you are high and mighty but the truth is that every pigeon in the Square can and does crap on you. What an accurate analogy.

In many ways I was lucky to be there at all. The years 1945-6 had seen a glut of babies as the men came back from the war and families felt confident enough to have children. Thus by the time of the 11plus examination there were more children than places at the grammar schools and similarly for university entrance. I thought I had no chance to get into Oxford or Cambridge and knew nothing about the London medical schools. Also, I wanted to be in a university with students of all faculties, not just medics. The demand for university places was so fierce that a clearing house had been designed – UCCA – University Central Council on Admissions (now known as UCAS) and we were only allowed to apply for four medical schools. Two rejected me without interview, one after interview and I was waiting for confirmation or rejection from Leeds. When applying I had no idea where to go but the careers master, Mr L C Hargreaves (Elsie) had asked me, "Have you thought of Leeds, fellar?" I had to confess that I had not thought of Leeds because I barely knew where it was. From my grammar school in Lancashire we did not know what went on on the other side of the Pennines. Coming to the north from the south had been difficult enough without extending my knowledge across the Pennines! So in September 1963 I was still awaiting my fate. Being just eighteen the stress had brought out a fine crop of acne to the extent that a visit to my family doctor was indicated. Doctor Kenneth Rostron was a fine family doctor, competent, reassuring and knowledgeable. I was shown into his surgery and waited. I do not know what case he had just seen but he walked in and said, "Any teenage girl who feels sick or is sick is pregnant until proved otherwise." What wonderful advice that turned out to be. Years later I watched colleagues refer young girls for hormone studies because of amenorrhoea, abdominal swelling and gastrointestinal issues. And these from the local estate where immaculate conception was the rule rather than exception!

For my first first term at university I was housed in a theological college at Rawdon, seven miles away from Leeds which was half occupied by theological students and half by university students. Frankly they were all a bit weird and I was the only medical student so had no-one to share problems with. I enhanced my singularity by taking the skull from my half skeleton and inserted a light bulb into it making it into a table lamp. Some of the students had been there for a year and survived the winter of 1962-3. It had been an awful winter and I remember in Southport the ice just got thicker for six weeks before warmer weather melted it. For the students it had been a nightmare and they regaled us with stories of ripping up carpets from the floor (they had carpets!) to put on the bed to keep warm. Thankfully our first winter was just normal.

I was eighteen, beer was cheap and Leeds beckoned. As it happened seven others from my grammar school went to Leeds in the same year so I was not short of old friends. I tried to cycle in at first from the place I was staying in Rawdon but the grimy Leeds air made my clothes filthy and my lungs cough. Then my fellow students and I tried a tiny old post office van painted green. At other times I used the Samuel

Legdard buses. These were legendary. They were blue and grey, old and cranky and driven by motoring psychopaths. I have no idea how they recruited their drivers. They raced and braked round the West Riding in a continuous white-knuckle ride reminiscent of the Night bus in Harry Potter. However, they were cheap and very quick. I do not remember ever seeing a Sam Legdard in an accident. These were the days before seat belts or breathalyser.

The students at the theological college fascinated me. They were half university students and half theological. The Baptist Theological College was winding down and moving to Manchester. The theological students were mature students. Some of them very so and had fine careers to look back on. Something had not fulfilled them and they had turned to the Baptist ministry. One had been a diamond merchant in Amsterdam and Berlin. It sounded so romantic – but clearly not enough. Others had had executive jobs in the City. I listened and learnt. The university students were a mixed bunch and it was here that I was introduced to young men from the North East. They could be identified easily by the way they talked but even then, it turned out they came from three separate tribes, the Tees, the Wear and the Tyne and to generalise as to their origin was asking for trouble.

At weekends we had time on our hands and mingled freely. There was a fives court there and one student had moved his old Riley into it. He was constantly repairing it and introduced us to pre-selector gears. The gear the car is to be in is pre-selected on the gear stick and the gear change completed by pressing and releasing the clutch. The change in gear was for those days incredibly smooth. His party trick was to drive the car into the fives court, put it in reverse and at the last second depress the clutch. The car would be smoothly making for the back wall of the court and then, equally smoothly, be reversing away from it. It was very impressive and he would repeat this trick until there would be a loud crunch indicating that the pre-selector gear box had fallen apart, whereupon he would start repairs and re-building until he could do his trick all over again.

Two characters there were Ian, a textile chemist, and Mervyn, an English student. Their penchant was for trivial excess whether it was eating crisps, which they would buy in grocery size, or drinking Pernod which they did with the usual result. They were larger than life and great fun. Mervyn had an old yellow car which we used from time to time.

After a term at the theological college I spent a term at a hall of residence. It was a fine place but far out and unimaginative. I had a friend from school (John) and my two friends from the theological college (Ian and Mervyn) and the four of us wanted a flat! They were wonderful people but not conducive to learning. John and Ian studied Textile Chemistry and Mervyn studied English. The flat was the upper two floors of a four story terraced building off Delph lane, with dire plumbing but habitable. Flushing the toilet would fill the bath.

Exploring the Leeds pubs was a priority and three, now long gone, I remember very well. The Yorkshire Hussar in the middle of the Headrow was magnificent but scary. It was unwise to look anyone in the eye else they would come across and ask your business! The Star and Garter at Kirkstall was also fine and had the added attraction of live music and dancing. The quantity of beer consumed was huge and what fascinated us was the barmen. They could all do this trick. As the drinking and wild dancing went on they would go round collecting glasses on a round tray. When full they would place another round tray on top of the first layer of glasses and collect another load of glasses. They would then do this a third time and having completed this wedding cake of tiered glasses, would hold them with one hand with splayed fingers supporting the bottom tray. But that was not the amazing bit. What was amazing was how they would then weave their way through the wild, heavily inebriated dancers back to the bar and never dropped one. They could all do this and defied the natural order of things which is normally from order to chaos. We watched mesmerised waiting for disaster which never came. The third pub I remember was the Robin Hood off Briggate. This was another sinister and dangerous pub frequented by locals and students rarely entered. I just had to and John and I went in one evening. After a pint or two a fight broke out on the empty dance floor which led to one man kicking another who was the worse for wear on the floor. It was brutal and for reasons that now make me cringe I got up and intervened. The pub became very hostile and the kicker confronted me. In unmistakeable terms he told me to clear off or he would hit me. With foolish courage I asked him with what. He pointed to his forehead. It was thick and scarred from many nuttings no doubt. I looked round for John. He was nowhere. I retreated to the exit and went down the wide corridor to Briggate. As the exit door beckoned I could see John's pale blue Ford Poplar, motor running and John waiting! We drove!

Drink played a large part of our recreation but we were also practical. We realised we had to eat and that potatoes were central to our diet. We therefore drove (John had a three gear Ford Poplar) out to a farm off the York Road and purchased a hundredweight of potatoes. The idea was that we should have a continuous supply of chips to throw in the fryer. To this end we had the bag of potatoes and two buckets full of water. When the inclination moved us we would peel a potato and throw it in the first bucket. Later another person would take the peeled potato and chip it and throw it in the second bucket. Therefore, there would always be a bucket of chipped potatoes ready for the fryer. It was a conveyor belt which served us well. However, we were aware that we were not cooks and Ian always had a supply of Neutradonna, an antacid, handy. To hone our culinary skills we decided, all of us, to watch the television chef, one Philip Harben, on BBC. How we would have loved Nigella Lawson and salivated over her delivery. Philip Harben was small, a bit overweight, bearded and bald. But we watched and listened with awe. I can't remember the first lesson but the second was on omelettes. There are four different types of omelette, said Philip, the French omelette, the souffle omelette, the Spanish omelette and the Mount St Michael omelette. The last one, said the twinkling Philip, was like the French omelette but the mixture had to be mixed by monks for three days! He liked his little joke and we tolerated it because we could now make omelettes! On the third lesson we were into stews and I have to say that I can still make a superb Lancashire Hot Pot. Philip the wit had another chuckle with us when he demonstrated the Irish stew. He opened the oven to reveal – nothing. There was, said the chef, no such thing as an Irish stew!

By the fourth lesson we were to make bread. We did our best but the combined effort of four undergraduates was to produce a small lump, which if thrown at a creature would have killed it. We tried again and produced something a little larger but equally lethal. We were not to be beaten and tried a third and then a fourth time. The last specimen was not very big and fairly hard but, and this was the thing, we could cut it with a knife! Then we buttered it and then, we all managed to eat a little. Having achieved this landmark we felt we had conquered bread making and thereafter went to the corner shop.

John had received an education in mechanics from his father and decided that his Ford Poplar with only three gears needed an overhaul. We collected newspaper and distributed it round the edges of what was quite a large kitchen/dining room. The engine from the said pale blue Poplar was then released and Ian, who was a gorilla of a man, lifted the whole thing out and up three flights of stairs. John then dismantled every part and each part was given its place, all on newspaper, around the room (with space left for the buckets of chips!) They were there for months for cleaning and general perusal. Eventually the time came to re-assemble and to John's credit there were only nine bits he could not find a place for. Luckily, they did not seem to have a role and the car ran beautifully. Unfortunately, the four of us were great friends and misspent many evenings exploring the pubs of Leeds. The film *'Withnail and I'* had no details in common with what we did but the ambience was perfectly accurate. The film captures exactly the climate of student life in Leeds during the nineteen sixties and made me tingle when I saw it.

We not only drank together but ate together which was so civilised. But having an English student as a flat mate had it's drawback. On one occasion Mervyn started choking during the meal. Our food was not good but it wasn't that bad. Then his lips began to part and to my horror blood began to seep from them. Then more and more blood frothed and dribbled down his chin until the point came when I honestly believed his number was up. At that point he wiped his face and smiled and chuckled at the petrified three of us. Evidently actors can use blood like capsules which they break in their mouths when horror is required. It sure worked with us. He also had some white ones in case froth was indicated during a fit or a seance!

So it was that I stumbled though the two pre-clinical years of humiliating vivas, life threatening physiology experiments and incomprehensible biochemistry. Apart from the continuous shortage of money I was enjoying life immensely. I had not chosen the best companions for studying but I was getting a university education by mingling with students of other faculties. There is a problem with something so closed as medicine that you only meet medical students but by flat sharing I met English students and engineers of all varieties. Leeds had them everywhere, Mechanical, Electrical, Civil (not literally,) Textile and probably others. They were needed to counter the huge loony left of the University. Leeds had a Marxist Society, Communist Society, Trotsky Society, Labour Society and probably others more secretive and subversive. The Great Unwashed. I loved going to the Debating Society which usually ended with a battle between the 'Great Unwashed' and the Conservative Society which was personified by a strange character who was proud to proclaim his oddness being due to centuries of inbreeding.

The psychology students were the weirdest and most out of kilter. They would have the most bizarre ploys to get through examinations. One would spend the whole examination session writing and repeating his own name in the hope of convincing the examiners that he was under severe stress. Whereas today, stress is a badge of honour and par for the course it carried no weight in the climate of the 1960s. Another when faced with a challenging question would write out everything he knew about the subject and put it all into one sentence with no end to give the impression that he was highly gifted but only hampered by lack of time. One of my flatmates, Ian, was himself rather odd and attracted other odd students such as the psychology students mentioned above. He had a photographic memory so sailed through his degree in textile chemistry but textiles were contracting in the north at that time so jobs were scarce and with a poor future. He eventually got a job on the buses as a conductor for Leeds City Transport. They soon recognised that he could memorise all the timetables so elevated him to inspector. It really was a marvel. He knew the lot.

My own flat mates, when we weren't drinking, would have sessions, directed by Mervyn, of King Lear with Ian as Sir Donald Wolfitt in the title role. When I should have been memorising the branches of the internal carotid artery I was bellowing Lear's curses to Goneril and Regan. "How sharper than a serpent's tooth it is to have a thankless child." Much of our medical learning was done using mnemonics. We learned those awful lists of branches of arteries using them - usually obscene - 'Please Can Soft Soap Remove Semen Stains From?' After all these years I can remember the mnemonics but haven't a clue what they alluded to.

Mervyn would take us to the avant guard cinema in Queen's square where we would watch films like Mondo Cane, Freaks, Kanal and Ashes and Diamonds.

I also had friends in other faculties and for some reason many of them were Geography students. Thus, I found myself on the coach to the Northern Universities Geographical Congress in Newcastle. I think I played football with them as well. The other Universities sent students interested in Geography but Leeds sent drinkers. And Newcastle was a treat. The Union there had five bars, one for men, one for women, one for men and women, a quiet bar and the 'Pit.' The Pit was a sunken bar where the real life and soul of the Union took place. Afterwards we went to some sort of dance. One of our number lost a contact lens and I remember seeing it floating off on a river of beer. When we returned to the coach we had lost five members but re-claimed one in Gateshead. There was no M1 then or toilets on the coach. The centre half, a tall Mancunian called Mick stood at the open door of the coach as it sped down the A1 at 50 mph. One by one we would go to the open door whereby he would grip our collar. We would then lean out and relieve our bursting bladder. Then "right Mick" and he would haul us back in for the next one to have a go. When I close my eyes I can still feel myself leaning out and see the tarmac of the A1 flying by below.

Whilst not being a good medical student I must have learnt something because I always seemed to scrape through. Maybe it was the art of scraping through I was good at. A good many of my fellow students were in a similar condition. In the first year everyone is above you. As the years go by there are students below you and however little you know, they know less which ironically is a stimulus for knowing more. You want to keep ahead of them.

Occasionally I'd return to Southport from time to time. It was and still is a fine town twenty miles down the electric train line from Liverpool and in the 1960s Liverpool was buzzing with music which went round the world. The Beatles came to the Floral Hall on the promenade. We would sometimes nip down on the electric train and see them on a Friday lunchtime at The Cavern for 1/6d. Later I saw the Bootleg Beatles at the Albert Hall. To be honest they were better because they had the whole repertoire (mostly unwritten when we saw them live,) and when they came to the Floral Hall John Lennon had a sore throat! The effect they had meant that four man beat groups abounded. It was possible to visit a dozen church halls on a Friday and Saturday night with first class groups for a dance, for next to nothing, and we did!

When in Leeds the student Union had dances on a Saturday night. They were wild as well as crowded. One favourite group, name forgotten after all these years, had a giant lead singer and a small organist. The use of the organ gave it a Gothic flavour. As the night wore on the organist would become more and more frenzied in his playing and the lead singer would follow his example. Eventually in a state of utter frenzy he would come up behind the organist and, as the music reached a crescendo, strangle him! He would then pick up the limp body and lay his lifeless body on top of the organ. As the rest of the band continued the frenzy to the horror of all, the lead singer would take a huge knife and plunge it into the moribund organist. With a thud. We believed, and let's face it good organists don't grow on trees, that he had on his belly a stout plank of wood for the knife to be plunged. To be fair it wasn't a trick you could keep on doing and although it was probably safer than some of our physiology experiments, there wasn't much room for error.

2006 Aged 61 Howard van Pelt and I on the stairs where we frequently did not see our names on the pass list!

The student who I shared the right side of our corpse with for two years was, as it happened. the student I met when we were interviewed months previously little knowing the turn our lives would take. He was the first medical student I ever met and we are still friends to this day. Many decades later we reminisced about those days and I confessed to him that I was the worst student (leaving out those who didn't make it.) Howard was amazed and insisted that he, not I, was the worst. We had a heated discussion for about half an hour until I conceded. Yes, he was pretty bad. Interestingly we both had long successful and hardworking careers.

I had applied through UCCA (the Universities central council on admissions,) where we were allowed to apply for four medical schools outside London and not including Oxford or Cambridge. Thanks to a bright idea from our Headmaster (King George V Southport) I was rejected by two before I had my A level results. To save money he thought that we could forego the O levels we would be taking at A level and would therefore have three years to prepare and thus get a better grade. This was fine for those who like him (he had been to Sandhurst) wanted to be scientists and took Maths, Physics and Chemistry. They had all the best teachers. But if you were going for Medicine or Dentistry and therefore had to take Biology instead of Maths you were thrown into outer darkness with the poorer teachers. As it happened one of our number who became a professor of neurosurgery used to help our physics master to solve the problems he had set! I may exaggerate when I say we were thrown into outer darkness but we were housed in the Geography Block which was outside the main school to emphasise that we were not of the science faculty. Having said that we had a remarkable Maths teacher in Mr Leciter, known as either lettuce or Neb. short for Nebuchadnezzar due to his great age and wisdom. If it was raining he would walk to the block at the optimum speed. Infinite speed would wet the front of the person to a maximum but no more. Infinite slowness would result in a soaking. The optimum was somewhere in between and Neb had found it. He taught me Joint Metriculation Board O26 Maths Pure and Applied and I passed with 80%. In fact I was furious it was not 100% but I think the examiners did not like my workings.

I was to take Biology, Physics, Chemistry and General Studies. The Headmaster, with another bright idea, thought that General Studies was another string to our bow. General Studies was often taken as a bit of a joke but conversely students rarely got good grades. There were two three hour papers the first being six essay questions. I remember one question asking an example of some feature of nature which had been enhanced by man. I was familiar with Thirlmere in the Lake District where the lake was manmade, a reservoir for Manchester Corporation, and the surrounding fells had been planted with firs. It was not natural or proper Lake District but it was beautiful so I wrote about it. Another wanted us to compare two newspapers. At home we took the *Sunday Graphic* which was a liberal paper (liberal then meaning having an open mind and nothing like liberal now,) and *The People*, which rough as it was, produced some genuine investigative journalism. I can't remember the other questions but had no trouble writing on the six subjects without preparation. The other paper had modules on Maths, English, French, Science, History and Geography. It was to be in the afternoon - I thought. At a quarter to nine one morning my stepmother came in with the news that the school was on the phone asking why I was not at the examination which was to start at nine! I cycled the three miles and was at my seat twenty minutes late. The invigilator, the scary Mr Leciter, stooped over me and asked me if I knew that the twenty minutes could be added on at the end. Joy! I told him I did not. "Good because you can't." Just his little joke.

Of the six sections you were obliged to do three, or more if you wanted. I finished them all with twenty minutes to spare. When the results came out I had got an A! Looking back maybe it was a sign that I should become a jack of all trades, a generalist. However, I think it must have helped at the University interview. One was at Liverpool and they rejected me which left Leeds. That day I took the train across the Pennines, changing at Rochdale, on to Todmorden, Sowerby Bridge and Halifax. These were names I am sorry to say I was less familiar with than Timbuktu or Khartoum. I walked out of the Leeds City station into Queen Square and up and across the Headrow, admiring the magnificent Town Hall, up Park Street and Thoresby Place. The Medical School was in front of me. I walked in and was put in a room outside the office of the Dean, who we were later to know as 'Daddy Walls,' a lovely avuncular man, to find myself sitting down next to Howard van Pelt. Our lives turned on that moment. He knows it too!

Through 'til two.

One of the characters in our year, John Charlesworth, fascinated me because on one hand he knew sweet FA about most things whilst on the other had a ready answer for everything. His repartee was famous. Replies that took me a day to formulate came instantly from him. I probably met Charlesworth properly during the second year and joined in his notorious "through 'til twos," drinking sessions that usually ended up at a greasy spoon transport café on the Kirkstall Road, the Tomato Dip. Gastro-intestinal disturbances the next day were always blamed on the food at the Tomato Dip and never on the large volume of Tetley's imbibed during the evening.

It was well known that he had joined the Navy, who sponsored his tuition, and spent most of his generous allowance from them on drink. Panic set in when he realised that part of that allowance was to furnish his uniform for various compulsory parades! It was the final year which cemented our friendship as JC, Geoff Slater, Flatmate John and myself went on huge pub crawls. These were the *'Withnail and I'* days before Mrs Castle introduced the breathalyser. During this time I got Geoff and John to play football for the local team. As part of my misspent student time I played a lot of football on Woodhouse Moor with the local boys. They were very disciplined having the example at that time of Leeds United under Don Revie but had a hopelessly dysfunctional manager. They had a team, the Woodhouse Wanderers which lost every game and asked me to manage them. They had some very good players so I took the best seven and added John Charlesworth, Geoff Slater, John Preshaw and myself. My plan was to have Geoff and JC as strong wide players to receive and hold the ball (Howard Kendall later did the same thing with Everton) whilst the ultra-fit youngsters would move forward to receive it. On one occasion the ball was hoofed up the field to Charlesworth on the left wing. Charlesworth, instead of holding the ball looked up and saw the goalkeeper off his line and from the halfway line hit the ball over the keeper's head for a wonderful surprise goal against the run of play. Pele did it later as did Wayne Rooney but Charlesworth did it first! He was supposed to be a rugby player but was just a natural athlete and a sportsman. The effect on the youngsters was electric. They knew they had a secret weapon. Confidence was high and we won most games and never lost. Alas, at the end of the season we split up and never saw each other again. Sundays were wonderful as after the game we would slip into the Bricklayers Arms for a couple of pints and then rest for most of the afternoon. In the evening Geoff's girlfriend, who had a job! would make us all a roast and we would watch the *Forsyth Saga* before going back to the Bricklayers for last orders.

The Bricklayers Arms – painted green in our day

Charlesworth would lead the singing and lead us out with choruses of 'goodnight Brickies' to the tune of Goodnight Ladies.

Charlesworth failed finals twice but eventually did pass and due to Charlesworth's luck landed the Professorial job due to no-one else wanting it! It was a crap job, of course with no responsibility, and taught him nothing which was saying a lot. As time went on the Professorial Unit realised what they had got and there was danger of him not being signed up. But then a perverse variety of Charlesworth's luck stepped in and he broke his leg. The Unit was now faced with Charlesworth absent for 3 months but then having to come back to complete his assignment for another 3 months; they signed him up!

We lost contact for a while but he did eventually pass and was obliged to fulfil his obligations to the Navy. I believe they virtually started him from scratch and taught him things like temperatures and blood pressure to make him functional. I have known Navy doctors who are sent to nuclear submarines and three months underwater, but Charlesworth's luck kicked in again and he was sent to Portland to a Royal Fleet Auxiliary helicopter support ship, the *Engadine* (later heavily involved in the Falklands war.) He contacted me and suggested he should come over as I was working in Poole. We were to meet in Bournemouth in the Square (which is a roundabout) and he would drive over. When the time came a black London taxi suddenly appeared. Why did Charlesworth have to have a London Taxi? Why couldn't he have a normal car like other people? The next time I went over to the *Engadine*. It was a very comfortable ship and it was clear that Dr Charlesworth was very popular. He had decided to get the crew fit and to do so had had the helicopters removed from the flight deck so they could play deck games. Drink was a serious issue on the *Engadine* which had a fine and comfortable bar for a 'naval' ship. Over the bar was a yellow light with some red letters and numbers on it. These were the latitude and longitude beyond which the *Engadine* was outside territorial waters and therefore permitted to release more Duty-Free booze. The *Engadine* was notorious for drifting off outside these limits when on manoeuvres. I went twice to this happy ship and there was no doubt that the new doctor had had a wonderful effect.

We lost contact for a while and as we all know, the years just slipped away. I became a GP Trainer and one day attended a course somewhere in Wiltshire, Urchfont I think, and got chatting to a doctor from Newark. I knew Charlesworth had gone into practice there and told him so. He revealed that Charlesworth was one of his partners. I was curious how he was performing and this doctor was eager to explain. I must now digress. One of my enduring interests has been the American Civil War and I have been to conferences and field trips there 20-25 times. Amongst my many books is one by John Worsham – *I Was One of Jackson's Foot Cavalry*. One day Worsham was put on sick parade duty. It was his job to get the sick soldiers and take them to the Surgeon. He observed that when each soldier came in the Surgeon would listen attentively and then say a few words and give the soldier some medicine. However, he also observed that the Surgeon only had three medicines, laudanum, Castor oil and something else. He would give these medicines out in turn and Worsham could detect no rhyme or reason as to which one or why. He also noted that the soldiers were content with this. They had been listened to and given something. As the Newark doctor described Charlesworth's performance I recognised Worsham's account. Charlesworth sat and listened, may have examined cursorily and then given a prescription. He said that the practice had at first been worried so they did an audit and found that in ninety percent of cases the outcomes were good and the patients were happy and content with this. They would identify the other ten percent and divert them elsewhere. I can believe that Charlesworth had the same inspiring and uplifting effect that he had on those footballing youngsters all those years ago. Balint called it 'the drug – Doctor.' I often wondered if Charlesworth needed to go to medical school to practice his arts.

As an aside, most student at Leeds would be aware of the Packhorse and the Eldon, opposite the Parkinson building. From our flat down Delph Lane we would sometimes visit the Chemic or the Swan with Two Necks where in the cold of winter I would take a medical book to sit by the coke fire. But our favourite was the Bricklayers Arms tucked secretly away off St Mark's Road. As in the clinical years we did not have vacations, we were the only students left and got to know the locals very well. They introduced me to an underclass of petty criminals for whom Armley jail was their second home when it wasn't their first!

First year survived

At the end of the first year I had scraped through and returned home. I needed work and money. Through my father I obtained a job at the hospital laundry in Southport. There were eleven hospitals in Southport, the Promenade, a general hospital with a spinal injuries unit, the Infirmary for more acute things, the Christina Hartley maternity hospital, New Hall for infectious diseases, a paediatric hospital and six other assorted convalescent hospitals. All the laundry went through the Promenade and the laundry was run by Tommy Rimmer. He was a little man, portly with a pink round face and eyes that seemed to want to pop out of his head. In fact, all of him seemed about to explode at any minute. He strutted around in a khaki boiler suit to make it clear that although he was the manager he was ready to get stuck in and get his hands dirty. He had a foot in both camps. To be fair he ran a tight ship and it all worked and behind the bluster was very kind to all his staff. It was he who instructed me to collect and deliver the laundry to Southport's eleven hospitals. It was wonderful. Jim, the boss, and I trundled around in a large Bedford van collecting the bags of soiled laundry and depositing the light aluminium boxes of clean laundry. It was hard and physical and at nineteen it was just what I needed. I had work and at weekends I had money. Jim was great company and after a seven o'clock start we were ready at ten for our 'baggin.' This was usually a meat and tattie pie from one of the many shops Jim was familiar with. There is something special about this culinary delight, a marker of the genius of English cooking. And yet, it is almost unknown in the south of England. Round the town we went, always welcome and then moving on. Southport then was a wonderful town. Its parks and gardens and its own Rotten Row were second to none. And it boasted the largest Summer Flower Show in the country.

After about six weeks, when I thought the job was my own, Mr Rimmer informed me that they were short in the laundry and I was to help. Apart from himself all the staff were girls and women and I was now one of them! The pressing, ironing, folding of clean laundry was now my duty. Those great boxes of clean linen that once I had slung around were now left for Jim to collect on his own. When he came we just looked at each other forlornly. He knew I was lost! Mr Rimmer, however, was not insensitive and realising that I was in the middle of about thirty predatory women decided to fish me out. The metaphor is not entirely inappropriate because piece of meat in a shark pool springs to mind! Mixing metaphors I now went from the frying pan into the fire; the foul linen laundry! All the contaminated linen with its urine, faeces, blood and pus was brought to the foul linen laundry. Instead of folding fine sheets I was now shovelling shit! It was ghastly but all done very efficiently. We just got on with it and I became friendly with a young West Indian man who worked there. One day I asked him how he felt coming from his Island home to the foul linen laundry; from paradise to hell on earth! I cannot remember his answer but all I can say is that West Indians always seem to be pathologically happy. He was content but I was not and pushed for a return to the vans. When I did return things were not the same. The spell of the wonderful summer had been broken. It reminded me that nothing goes on forever and soon I would be back in Leeds with Howard, John, Dave and our corpse for another year of dissection and vivas!

One other thing blighted the summer. My sister came home as well, this time to have a baby. Her first child was a boy but had triggered her Rhesus antibodies. She gave birth to a stillborn girl, nearly full term in the Christina Hartley Maternity Hospital. How she missed our mother then. A few years later Dr Cyril Clark hit on the idea of giving mothers anti D where appropriate to prevent the antibody reaction and Rhesus still births became history.

Beecher's brook

As the terms went by we came nearer to 2nd MB. The system was that 1st MB was the equivalent of A levels but could be taken within the aegis of the university. Then there were two pre-clinical years and the enormous hurdle of 2nd MB. This was the Beecher's Brook of the course and many would fall. If one was able to re-mount there would be 3rd MB (pharmacology, bacteriology and pathology,) 4th MB (forensic medicine and public health before finals, 5th MB which was Medicine, Surgery and Obstetrics. As Beecher's Brook approached I was nowhere near ready and failing was probably, looking back, a good thing. It was very unpleasant at the time. It should be said at this stage that the method of revealing our results was exquisite in its cruelty. The Secretary, a fine man, would come out of his office with a piece of paper and pin it to the notice board. It was a list of those who had passed. Thus, each candidate would strain to find their name going up and down the list in case nerves had made them miss. It was like when you lose a familiar article. You feel that if you look hard enough the article will magically reappear. In this case, of the eighty names in our year less the one who had fled the corpses, thirty-three names were missing including my own. The list contained only forty-four names! The arch villain was the Professor of Biochemistry, who flexing his academic muscles, failed thirty-three out of the eighty. The process was so exhausting that most of the forty-four who passed said they would not have retaken it.

Having said that, the Secretary was a wonderful man. He was slim, empathic and concerned. He was the nearest thing to counselling any of us experienced during our five years. He must have talked to thousands of desperate medical students quietly, deferentially and constructively, telling us what our next steps could and should be.

I now needed a plan. I briefly returned home but there was no sympathy there. My father and step-mother had had their own hard lives and were uncompromising in their opinion of the younger generation. My father had started work when he was thirteen as a pit messenger boy in the Rhondda Valley and after his working day had attended night school every weekday night. Whilst working in Southport he had attended Manchester University in the evenings and obtained a BA(Admin) with which he wanted to rule the world only foiled by Adolf Hitler who had interfered with his career. He actually took it personally. The idea that someone should have the luxury of a full-time education and fail was totally inexplicable to him.

More importantly, I realised they were going to be no use to me now. I had no one to rely on but myself. I scrutinised the calendar. There were twelve weeks before the start of the next term of which the last two would be solid examination re-sits. Therefore, I had to earn enough money to keep myself for twelve weeks from eight weeks of work leaving two weeks to revise and two weeks for the examination. I applied for and got a job at an offset litho factory making inks and solvents. I worked every day I could and fortunately paid no tax so knew that financially I could do it. At the end of the eight weeks I managed to look after a flat for some friends on holiday but to also care for their two budgerigars. The thing was that my two weeks revision was total. I would do nothing else but revise. It wasn't just that I wanted to do Medicine; it was that there was nothing else I wanted to do! Solitary confinement must be bad but I doubt if it is worse than solitary confinement with two budgerigars! They squawked and squawked for hours. As the days went by and my nemesis approached I became more and more dis-enamoured with those wretched creatures. I found that opening and closing a black umbrella was a good way of upsetting them. Eventually I managed to put a cork on the end of my air gun and took pot shots at them. Please do not worry. No budgerigars were injured in the making of this doctor. I just managed to survive with my sanity – I think.

As a belt and braces safety net we were advised to also apply for the London Conjoint examination which would also allow us through the gate of 2nd MB. They had their examinations on two Mondays, a week apart, in London. This meant that, as the Leeds examinations were on Tuesdays to Fridays also a week apart, I would have to go to London on the Sunday for an exam on the Monday, return that night for an exam on Tuesday and repeat the whole process the next Sunday. Two solid weeks of examinations. The main thing was – it could be done. The first Conjoint exam was anatomy and we were to be shown a body and questioned. All oral tests are nerve-wracking but this one was in a strange place. Mercifully, Howard who lived in London and who was in the same boat, put me up. Despite the tension of the situation because our careers depended on it we went to the pub on the Sunday night. We must have thought it was too late by then. Howard asked me if I would like a game of darts. I was very average at darts so agreed and was given the pub darts. That was when Howard pulled out his own personal darts. They were like javelins about a foot long. Never underestimate Howard van Pelt!

On the morning of the first examination I walked into the anatomy room, looked at the body and recognised - nothing! Sometimes when twins are born, one twin is the mirror image of the other. The body in front of me was such a mirror image! The heart was on the right, the appendix was on the left. The examiners must have scoured the morgues of London for such a body. I have no doubt it is possible with concentration and thought for the brain to cope with the changes but in those conditions? Only the glee at discomforting desperate medical students could have motivated them to do that. No doubt the examiners opened several bottles of claret that night as they enjoyed their trick. But it was not a good start!

The rest of that fortnight is now a blur. I have little remembrance of it apart from the surgical viva with surgeon with a fearsome reputation and with whom I had had little experience. He led me onto the spread of cancers through the lymphatic system. At one point I suggested a chest X-ray. This was a foolish move as being pre-clinical I had no knowledge of chest X-rays. The surgeon, the dreaded Henry knew this of course and immediately asked me what I knew about chest X-rays. He made it clear that I should not mention the subject again. Where else in the lymphatic system might cancer spread, he probed. I knew that although the lymphatics from the right lung and breast drained into the right subclavian vein all the rest of the lymphatics drained into the left subclavian vein passing through a large lymph node named after Virchow (pronounced ver cof.) "We should examine Virchow's node" said I groping for salvation. In those days all manner of anatomy, pathology and diseases were named after medical heroes from the past. The modern dumbing down recoils at such personality cult and all such names have been expunged. Those pioneers will soon be forgotten fostering the belief that everything has been discovered by the current generation. Henry pounced. "Who was Virchow?" I felt I had been pierced by that question. I had no idea. He then insisted that Virchow had died by cutting his own throat and asking me about branches of the carotid artery and whether the knife had gone in transversely or obliquely. I later found that this was pure mischief as Virchow died peacefully of heart failure aged 80! At the end of it all I retreated to the only sanctuary I had, the home of my sister in Dorset. Not for me the wait outside the Secretary's office for the list that may or may not have my name on it. Neither would I ring the Medical School. I had done enough. It was over. It was in the hands of God. One morning my little nephew appeared with a letter. "Letter for Uncle Charles." I opened it. I had passed. I had fallen at Beecher's Brook but remounted! And, with apologies for mixing metaphors, it was only the end of the beginning. A few days later we who remained gathered for our three years clinical work. There were twenty of our number who didn't make it. Even those who passed 2nd MB first time swore they would never take it again!

PART TWO
CLINICAL

CHAPTER 3
CROSSING THE ROAD

Leeds General Infirmary

Although still based in the Medical School we now crossed the road into Leeds General Infirmary. It was our Rubicon. We knew the future would be hard but those days of dissecting were now gone. My first experience was to be taught how to take a medical history by a Registrar who treated us as though we were people. It was so refreshing, stimulating – and revealing. Taking a history would be 70% of the journey to a diagnosis at the very least. We were on our way! We learnt a new language of the patients - making water, (passing urine,) costive, (constipated,) and physic, (passed a motion.) The downside was that every patient in Leeds had a chest problem from years of breathing polluted air and so by the side of each bed was a sputum pot whereby they would from time to time spit their thick green sputum. Blood, vomit and diarrhoea are not particularly pleasant, but for me, sputum was the worst. Talking about it makes me feel sick as does writing about it now. I had no portent that their sputum was to be my bread and butter!

A further progression was that I now shared a different flat with two other medical students. They were lovers of classical music and other things which I did not share so we had the advantage of not competing on the same ground. We got on well together and there were fewer distractions! One by one we were introduced to the different medical faculties and the consultants who ruled them. They were not exactly mini gods but not far off. Each one had a team or firm and each member of the team was expected to be utterly hostage to the wishes of the consultant. To be fair, they had all gone through World War Two and more than done their bit. The ones who went abroad had at times worked continuously, sometimes for years. The ones who stayed had to do all the work for the ones who had been called away. They had worked selflessly and expected their subordinates to do the same. Those subordinates were in the process of becoming our masters and had the same expectation of us. Also they had fought against fierce competition to get where they were. They were tough, some a bit unpleasant but we could live with that. We knew where we were with them.

At some stage those days disappeared and the power of the consultant with it. Probably it was the rising power and control of the NHS that did for them as it did for the family doctor. However, the power of the consultant was a stabilising influence on the aspiring doctor. They had the experience and we followed experience. This has now been replaced by guidelines and clinical governance. I know what I would like operating on me in the middle of the night.

Refreshing as the clinical work was we still plodded through lectures on pharmacology, bacteriology and pathology. The professor of pathology decided that lectures were not quite the thing. Instead we would have a *conversazione*. I think this meant that learning would be open with questions and answers and open discussion rather than the formal lecture. I don't remember any two-way discussion going on but there is no doubt he liked the word *conversazione*. The pathology department seemed to have limitless specimens of just about everything and just about everything was described in terms of food. There was the 'nutmeg liver,' the 'sago spleen,' the 'berry aneurysm,' the 'chocolate cyst,' the 'strawberry naevus,' and the 'walnut brain.' The normal prostate was the size of a horse chestnut. There were many more and very helpful they were.

When the pathologists wanted to show us an example of anything they would always find the biggest and most ghastly specimen they could find. I remember one proudly showing the enlarged spleen of Felty's syndrome. It was the size of a large marrow! In fact all the clinical people showed exaggerated examples of whatever disease they were demonstrating to the extent that one could have made the diagnosis from the other end of a football pitch. What a contrast years later in general practice where the patients would present long before signs were apparent.

One of the morbid delights of pathology was that we were obliged to attend post-mortems. They were frankly ghastly. One poor chap had died of empyema, a condition where after pneumonia the pleural cavities fill with pus. In this particular case the whole of the chest seemed to be pus and the pathologist was emptying it out into a bowl. The thing was he was doing it with a teacup! Yes a teacup. An ordinary teacup that you might use for having a cup of tea! I now always drink tea out of a mug. On another occasion we were filing in when there was some consternation and one of our ladies was being pushed to the rear. Her father had died in the hospital that night and it was his post-mortem we were to view! What crass thoughtlessness. But our medical masters had the empathy of a two-year-old. Another horror was a parachutist who had landed on a pylon. One side of his body had been seared and was a huge scab. He took ten days to die. One of several reasons I have never done a parachute jump.

I mentioned earlier that we created a conveyor belt of chips for frying. Food was always a problem. During our lunch times we would stroll the half mile down the Headrow to John Lewis which had a food department. They often had food tempters, mostly cheese and biscuits. We would amble in and take a sample and after a short wander in the store would come round again – and again. We would do anything for free samples. But one day Geoff Slater and I hit the jackpot. We were walking across Queen Square when a young lady asked us if we would drink some beer! Her people would pay us ten shillings for the favour! I daresay nowadays we would have been offered drugs or sex or worse but these were innocent times. We had to go to a room with several others, drink some Jubilee Stout (too sweet for me but hey!) and then give our opinion of it. For this we each walked away with a ten-bob note! It was not a dream but it never happened again.

Casualty

Great old hospitals like Leeds General Infirmary preceded the NHS. Some of the old traditions lingered and one was the hierarchy of the porters. At the front of the grand old building designed by the same architect who designed St Pancras station were the front door porters. They were top of the tree and as the consultants walked in they would slide their names across on a board indicating that Dr so-and-so or Mr so-and-so was in the building. These consultants had originally worked outside the Infirmary but held honorary appointments within the Infirmary whereby they worked for free but gained huge exposure to the human pathology of the time. They were therefore often referred to as 'honoraries.'

At the rear of the hospital was the back door manned by back door porters and these admitted the casual patients who arrived from the teeming back to backs of Leeds. Hence it was known as Casualty. No name is to be left unchanged by people whose only justification to existence is to change names, and Casualty is one such which has fallen by the wayside. Firstly it went to A & E (accident and emergency) except that not all the patients were accidents and certainly not emergencies. In America ER (emergency room) became the vogue and this country followed with ED (emergency department) which shares its initials with erectile dysfunction.

MISSION ACCOMPLISHED

To us it was Casualty and at Leeds it had its own patriarch in 'Father' Ellis. He was universally referred to as Father and was held in unalloyed respect. The reason for this was that he did the business. Most emergency departments are, due to the nature of the problems, chaotic. It took a special kind of orderly commander to make it otherwise and Father was that commander. As the 'casuals' were brought in Father would greet them from his chair, slightly raised as I remember, and assess the situation. Lacerations requiring suture would be referred to us, the students. Others would be sent to the appropriate department by putting the patient on a coloured line. Thus an ear nose and throat problem would follow one colour through the maze of the Infirmary until they would find the ENT section. Eye problems would follow another and so on. This was terribly efficient and probably unique at that time in the country. The ophthalmology track was a challenge to students and patient alike because it eventually ended up in the dark. When the ophthalmologist wished to get a really good view of the retina he or she adds drops to the eye which dilates the pupil. This gives them a good view but means the patient has blurred vision for several hours. This precludes driving although probably most patients did not arrive by car but it made crossing the Leeds roads a real danger. The simple way to dilate the pupils was to have the patient in the dark. So the eye department was always blacked out. We, the students, would find ourselves groping around in the dark with a load of patients who already had impaired vision. We used to speculate that there might be some who had been there for days still trying to find their way out!

Casualty was the poor relation of medicine then because consultants were not universally appointed to Casualty and there was no career structure. But we could see the potential and how easy it was if there was a leader and chain of command. Leeds had appointed such a leader and he was universally known as 'Father.' It all came from the military and although not suitable for the complex procedures today which function best in teams it was perfect for the time. Father was a great teacher as well. We were taught to suture and reduce fractures and above all to examine patients properly. Casualty was exciting and we loved it. We liked the excitement, the variety and the fact that we now had a place in the career we had chosen.

One strange thing happened then but was barely noticed at the time. Many of the patients attended with burns, some severe which would be treated in the Infirmary but came under the aegis of Casualty. They would be discharged as soon as possible but followed up in the burns clinic. Thus every week a long queue of patients would sit in the corridor waiting their turn. At the head of this queue would sit Father and next to him would sit the plastic surgeon. As the patient had his or her turn, Father would describe the problem and then turn to the plastic surgeon and ask him if there was any intervention he would like to make. Inevitably the surgeon, who had a long and unhappy face, would pause and then shake his head. The poor unfortunate would then move on to be replaced by another. We, the students, were witness to this most miserable of clinics. The patients, who had attended this clinic, possibly several times just in case there was anything that could be done, seemed to play their part in this miserable process.

Then one day appeared Jimmy Saville. How or why or by what permission or request he appeared no-one knew but the fact is he was welcome prancing around and entertaining this doleful queue. To be fair, such was the nature of the burns clinic, the intervention of the Black Death would have been a welcome alternative. The strange thing, in the light of the revelations about Jimmy Saville, was that at the time we never perceived any sexual motive to his performance. He just seemed weird. He was not the type of person you would approach because his whole persona seemed utterly superficial. I spoke to my colleagues and the overwhelming impression was of someone who was not interested in any form of sex. He appeared to be asexual.

General Surgery

I was lucky with the general surgeons I was attached to because they were blunt but funny. Sir Lancelot Spratt was not an imaginative invention. They were sexist but harmlessly so. "Women are all the same!" declared one surgeon one day, "they just have different faces so you can tell them apart." We speculated as to the cause of this statement. Trouble at home? They were Yorkshire. "Go East of Filey and you take your life in your hands!" They were one of us. One drank tea out of the saucer! They were also on top of their game. Surgery was physically hard in those days and still can be. But the philosophy of minimal invasion had not yet taken hold. The concept that the biggest complication of surgery was the surgery itself was yet to come. Speed was a priority, probably because of the risk of anaesthetic especially with the state of the lungs of our patients.

Our prize surgeon was the professor of surgery who had a worldwide reputation. His speciality was ulcerative colitis, an often-lethal condition which could be cured nevertheless by total removal of the colon. One of the complications of UC was cancer and sometimes if a rectal stump was left cancer could occur there. The solution was the abdo-perineal operation which meant total removal of colon, rectum and anus and an ileostomy bag. No patient liked the thought of such an operation but many had already nearly died from an exacerbation. The trick was to convince them when they were well. That was the best time to operate. The professor was a brilliant world-famous zealot and I remember him announcing to us one day that he would be doing a great disservice to a particular lady if he allowed her to leave the hospital with her colon. He clearly thought of people in terms of their colons. We were occasionally permitted into his research department. On the floor of this large room were large sheets of paper. On each piece of paper was carefully placed the colon of his patients. He was slim and lively and would skip round the room with a story about each one which he would refer to as though they were the actual person in the room. The truth is that quirky though it was we were mightily impressed.

I managed to avoid doing a rectal examination until my fifth year. I wanted to be a doctor not a person who inserted their gloved finger up other people's bottoms! How wrong could I be? The lady in question had intestinal obstruction and my examining finger felt a large obstructing cancer. She was operated on but died a week later. There is no doubt of the usefulness of the rectal examination but leaping forward I found it is not quite the same in general practice. Years later, being called out to a neighbouring village during a heavy night on call I was greeted by a very comfortable lady who offered me a cup tea. I was hungry and thirsty so accepted which delayed the history taking somewhat. Just as I was examining her husband she appeared with a plate of sandwiches which again I accepted. He needed admission and when on the phone to the admitting doctor I was asked, 'what did you find on rectal examination?' I had to sheepishly admit that I had not done one. I could hear our consultants at Leeds shouting at me. I decided never again to be caught out. A few years after that when on call I was called to a rather obese lady with diarrhoea. I insisted on performing a rectal examination but after insertion of the digit she explained that her diarrhoea was profuse, explosive and imminent! I was like the little boy with his finger in the dyke. I needed to remove the finger to continue with my visits but the consequences could be catastrophic. It is only a digression but don't ask any more!

Thoracic surgery

The thoracic surgeons were exciting because heart surgery was just taking off. Thanks to the dreaded streptococcus and rheumatic fever there were many damaged heart valves about and the surgery of valve replacement was developing. The first heart transplant had been done and emulated in the UK with poor results. But this was the frontier and it was moving all the time. The difficulty was, at that time before the heart-lung machine had been developed, that blood would go into one end of the patient as it bled out from the surgery. Blood donors from all over the West Riding would be called to make sure supplies were able to cope. And progress was made. When the heart-lung machines appeared the operations would last five hours with a team of technicians and helpers and, and this was the innovation, canned music in the theatre! So any connection we had with this frontier speciality was prized.

One of our teachers seemed to be sometimes the worse for wear when he gave his lectures as we noted when we arrived at the lecture theatre to find him sleeping in an ante room. Despite this he gave one of the best pieces of advice and one which the students of today might hear. He told us to go into the pubs and clubs of England. I can hear him saying it now and the point he was making (we did not need much encouragement for the substance of the advice) was that we should meet real people, see who they were, see how they lived, their aspirations and lives. An aphorism which I adopted years later with my GP Trainees was that people are our raw material; if you don't like them do something else! I found it extraordinary as the years went by to find doctors who don't actually like people! People live and so should the doctor. Now in the twilight of my life I have become a professional patient and have to receive the interrogation of junior doctors who analyse my drinking habits as though it is crack cocaine! Even my daughter who is a junior doctor herself says they haven't lived.

Infectious diseases

Leeds had an infectious diseases hospital at Seacroft with another inspiring consultant. His teaching interested me and gave me a lifelong interest in infectious diseases, ancient and modern. We are now locked in a pandemic whereby we follow the science. The history of infectious disease is the experience and I have no doubt that we should have been guided by experience. For a start our consultant would have recoiled at the practice of admitting an unevaluated infectious disease to a general hospital. Granted the old infectious disease hospitals have gone but we rapidly built isolation hospitals and failed to use them. The truth is as I write that 10,000 people have caught Covid 19 in hospital but our Government has closed the pubs where there has been little evidence, if any, of acquiring the virus there.

However, to return to the narrative, it was decided that we should all have a smallpox vaccine. The last outbreak, in this country I believe was in 1960, but the memory and tales of smallpox were the possession of every adult at that time. The vaccine was the live virus of cowpox known as vaccinia and hence the origin of the word vaccine and vaccination. It had allegedly been discovered by Jenner in 1798 but was certainly used by farmer Benjamin Jesty at Worth Matravers in Dorset in 1774. No doubt it had been used in Asia long before either of them.

I don't remember anybody else having the vaccine so I may have given consent. Volunteering would have been most unlike me. The vaccine was contained in a small polythene tube about one centimetre long and a millimetre thick which had to be cut. A small blob of vaccine was then dropped on the upper arm and pressed in with the flat of a needle so just the tip punctured the skin to the minimum degree. Primary vaccination needed no more than ten such pricks but boosters could go up to thirty or more. Each tube could produce four drops if required. Since smallpox was eradicated in 1977 all the above information is of historical interest only! The consequence of course was that I was now suffering from cowpox. Over the next few days my arm began to swell and my temperature went up. At one time it was 102*F. I showed the red and swollen arm to the consultant who was quite unimpressed. If he was not bothered then nor was I. The next day, a Saturday I played football as usual and as I remember it, it was a bitterly cold day and I was the only warm person on the pitch!

The time with infectious diseases must have had an effect on me because later when we had the opportunity to elect (it was known as the elective period) to do what we pleased I chose to go to Kenya. Undoubtedly those Jungle Doctor books, fed to me by Mrs Murgatroyd to occupy me when my mother was ill, by Paul White were the stimulation for this. The consultant Dr Stevenson at Seacroft was a superb teacher and brilliant doctor. I dread to think what he would be thinking now if he could know that during this curious Covid 19 pandemic that patients with infectious diseases were being admitted to general hospitals.

General Practice

One week accompanying a GP was considered a reasonable introduction to general practice in the 1960s. The profession was at a very low point and was revived by the Charter of 1966 none of which was known to me at the time. The thing I remember most is that the GP I was to accompany was one of the most hard-working doctors I have ever known. His name was Barry Colville and unbeknown to me was a bit if a legend. GPs could have up to 3,500 patients on their list which was near breaking point for workload. However, if the average number of patients for the practice was 3,500 the individual doctor could have more. Dr Colville had nearer 4,500 patients and he coped using one very simple technique. He worked and worked and worked! As a medical student this concept frightened me to death! We met and started at his surgery at 8 am and saw patients until they stopped coming. Each person clearly knew and trusted him. I wrote something down about every patient and after a few days ran out of paper. Then there were prescriptions and coffee and we then sped out and about Leeds. At about 1pm we arrived at his house where dinner was ready on the table. I was ready and hungry but at about 1.20pm he rose and once more we toured and visited the unwell of the district. At some stage, and by now my head was spinning, we returned for the evening surgery which ended at about 7pm. This process was repeated for each of the five days I was present. Dr Colville, of course, on top of this, had on-call duties some nights and weekends but I hadn't the courage to ask him about that. I wrote something down about each patient and he would always ask my opinion and congratulate me if he approved. I think I did pretty well but the sheer volume of problems was, at the time, overwhelming. I realise now that all new doctors to a list felt that feeling of being overwhelmed. The incumbent of course had built up knowledge over a long period. At the end of the week I had made up my mind that I would never become a General Practitioner. How strange that I spent thirty-eight years doing just that and subsequently followed it up for another seven years with assorted locums.

CHAPTER 4
3RD MB

At the end of the third year we had more examinations, this time in pathology, pharmacology and bacteriology. I remember very little about them except the bacteriology exam was preceded for me by three days of diarrhoea from presumably a bug. My flat mates observed that they had just seen a twenty-one-year-old man in out patients with bowel cancer! It was their way of taking my mind off things. So it was that on the day of the bacteriology viva as I bounded up six flights of stairs to the top of the pathology building, I was more concerned with my continence than bacteria. Slightly short of breath I walked in to be greeted, not by good morning or how are you but "what are the causes of venereal disease?" In my flustered state I replied, "promiscuity" which, although the correct answer, was one that I knew was not wanted by the examiners! I think I must have had to resit one of the examinations so took a job at an offset litho factory in south Leeds for the summer so had money and plenty of time for revision.

As a result in September I was ready to begin my fourth year at Leeds Medical School.

But first there was a respite holiday. I had joined the Boys Brigade when I was eleven and since leaving continued to attend the annual camps as an officer. This was 1966 and we camped east of Edinburgh. On the second Saturday we were there England were playing Germany for the Jules Rimet trophy and we were to play the local firemen – for glory. The first half was tricky as they were big and good and we went into half time at least three goals down. We then went into a nearby building and watched England win. There is no doubt it fired us up and we brought on Davy Brown, a fast and nippy left winger. I do not know why he did not play in the first half but he certainly did in the second and played out of his skin. At the end of the afternoon, England had won the Jules Rimet trophy and the 7th Southport Boys Brigade had beaten the local firemen by 5 goals to 4!

Public health

My summer vacation spent working at the offset litho factory had given me a taste for public health. It was a minefield of potential disasters. The etching solution consisted of a mixture of dilute hydrochloric acid, sulphuric acid and mainly chromic acid. The vats were huge and open. The fumes were awful, corrosive in fact. Worst of all was the cleaning of the vats with ammonia. This involved crawling along a plank across the vat with no safety rail or net. It was the only job I could not do; the ammonia was simply too strong. Part of the appeal was the history of public health which was also the history of our industrial revolution. We really are an extraordinary country. In 1911 the incidence of venereal disease in our cities was causing alarm. One person in ten had syphilis and the incidence of gonorrhoea disease was perhaps four times as common. A Royal Commission was set up which reported in1917 and as a result, VD clinics were set up. Patients were given money for the bus fare and a little more to buy beer to flush the bacteria away. Ironically in 2017, the hundredth anniversary was totally unknown to the GUM (Genito Urinary Medicine) clinics of today. I was realising that I had a love of history which played a huge part of the rest of my life.

Part of the training was to visit various industrial sites across the city. Leeds Fireclay was one and it was comical to see the rows of gents urinals stacked all over the place which was one of their products. The issue was the dust of the fine clay which our patients inhaled adding to the cause of that dreaded sputum which I hated. There was one top secret shed there where it was said the clay was so fine it floated as a colloid.

As part of the hands-on approach to learning that we had become used to we learnt that we were to visit a coal mine. This was particularly exciting to me as my father had been sent down the pit, in fact the Naval Colliery in the Rhondda valley, when he was thirteen. Many boys went to the coal face but his mother would not countenance it so he became a pit messenger boy. As a result she sacrificed several shillings a week. But as a consequence he went everywhere in the mine including the coal face and getting a much better idea of colliery life. He also recited the tales of his grandfather who had managed to retire in good health and died eventually aged 86. This colliery near Wakefield was said to be a model colliery and therefore suitable for us. We arrived, were briefed on safety and donned our helmets. We descended by a lift that seemed to go on forever. It cranked its way down until finally it stopped and we got out. Things did not look so bad. There was a large tunnel which I recollect to be the similar size to a London underground tunnel. We began to walk this dimly lit tunnel which had on the right-hand side a conveyor belt which continually transported newly hewn coal. We walked and walked for somewhere between half and one mile. It all seemed pretty harmless until it was clear we were coming to a dead end. In the gloom it was difficult to understand what was going on until our guide pointed to the bases of the tunnel, right and left. The seam was two to three feet thick and it was only this seam being mined so it would not mix with the rest of the rock. We were each taken to this small aperture on our knees. As I partly went in I could see men on their bellies with grinding machines almost as big as them, grinding away at the seam and shifting coal back onto the conveyor belt. Rock was above them and two to three feet lower, rock was below them. They were the meat in this ghastly sandwich. But it was a sandwich which had driven our machinery, our engines, our ships. We are still living on the legacy of those men. The whole of their day's work was spent like this – and this is what got me, this was a good colliery. Others were worse and the pits of my father and his grandfather's day would have not had machinery to grind the seam. For them it was a pickaxe. Hence his grandfather, Joseph Roberts, had become a hafter in retirement, a man who fixed the pick to the shaft.

Afterwards we went, well we really had to go, to the famous Dolphin at Wakefield. It was notorious for beer, music and strippers who were all transgender men. My first feeling was one of revulsion but after three pints they did not look so bad. I went to pass urine or as they say in Yorkshire, make water. The porcelain of the gents toilet was smeared with black, green and some red, sputum where the miners had spat into the stall. They breathed that dust all their working day and got rid of some of it in the pub. It said it all really. When mines were being closed my father could never understand why anyone would want to keep them open.

Forensic medicine

Our professor of forensic medicine (Polsen) was one of the giants of the age so our lectures were entertaining as well as educational and made well needed light relief. The notorious murders of the age were dealt with and we began to understand gunshot wounds and all manner of manifestations of death. Straight forward murder could look like suicide and vice versa. Occasionally pictures would appear of people we recognised from the newspapers and we would be told the real story. It was somewhere between Sherlock Holmes and *Silent Witness* without being near either of them!

One I remember was of a man lying in bed with the shotgun he had ostensibly killed himself propped up neatly in a corner. Was it suicide or was it murder? It was demonstrated that it was quite possible for the recoil of the shotgun to place it across the room.

Surgical Dresser

It was always considered at Leeds that we got stuck into our studies through practical application. One of these was to be a surgical dresser and we were fitted with pagers and called for new surgical admissions or urgent surgery. We would clerk the patients, shave them pubically as was the fashion then and assist with the operation, holding retractors and snipping sutures. All the time we would be learning, apprentice style, from the nurses the doctors and the patients. We would be on for sometimes days and nights at a time and in the quiet times could get into our books. At night there was always bacon and eggs in the refrigerator to help ourselves to.

Most of it was straightforward and repetitive but one interesting thing happened when dressing at St James's Hospital. It was a hot July Sunday and very quiet. We had pagers so four of us went out into the grounds and probably with others played football all day. We kicked the ball and ran and sweated and because the pagers stayed quiet we kept on until it was nearly 10pm and not only had it gone dark but we were seriously dehydrated. The pub opposite St James's was called the Cemetery probably because there was a cemetery there so possibly not the best name for a pub next to a hospital, especially as, at that time, St James's tended to be the last stop for the elderly. We ran in and being mischievous, as I can be, I downed my pint in one. Duncan, did not drink but had a pint of orange and downed that in one as well. We bought fresh pints and mine went down quickly as did his pint of lime juice. We bought a third and this time Duncan downed his pint of Peppermint in one before I had started. Down it went and there was still time for last orders. We used to say that happiness was a pint at closing time and I drank my fourth pint and he drank his fourth pint of cordial, this time blackcurrant. There is no doubt that we were seriously short of fluid and no doubt that we had replaced it expeditiously. But here was the point. The next morning when we reported for duty once more, Duncan had a prize hangover. I was fine and fresh. His hangover was certainly not due to alcohol. I suppose the logical inference would be to avoid soft drinks but it taught me that there are many other causes of hangover than just alcohol. My only alcoholic drink was beer; I never had wine until I was thirty or spirits until I was thirty-five.

CHAPTER 5
4TH MB

THE EXAMINATIONS AT THE END of the year were in public health and forensic medicine and I passed. It could have been because I actually knew the stuff or because I had serious plans for the holidays and did not want to re-sit. The actual examination was unremarkable but I remember the forensic medicine viva well. I had been shown a picture of the deceased with froth coming out of his mouth. What were the causes of such a phenomenon was the question. I knew that it could occur during a fit and frothy sputum was a feature of heart failure. It could also occur in respiratory failure particularly due to barbiturates. The exquisite torture of the viva is that the interrogator always wants a little more, sometimes and perhaps especially when there isn't any more! The interrogator was one of our lecturers but with him was an external examiner from Norway. I had exhausted all causes known to me. They were looking at me expectantly as though they could see me scouring the depths of my memory banks. "Ectoplasm," I blurted in desperation. The Norwegian appealed to our lecturer for explanation. In the victim, persecutor, rescuer triangle I had found my rescuer. No-one knew the Norwegian for ectoplasm. "As in a seance," I threw in for good measure. This muddied the waters nicely as now ectoplasm and seances swirled round in Anglo/Norwegian. The rest of the viva was taken up and literally lost in translation. I think they enjoyed it because they passed me and I could execute my plans for the summer.

Elective period – Kenya

At the end of the fourth year, although in the three clinical years we did not officially have holidays, we were given the opportunity to elect to do something and go somewhere entirely different for our medical education. I had a sister in Kenya and so Kenya would be my target. She had gone to become a hairdresser in Nairobi in 1958. The flight had taken two days but the tales of that wonderful country had enchanted me. It was strange on landing to see ostriches wandering near the runway. The first day on arrival I went for a walk over a nearby hill and into a small village. I was a curiosity but so were they to me. I stood for about an hour while I was questioned and I questioned the villagers. Goodness knows what they made of my naivety but I was only ever used to talking to people straightly as equals or in my case, subordinate to my medical masters. Then I walked back. The first evening I was there my sister invited all her friends round for a party and to show me off to them. I remember talking to them. There were twelve men present and six of them had bilharzia. To swim in an East African lake meant that you would have bilharzia, a parasite which eventually lodged in the bladder causing loss of blood and anaemia. At that time there was no cure. I had read about the colonial history of East Africa. There was adventure. It was exotic. It was romantic. It was exciting but the disease element was shocking. So many young men went out there only to acquire chronic illness or die young. But the temptation was too much. I wondered what had motivated those young men. During the course of the evening I casually mentioned that I had walked over the hill to the village nearby and talked to the people there. There was silence. No-one had ever done that or thought of it. They had roamed and flown all over East Africa but never wandered locally.

I had arranged to be attached to the Kenyatta National Hospital in Nairobi, previously the King George V hospital but renamed after independence in 1963. I was entranced. There were a few English students there but mostly from the three East African countries, Kenya, Uganda and Tanganikya, (renamed Tanzania.). Between them they had formed the Makerere Medical School. The pathology was overwhelming. All the patients had five conditions before they attended.

They all had some form of chronic malaria, bilharzia, hookworm, (these last two caused chronic blood loss) trachoma (an eye disease causing corneal scarring and blindness) and something else, which after fifty-three years, for the life of me I cannot remember. The registrar explained that myocardial infarction was very unusual there and gall bladder conditions a curiosity. Diabetes was almost unknown because the Type 1 patients died quickly and the population was too thin for Type 2 to be an issue. These were the days before HIV but malaria and tuberculosis were huge problems. There were people with leprosy on the roads and I thought it the biggest scourge until I was in general practice later and saw the effects of rheumatoid arthritis. Every few days lorries would arrive with wounded men. They had been fighting in the north against the Shifta, a local name for insurgents from Somalia. Some of the patients had walked up to fifty miles to get hospital treatment despite their five basic conditions and associated anaemia. One man had gone into heart failure and treated his swollen legs by taking slices out with his panga. The oedematous fluid leaked out but so also did the plasma proteins which osmotically kept the fluid in his blood vessels. Thus although it worked in the short term he was also losing precious protein. In the event the lacerations had become infected which was the reason for his attendance. Each patient had the most extraordinary story and pathology. I attended the hospital all day for a month before waking one day and thinking 'I am in a wonderful country and haven't seen it yet!'

Having been brought up in an exclusively white Anglo-Saxon/Celtic Protestant environment I had never had acquired racial prejudice. There was no-one to be prejudiced about so the undercurrent of racism was completely new to me. One of the pharmacy students at Leeds was a native of Nairobi, of Indian origin. We made contact and decided to meet in a bar in the centre of town. It was quite exciting to travel five thousand miles to meet a friend for a drink just as we might have in Leeds. Kenya had become independent four years before so I asked Ramesh what had changed. "Well, the first thing is that I am in here with you!" This was a shock to me and I said so. He was good enough to take me to his house. It was by my standards a huge mansion. As we walked inside we looked through an open door where six or seven women were on the floor doing things with food. "That's my mother over there," he said, "those are my sisters and there is my aunt." We moved on upstairs where there were rows of high beds on each of which was a man lying on his back. We walked round them as Ramesh pointed out his father and uncles clearly having an afternoon nap and oblivious to us. This was a real culture shock to me but it then occurred to me that Ramesh would have endured a similar culture shock when he arrived in Leeds to do pharmacology.

At the medical school I became friendly with many of the African students from the three countries. They were a jolly lot and I got on well with them. There were some English students there and they were somewhat severe and aloof. Something had clearly happened because I came in one morning to find agitation amongst the Africans who approached me. "We have had a meeting Charlie," they said, "and decided to ban all the white students from our lectures." I was aghast. "But you don't mean me do you?" I said with a mixture of temerity and confidence. "Oh no, of course not," they replied. Nothing more was said so for the ensuing weeks I was the only white person there. Sometimes events are labelled as racism when the real reason has nothing to do with racism. They did not like stuck up, pompous arrogant people. Neither did I!

I had heard that there was a VD clinic in one of the shanty towns I should attend. Nairobi had two shanty towns at that time, Pumwani and Eastleigh. Shortly after I left the government decided that shanty towns were undesirable and bulldozed Eastleigh making twenty-five thousand people homeless. But the clinic I was visiting was in Pumwani. I trundled in using the Fiat 600 that my sister had lent me without ever thinking that such a thing might be dangerous. The most important thing with naivety is luck. The doctor running the clinic was one of those unsung heroes. The government did not want to acknowledge venereal disease so the clinic was starved of funds. Da Costa, for that was his name, ran his clinic on a shoestring in the most efficient way he could. He knew the clinic had to function with or without official approval. Every member of staff, therefore, was trained to do all roles and rotated every three months. So today's receptionist may have been taking swabs last week. Someone examining specimens under the microscope may soon have found themselves on admin duties. They all seemed content with this and it meant that if one was sick and unable to come in the clinic still functioned. So the patients arrived and arrived with their syphilis, chancres, chancroid, gonorrhoea and a host of non-venereal infections that those clinics attract. I was mesmerised and learnt so much, but not only about diseases. I learnt about people, their resolution and resilience. Ever since my mother had been ill when I was eleven and the lady who looked after me, the saintly Mrs Murgatroyd, had given me books about mission doctors in Tanganyika I had wanted to do mission work. Alas I was to learn that these countries were now independent and did not want help from anyone but themselves. My road was to be a different one but in the meantime I had my eyes on a flight to a mission hospital!

Flights from Wilson airport, Nairobi kept the mission hospitals supplied with essentials, in this case, radio equipment. I was twenty-two at the time and the oldest person on board. The pilot and the radio operator were younger. The hospital we were to go to was just over the border with Tanzania. As we flew the bush below revealed small villages but few roads. Years later when climbing Kilimanjaro I flew over the same area. There were roads lights, towns everywhere. The saintly Attenborough pontificates to the United Nations on the dangers of climate change but in his wonderful programmes he never mentions it. Human encroachment, not climate change, is the phrase he repeats. It is the real enemy of wildlife. The population of Kenya in 1967 was ten million. It is now forty-five million. Overpopulation always was and is the problem. Ironically the alleviation of poverty has eased one problem whilst making another one worse. The only solution is good education for young girls and contraception.

The landing strip was on a plateau which was jutting out over a plain like the prow of a ship. The hospital was in walking distance. I had no specific role so did my usual walkabout. I went inside and the thing I noticed was the smell, mainly of sweating bodies. But everybody worked and had a role. They were on the front line of fighting so much disease. As I walked outside I was almost overwhelmed by the beauty of the place. It was eventually time to go and we went slightly north. With Kilimanjaro on one side and the distant apparently endless

Serengeti on the other and the great soda lakes below, navigation aids were unnecessary. Those soda lakes, blue on the map were any colour but blue in fact. Greens, browns and the pink of the flamingos were like an artist's pallet. As we turned for home there was what looked like a star on the horizon. It was the reflection of the late sun from the drive-in cinema screen guiding us back.

By now I was wanting to see the country and what a country it was. The game parks were incredible. In those days even the Nairobi game park had lion but not now. In Tsavo we drove until we were stopped by three black rhino. When we tried to reverse there were four more behind us. There are no black rhino in Kenya now and even the white rhino have been transferred from South Africa. In Amboseli with Kilimanjaro looming in the south we were seen off by the senior matriarch of a herd of elephant. She was followed by a trio of teenagers. When she had seen us off she turned and lashed them with her trunk and shooed them back to the herd. At the water holes a solitary male would drink alone. About a hundred yards away another solitary male would wait, swinging his trunk waiting for his turn to be the solitary male at the water hole. Another hundred yards beyond him, through the haze another would stand patiently and another hundred yards beyond him would be another. As the first moved off each one would come closer, patiently waiting their turn. There were huge herds of buffalo, standing menacingly. Giraffe and zebra, so comical out of context were perfectly camouflaged in the haze. The country was magic. I wish in retrospect that I had taken photographs of these wonderful spectacles but I had become obsessed with warthogs. The idea of these relatively small, ugly, pugnacious and above all tasty creatures strutting round amongst the predators fascinated me. It was like roast pork being paraded in front of ravenous teenagers. They seemed out of place and yet very successful. So my 'holiday snaps' of Kenya were mostly of warthogs!

The beach was white, the sand not as good as Sandbanks in Dorset but good for all that. I met some friends and we slept on the beach for a few nights just north of Mombasa and next to the beach home of Jomo Kenyatta. We avoided the armed guards on the beach. My closest companion at night was a Dobermann Pincher bitch. A wonderful dog but one morning I woke with a huge blood-sucking tick on my chest.

I ripped it off instinctively. If you did that with a tick here it leaves the head in but this one took a significant bit of my chest with it! Having learnt all the unpleasant diseases that ticks carried in Kenya it never bothered me that I might catch any.

The planes used for our student flight flew pretty low and on the return journey to Cairo we flew through a thunderstorm which was a bit of a white-knuckle ride for those who did not like being in the middle of thunder and lightning. It was decided that we should stop in Cairo to give Egypt some tourists. As if a load of students had any money! This was 1967 and the war between Egypt and Israel had ceased and we were to be the first tourists to visit. There were Russian MiGs zooming around the skies and sandbags in front of all the hotels. I had never felt heat or humidity like it. I just took a cold shower and stood in front of a large fan and tried to cool off. This I had to do every few hours at night to get any sleep.

The next day we drove the seven miles to Giza to see the great pyramid and Sphynx. Years later when I did a detailed tour, Cairo had spread to Giza. I could see the pyramids from my hotel window. I can never see a hill without wanting to get to the top and immediately started climbing the great pyramid of Cheops. I was soon called down. Security!

Midder

It was a happy and confident student who returned to Leeds Medical School for the last year. One of our assignments was obstetrics or midwifery (midder for short) and it defined those who went to Leeds Medical School in those days. My friend who I met in the 1970s, Tommy Haw, had been a student at Leeds qualifying thirty years before I did. They too, had to do midder but for them it meant doing hundred home deliveries which they could all do within biking distance of the medical school to the north. It is now the University campus but in my day it was rubble from slum clearance. In Tommy's day it had been a teeming warren of back to backs with enough children born to furnish the needs of all the medical students and then some. Clearly this sort of experience was neither desirable or appropriate for us but our professor of obstetrics had his own agenda. He believed that the only way we could understand what labour meant was to be alongside the lady in labour. Ten such labours were to be observed during the four months we were resident in Croft House next to Leeds Maternity Hospital. Thus at some stage each group would be incarcerated in this place. We would wait for our call and when called sit with our patient until the labour was over, the baby born and the afterbirth removed. All the deliveries at LMH were potentially difficult. That is why they were sent there from all over the West Riding. The labour could last from any time up to 10 hours and we had to witness it throughout. I well remember my wife, who had four children herself explaining to her daughters, "there is no way you can wrap it up – it is just bl—dy painful!" Obviously if you have not had a baby there is no way you can appreciate fully what it is like but I think we did the next best thing. Also it was before the age of mass Caesarean section. Long labours ending with forceps or Ventouse was common. But undoubtedly the best thing about obstetrics was the happy ending. The worst thing was when it did not end happily.

One piece of excitement to liven up the day was to be asked to join the flying squad. I was watching *Call the Midwife* on television the other night and they mentioned fleetingly the 'flying squad' but with no explanation. The year they were covering was the same year I was doing midder in Leeds so I perked my ears up. However there was no embellishment of what this meant. In those days only difficult deliveries went to hospital. However, crises still occurred but they were at home. Hence the hospital doctors would sometimes go to the home instead of the patient coming to hospital. Home deliveries, if selected properly are very safe and there is something sublime about a lady giving birth in her own home. When it goes well it is so easy. One common crisis was the retained placenta. On this occasion the Registrar, the Senior House Officer and myself went off in the Registrar's car to somewhere in Leeds and went upstairs to a lady who had given birth successfully with the afterbirth stubbornly refusing to budge. She required anaesthetic and this was administered, by me, by sprinkling chloroform on to a gauze held in a wire frame. Chloroform and ether are both very good and safe anaesthetics. The placenta was duly removed producing relief in the team especially as there was no bleeding due to an injection which constricted the womb. As usual at the point of relief the more experienced doctor would reminisce about the old days. In this case it was when they had used ether, which is highly inflammable, and how the tension was at its highest when there was a burning coal fire in the room. What? They actually did that. How they did not blow up a few houses must have only been due to incredible luck. When they talk of medical advances they don't mention avoidance of destroying the neighbourhood!

So when we were not doing lectures or some other clinical obligation we would sit or lie in our rooms waiting. Waiting. My roommate was Yorkshire through and through. He was a man of few words. After a few years of close friendship with our group he announced that he was married. Since most of us had come straight from school this was a bit of a shock. After another year or so he announced he had a son! Few words! He would often take a breath as though he was going to speak and then think better of it and breath out. We would often lie on our beds next to each other, me trying to revise and he reading Dostoevsky. He would read *Crime and Punishment* hour after hour. After half an hour of intense concentration he would look up and say, "the cossacks have come into the village and raped all the women," and then sink back into intense reading again. Maybe another half hour would go by before he would stop to recite some atrocity or other. I used to wonder what he got out of Dostoevsky! The waiting for some poor lady to be admitted in labour led to much boredom on occasions. We found relief by pinning the picture of a naked, large-busted women to a cardboard grocery box and trying to hit her nipples with our airgun pellets.

One great thing about Croft House was that it had its own bar and I became the bar-cellarman. I ran a tight ship and documented everything and thanks to the honesty of the drinkers there it all went very smoothly. One Sunday morning I was called to the bar to be presented with an alien tankard! Our rugby team had played Manchester the day before. Manchester Union was two or three floors up in the Union building which meant that the 'cellar' to the bar was not in the basement but on the first floor. Therefore, as our team vacated the bar at throwing out time they had to go downstairs past the 'cellar.' On this occasion the cellar door had been left open and someone (probably all) had thought it was a good idea to pinch one of the casks. These casks were pretty heavy but it turned out thanks to drink that they could each take it in turns and carry it alone. Funny because the next day they could hardly lift it at all. It was Bonfire night and as they transported the cask up and down in the lift Charlesworth wrapped it in a coat and asked for a penny for the guy. Slater, Beresford, Papworth, Lishman and Saunders were undoubtedly accessories and others who know who they are! Anyway it was decided that my bar was the only safe place for this beer bonanza!

I was horrified. This was stolen property and was firmly ensconced in my bar. I was an accessory! It is a strange thing how one's view of a problem can change in an instant. In this case the instant occurred when it turned out that the connection equipment for my beer did not fit the connection of this beer. It suddenly became a problem and there is nothing men like more than being given a problem. I found years later that when women talk to men just wanting to express themselves men believe they are being asked to problem solve and respond accordingly much to the annoyance of the said women! The brains of Croft House including the perpetrators were taxed with the issue of how to get the beer out. OK, it was messy but we did it and having done it realised there was no way of storing it and by next day it was all gone.

The thing about the Croft House experience was that it was something that could only be shared by our medical school. I don't think any other medical school did it like that. Our professor was a humourless Scot whereas his successor, who I never knew well was a marvellous wit.

CHAPTER 6
THE FINAL YEAR

By now I was enjoying medicine. Amongst other things I did a locum for the professorial surgical team. The Reader in Surgery said I had performed with great panache. The truth was that I was in my element working but was still not a good student. I liked learning the things I liked learning and not what was supposed to be learnt. I visited the medical school library a lot but always discovered the wrong books. One such book was about Islamic medicine in which the physician, for reasons of decorum, was only permitted to examine the lady's hand. She would proffer a hand and he was supposed to diagnose pathology from any system of the body. This concept fascinated me. The hand like the face (ruled out in this case) tells us so much about the individual. Heart and lung disease may have signs in the hand. Neurological problems may be diagnosed from tremors, numbness or paralysis. So if you wanted a student who knew ten signs of liver disease or six signs of scleroderma in the hands, I was your man. Alas, medical requirements went beyond this and I was found wanting.

I also spent far too much time playing football. Apart from the Medical School matches and University league games I would be out on Woodhouse Moor on a Sunday playing all day with the locals in a huge game which continued as one group would arrive and another leave. The Irish contingent would be there, all trying to play like George Best. Then the Pakistani boys would arrive, slim, fit and skilful. There were the local Yorkshire boys, hard and unyielding. And amongst them all for most of the day a young medical student who should have been elsewhere. I should have been studying medical books but the outdoors and physical activity was what I craved. Eventually I took over a local side, mentioned above, the Woodhouse Wanderers. In my head I had decided that I would enjoy the physicality of life until I was aged 30, (a target which seemed a universe away,) after which I would knuckle down and be academic. In fact I managed to be eventually academic without ever giving up the physical. At the time I thought it was wrong but maybe I was right. At seventy-five I still run, cycle, windsurf, swim, and yes, play six-a-side football when picked!

There were other things happening in my life at the time which undoubtedly contributed but the chief one was lack of focus. Ironically despite wanting to exchange being a student for a doctor I prolonged the student bit a bit too much! As a result when the pass list went up, my name was not on it. At the time it was a great blow but the solution was to simply add another term. After a return home and more frost I needed a job and this opened up one of the most remarkable experiences of my life. I started work as a male nurse at High Royds Hospital, Menston, one of the great old Victorian asylums.

High Royds Hospital Menston

MISSION ACCOMPLISHED

Anyway, it was to this historical establishment that I was to work the summer. Most of the patients were taking phenothiazines, psychotropic drugs which produced Parkinsonian like side effects. They walked as though they were going to fall forward and had no facial expression. These zombie-like patients walked the huge, long corridors making it look like some horror film. The other side was that the place was a place of safety for people who needed asylum in the true sense of the word. It was relatively cheap to run and frankly, the life was not bad. In its day it had its own railway connection to the main line. The wards would be run by husband and wife who lived on the wards.

I was placed on the admission ward. This was real excitement and several times a day a new patient would arrive. They were all interesting and attracted my total attention. When patients become really high, they are termed manic and can be a huge problem. We had heard on the news of a man who had stolen a bus in the centre of Leeds and been driving it around wildly. A day later a man was brought in for stealing a bus and driving it around Leeds! It was that man. When he came in, he was as high as a kite and would not listen to, let alone, accept any treatment or management. How does one deal with such a problem? This is where experience counts. The charge nurse had dealt with such a situation before. I watched his technique in awe because the man in question was also on the edge of violence. First, he chatted with the patient, and in no time, they were the best of mates. This went on for about an hour until the charge nurse suggested they have something to eat – Asylum Duff! The food was good at High Royds, but was traditional English and heavy with old-fashioned puddings like Spotted Dick. A plate-load of a heavy suet pudding was brought in (known in the hospital as Asylum Duff and made for this very purpose), and they ate together. The charge nurse encouraged, and the patient agreed, on seconds, which he devoured. This was followed by thirds! The charge nurse himself, of course, only had a very small portion. He knew that, however manic you are, three large portions of Asylum Duff would calm even the wildest patient. Very soon, treatment was accepted and order restored. Goodness knows what they do now!

One interesting young man appeared one day who seemed entirely normal when I interviewed him. The first thing he asked me was what films were on and if the cricket team was still going. He seemed to be very familiar with High Royds. He revealed he was just back from the Netherlands where he had been in prison as a result of which he was going to write a book about the prison system there. This seemed a bit over the top and it was not quite clear why he had been imprisoned. It seemed to transpire that after that experience he fancied a more restful experience for the summer and had chosen High Royds. He had clearly been there before and knew all the facilities which were, in fact, very good. They played games, had teams and the grounds leant themselves to this. There was entertainment in the evenings and frequent films. The food was good and abundant. It was still not apparent why he was there or how he came to be admitted. I remember in my general practice career how difficult it could be to get quite seriously disturbed people admitted and here was this man able to walk into what was for him, summer camp. The way to do it, he said, was to arrive in the evening and tell a story that intrigued the psychiatrist on duty. In this case he had produced a story of domestic dysfunction in which he had slept with his mother. That always gets them, he revealed and they can't touch you for it. You have to hint at the possibility of more to come. Apart from the fact that spending your life in prisons and mental hospitals instead of working is probably not normal I could never put my finger on any aspect of mental illness in this man. Indeed, we got on very well and would often slip out at lunchtime or after work for a pint and darts at the nearby pub.

After a month of this very pleasant and stimulating existence the wheel of fortune took a dip and I was moved to Ward Five! Ward Five was the worst male psychogeriatric ward in the hospital. There were seventy beds to the ward, many pushed against each other with patients of the type I had never seen. I was unlucky enough to arrive on the alternate Tuesday that was bath and hair washing day. I took my duties seriously and was determined that every one of the seventy patients should be bathed and have their hair washed. Thus I was introduced to all of them in the space of a few hours in their mental and physical nakedness. To bathe each one was a battle and to wash their hair was another. One man was brought in by two male nurses. He was in the advanced stage of Huntington's chorea. He was once a man like me but was now brought in with as much voluntary movement as a scarecrow, his legs thrown forward in front of him. From his rectum hung the largest turd I have ever seen hanging, apparently unable to detach itself or be detached by the nurses. Another swore and spat continuously throughout the day but especially at bath time. Another entered the bath eagerly but once in fingered faeces from his rectum which he threw round the room. Another had suffered from severe hydrocephalus so his head was huge taking twice as long to wash his hair.

The effect of failing finals which I had thought I had coped with until now took its toll. At the sight of these poor souls my heart sank. They were wretched and I was joining them albeit to care for them. One of the features of depression is getting things out of proportion. Mountains out of molehills. And yet the young male nurses there were inspirational. They all felt that there was a chance however remote that these men would one day be returned to normality. The charge nurse of Ward Five was even more inspirational. Every time I hear the honours list with so many time servers honoured I wonder, angrily, why people like him were not recognised. He was kind, smart, efficient, caring and creating order and compassion in what I felt was hell upon earth.

I asked to see the Medical Superintendent. He asked me what the problem was. He knew I was distressed. "I think they ought to be put down," I said quietly. After a pause he said, "you don't really mean that." I repeated that I did and then gave him five names of the worst and most wretched patients there. He was very tolerant and I was moved to a manic-depressive research ward. Ward Five was an awful experience and probably I was not ready for it at that time but the uplifting experience was the selfless male nurses and charge nurse. They were the unsung heroes, the most extraordinary role models. I will never forget them. Strangely they were not the only unforgettable people. Years later I met one of the male nurses in a Leeds bar. We could each vividly remember all of those poor patients and cheerfully reminisce on our experiences.

The manic-depressive research was interesting. Manic depressive psychosis produces mood swings over weeks or months or years. It is debilitating when severe. It is often referred to as bipolar now and people only mildly depressed claim to be bipolar. This is not to be confused with those people who blow hot and cold with frightening speed to the dismay of those around them. They are cyclothymic and rarely fall into the hands of the psychiatrists. The patients we had were true manic-depressives and were given lithium. It would pass quickly through the body of most of us but would be absorbed in large quantities in these patients. When they were high they would resist treatment because they knew that sooner or later they would plunge into depression and were afraid that the lithium would precipitate this. One of the male patients had had a mother with the same condition. One day when he was low and she was high, his nerve had broken and he killed her. Years later a not dissimilar thing happened to one of my patients which haunts me still.

The last hurdle

At the end of what was in fact, despite the dip, a rather pleasant summer, I returned to medical school. There were about thirteen of us for re-sit and as far as I am aware we all had long and fruitful careers so maybe it was for the best. This time I behaved and worked and prepared myself for finals. They were duly taken but there was one twist in the tail. I decided to attend for the ceremony of the list, (that awful moment when the secretary pinned up the pass list which may or may not have your name on it.) and drove over from Southport to Leeds one December night. I had hired a car and in Oldham it broke down. I had no choice but to spend the night in the car outside a garage. Luckily I had a coat but nearly froze. Nevertheless I saw the list come out and my name was on it!

Bathos is a feeling of anti-climax and I was to have it in shed loads. The Medical pre-registration jobs ran from August to the end of January so there would still be five to six weeks to wait before I was able to work. Qualified as a doctor? Yes. But it was still back on the Christmas post once more for me. At least experience meant something there! Initially I had started delivering letters but quickly advanced the following year to parcels. This was much more fun. It meant travelling round Southport in a big van with a team. The van would trundle along and we would jump off with our parcels and on again. The postman was conducting operations and did little apart from cope with the large dogs. In my final year I had graduated as postman to Lord Street. Southport is a magnificent town and Lord Street was its jewel. More than a mile of boulevards and gardens with verandas along its length. Southport people loved to stroll from one end to the other just to see who they could meet. It was very convivial and as postman, I did just that but also pushing a smart cart full of parcels.

Somehow I was appointed houseman to the Orthopaedic department at Leeds General Infirmary. I was keen, a lot cleverer than I had so far revealed and physically very fit. I had no idea how that fitness would be so important. The main thing was that I would at last be able to work. The student days were over but I had milked all I could out of them. Now I would be a working doctor. I never looked back!

Our five years training had filtered out twenty five percent of our number. Today barely anyone fails. The great contrast is that our group was so robust and resilient. Today's batch does not fail but so many are fragile and precious. They are nurtured by their hospitals; not exploited. Their clinical assessors are carefully chosen and told which ones not to upset. At my local hospital, one new graduate is excused nights and weekends as it might upset her! To be fair they are assailed on all sides, by the non-clinical demands of NHS England, the doomsday scenario painted by the defence organisations, and working for a sacred cow pretending to be a Health Service.

BLUNT BUT GOOD

MISSION ACCOMPLISHED BOOK 2
BY DR CHARLES REES

CHAPTER 1
LEEDS

Had I been starting work on 1st February 2021 I would first have been vetted by Occupational Health. This would have been followed by a welcome from the Hospital Trust and the beginning of a week of induction. My colleagues and I would have been registered and given ID and basic information. We would have been advised on self-directed learning and how to get the most from our training. This was not work it was training. God knows what we were doing for the last five years! There would have been Core teaching, a Care/ Health support scheme, instruction on record keeping, the structure of notes and discharge letters. There would have been advice on medico-legal issues, mentoring and advice from the Guardian of Safe Working. We would have been told what to say to the microbiologists, given a talk on how to use the library, and introduction to Radiology services and Diabetes and Endocrine. Then there would have been a tour of the hospital which would include the Doctors' Mess, the Pathology laboratory, the General Office, the Mortuary, the Clinical Site Team, Emergency department and Acute Medical Unit. There would have been more instruction on Exception reporting. After lunch group sessions would advise on blood competencies, prescriptions, consent, death certificates and EIDF, (Edinburgh International Data Facility.)

The next day there would have been teaching on Acute Illness Management with a talk on the hospital at night, patient flow and the role of CST. The next day there would have been defibrillator training at the Clinical Simulation suite. The afternoon would have been given to an introduction to the numerous IT systems in use at the hospital. The following day time would be spent on the wards at last but not actually doing anything. We would have shadowed the present incumbent of our role because for a week the hospital employed twice as many doctors. Then there would be a talk from the Coroner and a discussion on bereavement. Then would follow a talk on fluid balance and NG tube replacement, anticoagulation training and to cope with it all, Resilience Training! At some stage there would be a course in survival skills which begs the question, surviving what! At some stage that I may have overlooked in the above programme, we would have been introduced to the virtual learning environment and Training Overview and Staff Wellbeing.

There would have been more teaching in infection control, (from the hospital environment which nurtured Norovirus and MRSA.) Basic life support and sepsis would come at some stage. An hour would have been spent on fire evacuation, and how to manage major incidents. There would have been advice on Personalised Care Plans and Compassionate Communication and of course at various stages there would have been evaluation of all the things that had been done. Modules would then be completed on Fire Awareness, Infection Control, Information Governance, Equality and Diversity and Human Resources, Moving and Handling, Health Safety and Welfare, Safeguarding Adults, Safeguarding Children, Security, Violence and Fraud and some more on sepsis. I may have forgotten Dementia Awareness so please forgive me. I may have also forgotten to say that at every stage we would have been reminded of the Values, Objectives, Strategy and Vision of the Trust.

One may have noticed that at no stage in the week have the thirty or so of my colleagues seen one patient. The cost to the NHS, and do not forget the poor old taxpayer, of all this is huge. But it is not just the cost of paying doctors for a week to be unproductive. The administrative machinery, the specialist input of all this is huge – and not one patient will have benefited one iota so far. When they made *Yes, Minister* at least it was a comedy programme!

MISSION ACCOMPLISHED

On 1st February 1969 I walked to Leeds General Infirmary as a doctor. That was it. No interest in my health or any other record. I had my stethoscope, was given a pager and that was it. What we did have was apprenticeship. We learnt, mighty quick, on the job from our seniors. I did not care about what conditions or challenges faced me. After five years of hard learning, I was twenty-three years old and a doctor. The terms and conditions of how I was going to work did not concern me – then! The job was as a houseman in Orthopaedics and Trauma. I had wanted a Medical job but found it had been taken leaving a choice of Neurology or Orthopaedics. I chose the latter which I never regretted. There would be every other weekend off and a half day a week. Apart from that I was on-call all the time and would be working for all that time if required. As the weeks went by I calculated it to be on average a hundred and four hour week. My Seniors thought that perfectly reasonable if not a bit lucky. On one trip back to Southport in the bar of the Hesketh Casuals Football club an old school friend informed me that a hundred and four was rubbish because there weren't that many hours in the week. He could not have been very good at sums because there are 168.

Work was very busy and we had a take-day of new patients every other day. This meant that every other day I would be working the day, then through the night and then the following day. The only way I knew I would survive was to go to my room which was in the hospital, at any quiet moment and try to sleep. The pager was always with me so it didn't really matter. On the non-take day in the evening I would step outside to the Victoria just a bit further down St George's Street for a pint or two in the evening. The bar on the left as you go in, (now closed) was an annex to the hospital and seemed to have a line to the switch board. All the junior doctors slipped in there at some stage so it was a good place to compare and catch up. Closing time then was 10 pm whereby I would return and in the quiet of the non-take night do a ward round. It was the only time quiet enough to reflect sensibly about all the problems.

The Victoria – our haven.

Although I had patients all over the hospital my main ward was Ward 16. It was big and had wooden planked floors which made it somewhat noisy when walking. This was a large Florence Nightingale ward with large bays at the centre where the Nursing Station was. From this point the nurses, and Sister in particular, could see it all. Nothing missed their eyes. The nurses themselves were lovely. They were slim and neat with those waspy belts and very competent. They too had been very well trained and we made a good team.

In the hurly burly of the life of Ward 16 one incident deserves remembrance. Not all the patients on Ward 16 were mine but most of them were. One man was brought in after driving into a tree and breaking his neck. There was a clear fracture dislocation between, as I remember it, the sixth and seventh cervical vertebrae. He had some quadriplegia but by no means complete and with hope of a good recovery. But first his neck had to be stabilised. It was decided to do this by distracting his neck whilst he was on a special bed which could be manoeuvred in all positions for comfort. While the weight of his own body would provide the downward pull, the head would be pulled upwards by weights fixed to his head. The way this was done was to insert pins into the petrous bones on either side. The hearing mechanism is contained in the petrous bones which like the name suggests is solid (stone like) enough to take pin insertion. The pins would then be attached to a sort of wishbone and to this, by cord over a pulley, would be added the appropriate weights. It was my job with a Senior Registrar, each day to pull his shoulders down so that an X-ray of the fracture could be taken. Alas, each day the X-ray revealed that the fracture had not been fully reduced and another weight would then be added.

Meanwhile in the dead of night an intriguing thing happened. In the opposite bay to my patient, there was a mysterious arrival. He was mostly curtained off but not always and with him were two policemen. Other policemen came and went and the rumour was that he was a criminal who had been involved in an armed robbery and so was potentially dangerous. Dangerous or not he looked to be in a bad way, perhaps because of his arrest. My patient was opposite this exciting character and because of his own suspension could do nothing but watch. He was like James Stewart in *Rear Window*, unable to do anything other than be a voyeur to the potential drama in front of him. Gaps in the curtains sometimes appeared when staff went in and out. In view of his incarceration it was a welcome relief and I took opportunity to visit him for news of the latest happenings across the ward.

Meanwhile my patient continued to defy the medical plan and his fracture dislocation refused to reduce sufficiently. I continued to buzz around the wards but one quiet time of the day was visiting time. The nurses were busy and all was taken up with the visitors. Visiting time then was short but usually between 2 and 4 pm with Sunday being the busiest day. I was trying to nap one Sunday afternoon when my pager went off at 3 pm. Emergency on Ward 16! When seconds later I arrived there was pandemonium. Whilst the weights had been added to my patient's suspension no thought had been given to the suspension cord. It was simply window cord! The weights had reached 36lbs and at 3pm on that Sunday afternoon when visiting was at its maximum the cord had snapped - 36lbs had plummeted to those noisy plank floors with a great reverberating bang. Visitors had jumped out of their skins.

Some had collapsed. The policemen opposite had jumped into action suspecting an armed escape. Nurses had rushed round trying to calm everybody whilst not knowing what had happened. And through it all, rigid and petrified was my patient, fearful that if he looked right or left even slightly, his head would fall off!

For completion of the story, no visitors or patients died, my patient's fracture dislocation was reduced and united and he walked out. The mysterious guest opposite ended up in Armley jail.

The job was a mixture of cold orthopaedics and trauma but it was the trauma I loved. I loved stalking Casualty at night looking for work before it had been admitted. No-one seemed to mind the lack of experience. We all, doctors and nurses, at the sharp end at night did not have a lot of experience between us but we just had to get on with it and we did. One night I saw a man on a trolley and asked him his name to see if I could speed things up. He barely replied. I asked him again and it was clear that he did not have the breath to reply. There were no external signs of trauma and I could not make much sense of his breath sounds so I ordered an immediate chest X-ray. It was done quickly and showed the contents of his abdomen in his chest. He had been involved in a head on car collision and his stomach had taken the brunt. His diaphragm had ruptured allowing his guts to burst through into the thorax. The thoracic surgeons were called, operated, put his guts back and sewed up his diaphragm. I saw him the next day and he was fine. We had a number of surgical specialities at the Infirmary and I noticed that whereas, to people outside their speciality who saw their problems as huge, the specific specialist would regard the problem as bread and butter. Trauma involving the brain was a fearful no-go area to us but to the neurosurgeons all in a days work.-I was getting experience and meeting many other specialities.

One wonderful thing occurred. That June was the first June I could remember without a crucial life dependant examination. Every June when the weather had perked up and people were out enjoying the summer, I had been indoors with the books involved in some life and death struggle and another examination hurdle. Not so this year! At twenty-four years old I had a stress-free June! I went out with my pay packet and bought two pairs of shoes. I still have one of those pairs.

MISSION ACCOMPLISHED

As the six months came to a close I arranged a Medical job at Chapel Allerton hospital in north Leeds. The time came for transition. However, no time was allotted for transition! One was expected to leave one job at the last minute and begin the next, wherever it was, an instant later. On the Friday morning of transition when I was expected to start my new job and be on the 8 am ward round I went into the Consultants' room at Leeds. There were several consultants there and I actually was responsible to several of them. I addressed for politeness the Professor of Orthopaedics to ask him if he would allow me to leave. He started by dressing me down. In fact the only thing I did for him was arrange his surgery lists twice a week which I had done perfectly apart from a single hiccup on the last one. It was that to which he was referring. I stood there fuming. It was plain he thought I would be asking for a reference and would be prepared to grovel! In front of the gathering I observed that I had arranged his list twice a week for six months without fail until the last one and had received nothing in return. No teaching; no thanks. I added for good measure that I would not be asking for a reference and left. At 8.30 am I had driven across Leeds and was on a medical ward round at Chapel Allerton. In fact the white haired red faced professor had achieved his high status by writing critical documents of others who had done the research. He had never written anything original himself. I could do without him.

CHAPTER 2

CHAPEL ALLERTON

So it was that I left Leeds General Infirmary shortly after 8 am and was on the wards for a round at 8.30am the roads in Leeds being relatively quiet in 1969. I was looking forward to Chapel Allerton. Apart from anything else I had got married and Chapel Allerton had married quarters. Virtually all the junior doctors there were in my year or above and we were all friends. The hospital, like so many of these early NHS hospitals consisted of blocks of wards in the grounds of what once must have been a fine estate. The grounds were beautiful to one who had been virtually confined indoors apart from the evening visits to the Victoria for six months. The work was busy and the take night was on alternate nights but I was not on-call on the other night in between. This was luxury! The evenings were very pleasant in the late summer months and the other junior doctors and I would use the grounds for a game of football. The hospital had been the site of the Gledhow Grove mansion with spacious grounds off the Chapeltown Road. One evening we were well into a game even playing with one of the patients in his dressing gown. Suddenly the surgical Senior House Officer yelled, "hey, stop the game!" He looked meaningfully at the gowned patient and said, "didn't I take your appendix out yesterday?" Indeed he had and the chastened man was banished back to his ward.

It was all pleasant and very busy. Inevitably in Leeds there was the continuous stream of chest infections with all patients having their own, often overflowing, sputum pots. The admissions would stream in each take night throughout the night but the other main problem which exercised me far more was haematemesis or the vomiting of blood. Whereas the chest infections would simply involve the usual clerking and prescribing, haematemesis was a medical emergency. The cause was nearly always the bleeding duodenal ulcer. For years it had been known that a bacterium was able to survive the dilute hydrochloric acid of the stomach but its presence under the gastric mucosa had been thought to be coincidental. Therefore the treatment of duodenal ulcers was antacids and when appropriate, operation. The operations had become steadily more sophisticated until, at the moment of maximum sophistication it was realised that the eradication of this bacterium, the helicobacter pylori, with three sorts of tablets for two weeks, would solve the problem. None of this was known to me or accepted by the medical establishment at that time. I was faced with urgent cross matching and transfusion as these poor patients vomited blood and passed it per rectum steadily exsanguinating themselves. Sometimes the blood would have to be forced in under pressure to prevent shock and I would have several on the go at once. It was often touch and go but we never lost one person in my six months there.

It should be said that these poor patients, before helicobacter was accused and found guilty, would have been accused themselves of personal negligence. People with duodenal ulcers were told they had poor living habits amounting almost to self-abuse. They would be smokers, (bad but not the cause,) they drank too much, ate too much, didn't eat the right things, and generally were a bad lot. The concept of blame for the illnesses you had was medieval in its basis and applied to many things in medicine at that time. Then came helicobacter and suddenly all were blameless. The medical 'witchfinders general' were unrepentant.

Two incidents which emphasised the huge changes in medical management compared to today occurred whilst I was there. The more serious one was this. A lady in her mid 40s was admitted with a profound cerebral haemorrhage. Readers may be aware that stroke can come in several forms but some are due to thrombosis which although bad can be managed and haemorrhage which tends to be more devastating. This lady had a huge haemorrhage. There were no CT scans at that time. As the hours went by and her intracranial pressure increased her respiration was depressed. It was apparent that sooner or later she would stop breathing. The SHO I was working with remembered that the ward had a respirator. We intubated her and she was now unconscious and on assisted breathing. This took many hours through the night but on the ward round first thing we were pleased with ourselves as we presented the situation to the Consultant. He listened, looked and then said "turn it off." That was it. No discussion, counselling for the lady's family or the inexperienced junior Doctors! Just turn it off. He was right of course. There was no future for this lady and it would have simply kept her brain dead body alive and prevented the family mourning and achieving closure. Explaining things to the husband and sixteen year old daughter was unpleasant.

On a lighter note was the man with heart block. One of our duties was to minister to the war veterans housed nearby. Not all of them had war injuries; many just had conditions which they had acquired in service. One afternoon I had a call that a gentleman had collapsed. In fact he had gone into heart block. Without a pacemaker, natural or artificial the heart will beat at about 40 beats per minute. If the pacemaker stops, the drop in heart rate from, say, 80bpm to 40 bpm can cause collapse. Pacemakers then were primitive and comprised wires into the ventricles attached to a receiver under the skin of the chest. On the outer skin of the chest was a device delivering the pulse. This was driven by a battery. What had happened was that the battery, one of those old twin EverReady batteries had been short circuited because the gentleman had been incontinent. My solution was to get a new battery, house it in a polythene bag and seal it with sellotape! It worked. Comparing modern pacemakers with this is comparable to comparing modern life with the stone age!

The 'house', the resident junior doctors, was the best I ever enjoyed and we gelled. There was Geoff who had played for the Woodhouse Wanderers and Howard, my dissection partner and many others. When it came to Bonfire Night we had a bonfire in the grounds and after lubricating at the Shoulder of Mutton went back for fireworks. It developed into a war of rockets which we fired at each other with some success but no harm. As the children of men who had done their bit in World War Two it seemed mild stuff. Years later when I worked in

Casualty at Poole I was on duty for two Bonfire Nights. I attended one mild injury. Fireworks were easily bought over the counter by children and families had their own displays. How things have changed. How did the current generation become so 'precious'? Dare I point at the lack of male role models?

The six month tenure went quickly and I learnt. The two consultants I worked for were excellent teachers and treated me with respect and I repaid them with hard work. Christmas on the wards was great fun and by now I was thinking of my next job. Work, by and large, at that time consisted of six-month contracts. If one was lucky enough to get on a training scheme as many as three such contracts might be linked giving a very short element of security. For reasons which I now cannot remember I applied and was appointed as SHO to Leeds Maternity Hospital.

CHAPTER 3
MATERNITY

WITH THE SAME PRINCIPAL OF leaving one job and starting at another at the same instant so there would be no break, however minor, in continuity of patient care, I started at Leeds Maternity Hospital. I don't know, looking back why I wanted to do this job but I think it was to do with my original core wish to be, what I had conceived in my mind as, a 'proper doctor.' To me a proper doctor, brought people into the world, eased their transition out of it, and dealt with all their problems in between. He or she would, diagnose measles, mumps and chicken pox; would manage heart attacks, strokes, diabetes; and nurture suffering humanity through the trials and tribulations of life. In this respect an obstetric job was mandatory. In the event it was towards the late 1990s that I ceased managing home deliveries.

It turned out to be one of the most rewarding things I have done. I loved obstetrics and I believed I was good at it. Ultrasound only really got going in maternity hospitals in 1970 thanks to Ian Donald and his team at Edinburgh so we had to rely on our hands and particularly our fingers. In this respect I learnt to 'see through the tips of my fingers.' The lie of a baby is of crucial importance for vaginal delivery and if your fingers are confident of the suture lines of the baby's head or whatever else is presenting, you will know what you are doing. It was not fashionable then to do Caesarean sections for many reasons. For one it is a very bloody operation and the blood loss scars the kidneys. It quadruples maternal mortality, mercifully very low anyway, and also the babies were much smaller then. We often had to assist the delivery with forceps or Ventouse. The function of the forceps is to guard the baby's head, (Wrigley's forceps) or to turn the head to the face posterior position as well as protect the baby's head. (Keilland's forceps.) I thought I was pretty good at both mainly because, thanks to my fingers, I started from the right place! Twins were my speciality and I am glad to say, and thank God, that all my procedures were successful and uneventful. I was never fond of the Ventouse which was a sort of suction cap that you fitted to the baby's head to pull it out. It seemed to me more like *All Creatures Great and Small* rather than *Call the Midwife*.

You will have gathered by now that we had very little supervision after the first week or so. It never occurred to us to call for help except in the most dire of circumstances and one, I will relate later. On the first day we were called to be instructed on how to intubate a baby. Most babies as we know from *Call The Midwife*, a truly remarkable programme, cry within a few minutes whereby the tension goes and there are smiles all round. The baby is put on the breast and the delivery of the placenta is hardly noticed by the mother. The haemoglobin in a baby's blood can keep its brain oxygenated for seven minutes but beyond that it will suffer damage. Using a plastic baby, the size of a doll, we received instruction on intubating a baby. I never thought I would have to do it personally but a few weeks later after a straightforward delivery there had been no response for several minutes. We always had the clock ticking for this situation. The minutes went by and we were all on edge but on six minutes I said intubate and the midwife handed me the tube. You never know how you will react to this sort of thing until it happens but I just went ice cool and intubated perfectly. The baby was oxygenated and began to breath normally. I never had to intubate a baby again. Looking back as I am now I wonder if the baby would have died if I had not done the job properly. Would there have been brain damage? Would it have eventually breathed spontaneously. And after all these years, does it matter? My records showed that I delivered eleven breeches, five sets of twins, fifteen babies using Wrigley's forceps, rotated and delivered twelve babies face to pubes using Keilland's forceps, one Ventouse and assisted at nine Caesarean sections.

I was usually on call on alternate nights so slept those nights in the hospital. Thoughtfully they had put our bedrooms over the neonatal ward so I fell asleep and woke to the sound of crying babies! But I did not mind. I was being paid 5/- an hour. For comparison my cleaner was paid 4/- an hour but she earned 6/- an hour for overtime. Most of my hours were overtime! There was one curious thing about the post-natal ward where all the new mothers lived in that in the morning when their babies had been returned to them I would do a quick ward round. Usually there would be great joy with the mothers all laughing and joking as one thought they should be. But on some occasions they were all weeping bitterly. They all did either one thing or the other. I realised that they must have huge mood swings after all those hormonal changes but the herd either laughed or cried together.

To facilitate the birth vaginally and avoid tears, we often performed an episiotomy. This was a cut from the fourchette (the lowest part of the vulva,) towards the buttock. In the case of the Keilland's forceps where the baby's head would be rotated to face posterior the episiotomy had to be quite big. I do not know who trained me because there were various ways of sewing them up but I developed my own way using a single strand of catgut which ended with a subcuticular suture finishing at the fourchette. It did the job well and needed no removal of sutures so the lady could forget her nether parts for the foreseeable future. I reckoned I was pretty slick, and a good job too, as it was not uncommon to repair three before breakfast!

I was lucky in my consultant. Our job, and there were four SHOs working for four consultants, was mainly obstetrics but we had some gynaecology and when on call dealt with all the gynaecology emergencies. My consultant was considered cautious by the standards of the day. The others often did complex or heroic surgery which led to complex and heroic after-problems! My colleagues were always having to contend with these problems, many of them insoluble. I, on the other hand, was rarely called on my non-take nights for these challenges. My consultant was very much old school. But he was polite and respectful and utterly charming to the ladies, which some of the others were not! However, on one ward round he was denigrating men who wore jewellery, (goodness knows what he would have made of tattoos,) and I found myself slipping my wedding ring off lest it condemned me.

MISSION ACCOMPLISHED

One wonderful character who influenced me was John Philips. He was a Senior Registrar awaiting his own consultant appointment. As a result he dared not put a foot wrong with the current consultants. One bad word could blight a career. In fact he always did far more than required because he simply loved obstetrics. As an SHO on call, the right place to be was hovering about the delivery wards. But most evenings, hovering as well was John Philips. He would look for the difficult delivery, the long labour, the distressed mother to be. He would talk to her with his soft Welsh voice (come to think he would have made a great shepherd,) and soon the anxiety would have been soothed out of her. Then he gently went to Ventouse or forceps or a little more Syntocinon and order would have been restored. When all was well, the baby on the breast and mother tired but content, he would fade from the delivery room with a comment to the mother, "you won't realise the significance of this event tonight for another eighteen years!" When he wasn't delivering he would tell us tales of the history of obstetrics, some real horror stories. The problem is that because humans have such large heads there are inevitably going to be problems of getting the head through the pelvis. Babies do not really come to life until six to seven months which is probably the time they should be born. Because of the size of the pelvis they have to be born at nine months but it can be a close run thing. Hence the horror stories of disproportion and stuck babies.

John Philips loved obstetrics and also had an interest in gynaecology. Early in his training he had been obliged to do National Service and had chosen the Royal Navy. He had been stationed at the naval base at Rosyth where there was an uncontrolled population of cats. To hone his skills in gynaecology and control the cat population, thus killing two birds with one stone, he decided to sterilise the female cats. Some would have a tubal ligation, some a hysterectomy. As anaesthetic he used Omnopon and Scolpolamine injected into the abdomen. Omnopon is an opioid and Scopolamine dries up secretions. It came as a single phial and he found it simple and effective. Unfortunately, one weekend he went back home having left the pharmacy unlocked. When he returned he faced charges of leaving the pharmacy unlocked and more serious, a question of where was the Om and Scop! He was thus Court Martialled as was the normal procedure. This was a shock to the young lieutenant but on full acquittal (and acknowledgement of the solution to the cat problem) there was another one to come. His commanding officer called for him and told him he had gone through the ordeal with flying colours, was clearly officer material and would he like to sign on for ten years!

John was likely to get a job at the new Airedale hospital near Keighley which had given me an idea for my next step. I was leaning towards a career in Casualty even though at that time there was no career path, but to start I would need a surgical rotation and there was an eighteen month one at Airedale. We visited the unfinished hospital and I was impressed. I also spoke to some of the surgeons and things looked hopeful with a reference from John.

LMH had its share of disasters and like most disasters you don't see them coming because if you did they would have been averted. One such was not my patient but I was aware that there was a difficult breech (bottom first) birth in one of the rooms. In one of those moments when all had taken their eye off the ball there was a scream. When we went in there was blood all over the delivery suite. The baby had been born, had died, the umbilical cord had ruptured and squirted blood all over the room. Someone who should have been with the lady was not, for reasons never revealed. The incident was hushed up and supressed but the word was that the price of silence was more staff on the ward.

Another important incident occurred at this time. The consultants were yet again in dispute with the Government. All this was part of a continuing process since the advent of the NHS for the Government (NHS England etc) to take control of the doctors who worked for it. The power of the consultants had been huge but now occurred another step down. To further their cause they decided that there should be a strike of junior doctors! Not the consultants whose cause it was but the minions with no power and little money. We told them to get stuffed and astonishingly they were shocked. Things were changing. Junior doctors had been so dependent on the references of their seniors in the past but things were changing.

The change in relationship between junior doctors and the consultants must have seeped through to me although as a fiesty young man there was no shortage of fight in me. I had already ended my first job with a consultant I had no time for and who had no time for me. So when it came to the interview at Airedale I knew what I wanted and although I did not realise it when I went in, was not ready to compromise. I had done all the necessary groundwork and was reasonably confident. Unbeknown to me there were others who had also done their homework and knew what they wanted. After the interview there was clearly a long discussion and a messenger consultant kept coming in and out for confidential discussion with the candidates including me. Eventually the messenger came out and said I had been offered the three jobs in rotation. He then gave me the order of the jobs and they were not in the order I wanted. I was aware that the surgical job I had done was mainly trauma so wanted general surgery as my first job to make up for it. They were offering me general surgery as my third job! I told them I declined the offer. I don't think such a thing had occurred before and the messenger went back and forth. But they would not budge and nor would I. I walked out full of righteous indignation. I am not sure how long righteous indignation kept me going but I think it was until I realised that with a few weeks to go I had no job to go to!

Righteous indignation then gave way to desperation as I scanned the back pages of the British Medical Journal where the jobs were advertised. In those days they were all in small print with no big black lines around them or large print or any type of emphasis as they have today. Bar one! Right in the middle of a page was an advertisement surrounded by thick black lines, the only advert with such emphasis, for a Casualty Officer at Poole General Hospital. I had been born in Bournemouth nearby at the old Boscombe Hospital. The current Secretary of Poole Hospital had been appointed by my father and I knew him well. I phoned immediately and spoke to the Hospital Secretary's secretary, Mrs Winter. She was delightful. She seemed pleased to hear from me. It was settled. My future after seven years in Leeds would be back on the south coast. All I had to do was get through the last week at LMH.

It promised to be a normal week with on call Tuesday and Thursday nights. I would then leave on the Friday evening, stay with my sister just outside Poole and start work there first thing Saturday morning. That was the plan. Monday was a fairly normal day. All the deliveries were difficult but that was normal and what we were there for. Tuesday was much the same but in the evening a lady came in with a missed abortion. In other words the baby had died but as she was about thirty weeks she still had to deliver the dead baby. She was in her late thirties with other children and like so many of the Yorkshire people I got to know was stoical and resilient. The dead baby was delivered without problem but a little later the midwife called me to say that she was bleeding heavily and her blood pressure had dropped. Blood was always ready and cross-matched and I began transfusion. With experience of those exsanguinating duodenal ulcers I began pumping blood in. After two pints there was no improvement in blood pressure and I ordered more blood. I had examined the lady and called the Senior Registrar on call. I told him of the blood pressure and also that when I examined her there seemed a large hole but I didn't really know what I was feeling. He was not long and on examination just said "ruptured uterus!" More blood was ordered, an anaesthetist called and preparation made for emergency hysterectomy. The senior registrar worked away with me assisting and the ruptured uterus was removed nicely but sewing up was delayed by bleeding. The hours went by and more blood was transfused. It was apparent to me that the anaesthetist was a highly capable hero, unfazed by the potential disaster in front of us.

At 3 am the Senior Registrar asked me to call the consultant. He too arrived quickly, assessed the situation and called for hot towels. The lady seemed to be oozing blood from everywhere in her open abdomen. The likelihood was that the anticoagulant in the transfused blood was simply aggravating the situation and preventing clotting but we just wanted her to stop bleeding. The consultant pressed the hot towels into the abdomen and waited. His calmness was priceless. I was feeling very light-headed for a while as mini-sleeps overcame me. At about 4 am the consultant began to remove the towels one by one. After each removal he would cauterise or suture every bleeding point as they appeared and there seemed to be an awful lot of them. This went on for at least another hour, painstakingly, bit by bit. Eventually he looked at the open abdomen, saw no new bleeding and we closed up. The anaesthetist had transfused the twenty-third pint by this time and as it completed the lady began to rouse. She was fine. She had no idea of the drama, that we had nearly lost her, that we had worked through the night. Later that morning when I went to see her she was sitting up in bed and looked so well. I was still in awe of the team of people I had been working with performing miracles as part of their daily (and nightly) job.

I had Wednesday night off! All there was left was Thursday, Thursday night and Friday. Everything I had was loaded into a minivan ready for off the moment I was permitted to leave on Friday evening. All was well until the Thursday evening. A lady who was on her fifth or sixth pregnancy had been causing anxiety for a few months and I had seen her in the ante-natal clinic. She was not just obese, her belly hung low. Indeed, we had done an X-ray of her abdomen only to see that there was no baby there. The baby was somewhere between pelvis and knees and had not shown up on the abdominal X-ray. Nowadays she would have gone to Caesarean section quite rightly but vaginal delivery then, was nearly always attempted first. She appeared in labour in the middle of the night. The whole thing was dysfunctional and she lost the baby. It was awful because it could have been prevented.

Friday, therefore, began with little sleep and another hard day ahead. At some time before 6 pm I slipped away for the last time from Leeds, jumped in the van borrowed from John Belstead and sped south. I arrived at my sister's, slept, woke and drove down to Poole. The habit of leaving one job and starting the next without break was instilled into me. I walked through the door of Poole Casualty at 8am and a nice lady asked me to sit down. There was no-one there. It was quiet. I wasn't used to quiet. At some time before 9am a tall, good looking charge nurse came up to me and asked what my problem was and told me that the doctors may not be around for a while. It was clear that he thought I was a patient, and come to that, a patient without much wrong with him! I blurted out that I was the new doctor! "Oh," he said, "I don't think they were expecting you. I think they thought you would want the weekend off!" As I write now fifty years later I can almost cry as I nearly did then. They did not want or expect me to get stuck in, day and night, as they did in Leeds. Relief! Rest! Sleep! They had no idea of the week I had just had! The charge nurse was Ray Matthews, who became one of my closest friends until his sudden death from a cerebral haemorrhage many years later.

As a sequel I might add that I decided to take the Diploma in Obstetrics. Whether it was because I loved obstetrics, or whether I was good at it, or whether it was because I had to pay for this examination for the first time in my life, or all three, I do know I passed this first time!

CHAPTER 4
POOLE

Blunt but Good!

Ray Matthews, the charge nurse on Casualty, and I became close friends. He was one of the funniest people I have ever known. His persona was one of camp indignation. He would impersonate the many nursing and other female workers in the hospital. He would become Sister Prout adjusting her bosoms strutting round like a mother hen. He would become one of the squinty eyed senior nurses making life uncomfortable for a junior. On one occasion I overheard him on the phone presumably conversing with someone who wanted to know what the new doctor (me) was like. "Blunt but good," was his response. Hmm. Well of course I was blunt. I had been trained in Yorkshire. Blunt was normal. But not in the south of England where saying things as they were was considered almost rude. I sadly learnt that in the north people talked to their neighbours: in the south they sent them solicitor's letters! Despite having been born and lived in Bournemouth for the first ten years of my life I had adopted northern ways. The so- called northern bluntness had its advantages. So a conversation with the doctor may go like this. "Is there anything you can do for me, Doctor." "No." "Right then" This acceptance not only saved time it had more subtle advantages. Sometimes the most difficult thing to do in medicine, indeed in life, is to do nothing, even when it is the right thing and even when it is the only thing. To be told that nothing is to be done and that is the correct thing and accept it has enormous advantages for the patient.

Later as a GP I used to warn my patients that if they keep demanding that something must be done – eventually it will be done – and they may not like it! I learnt slowly that to tell someone in the south that nothing could be done and that their condition would get better of its own accord was considered an affront. Thus, so much unnecessary work is done by physiotherapists, chiropractors, counsellors and others. To be fair they make a living from it and of course, the patient gets better!

It was the 'blunt *but* good' which concerned me. Why not 'blunt *and* good?' It was the BUT instead of the AND which exercised me. Forty years later when I retired from the practice about two hundred of my patients actually wrote me letters. Probably half of them used the word 'forthright.' They had admired, relied on, approved of, my forthright attitude. If they had only said it to me at the time and not after I had gone I may still be working now! The effort, decade after decade, of having patients argue with you as you try and save their lives, save them from pain, save their organs, takes its toll. And yet it turns out that they had appreciated and respected my attempts. 'Forthright *but* good' would have been better but I think for my epitaph I would prefer, 'Forthright *and* Good!'

Having enjoyed the first weekend off and started work it was apparent to me that the organisation of the four SHOs was poor. We were the medical core of Casualty with backup from the Registrars. But, we needed to be there so I produced a rota in which one of us would always be there. This meant working more hours that the incumbent SHOs had been used to but they saw the sense and Casualty worked much better for it. Also it meant that whilst working the days I only worked one night in four. Three nights out of four off! After the previous eighteen months this was glorious especially as I was newly married. But it meant that one weekend in four the SHO on call worked from Friday morning to the following Monday evening. It was usual to get some sleep most nights. The department saw thirty thousand patients a year with seasonal variation so in August the rate leapt to the equivalent of fifty thousand.

Having been in a great city in their busy hospitals I was amazed at how rural Poole and Dorset were in those days. West of Poole was a large county of tiny villages and a lot of sheep. There seemed to be a

MISSION ACCOMPLISHED

great deal of inbreeding and a different sort of poverty to the city I had been used to. The ambulances were driven by husband-and-wife teams or a father and son in one case. There were no paramedics but because of light traffic the injured arrived more quickly and clerking was kept to a minimum so things happened quicker. We rapidly developed the art of 'shifting a queue.' It was possible to take short cuts which would never be done today which is one of the many reasons patients wait so long. Far from compromising patient care it enhanced it. Having been born in Bournemouth and lived there until I was ten I felt that I was coming back home. I had spent seven years in Lancashire and seven in Yorkshire. I was not prepared for the parochialness of Poole and the south of England generally. The local knowledge of anything north of Fordingbridge was miniscule. Occasionally I would phone my father in Southport and had to go through the hospital switchboard. "Did you want to be put through to Southborne?" said the operator on every occasion, apart from the geography expert who asked me if it was Stockport I wanted. All my phone calls were billed as calls to Southborne! When I told them what I had done in Leeds I could have been talking about another planet.

The consultant I worked for was the senior of four and a fine and meticulous surgeon. Often in theatre the registrar would saunter in with the score from the current test match. I began to realise that he had been a fine cricketer. (So was the registrar who later lost an eye from a cricket ball.) As he warmed to me one day in the middle of a menisectomy he said, "did I ever tell you about the time I scored fifty against Harold Larwood? It was 1939 and I was opening for Essex." Harold Larwood was a legend and one of the world's great fast bowlers. I listened spellbound. "The first ball was so fast I didn't see it, or the second or the third. So, I thought, he's fast but I'm still here, I'm going to go for him! The next ball I kept a straight bat and smacked it straight over his head. Came down and never reached the boundary. The thing was, Larwood was the great fast bowler at the end of his career and didn't do any fielding. All the fielders were behind the bat and someone had to run to the other end of the pitch so we ran four!" And so he went on relating each stroke and score until he was out for fifty. Years later I checked Wisden – it was all as he said.

He was a fine batsman evidently and had gone to Cambridge where this had been recognised immediately. As a result he was excused looking down microscopes in case it ruined his eye! How things change. I remember some of our year asking the cardiology consultant if they could have Wednesday afternoon off to play for the Medical School. They were asked in pointed terms if they really wanted to become doctors!

I worked hard and we worked well. The whole team did and there was the feeling that you knew everyone in the hospital. I began to play for the hospital football team. We had some really good players and I was glad to be with them. Strangely, whereas in Leeds, the big pond, I was encouraged to do almost anything. Here in the little pond I was held back. I think they had been used to a different sort of junior doctor. This changed with the advent of Southampton Medical School. Then British graduates began to flow in.

My consultant was fair but very blunt in outpatients. The obese were clearly informed by making them walk round outpatients with two heavy bags round their shoulders marked 'SUGAR' in big letters. Smokers were commanded to stop and exercise encouraged. "Put their breakfast in the day room Sister," was the order to patients who did not mobilise quickly enough. Patients would have all their teeth tapped as he looked for signs of infection. "Bad teeth stops your bones uniting." He automatically stereotyped people. It is considered unfashionable today but was harmless and even reassuring. To him all Dutch people grew tulips, all Australians talked to kangaroos, all Italians made spaghetti and all West Indians played cricket. How different to the PC (pernicious censorship) we have today that makes otherwise sane people hesitate whether to order coffee black or white! But the patients responded to these idiosyncrasies and if he had one fault it was that he would never discharge patients until they were completely better. The trouble is that very few people are 'completely' better so outpatients was often a dreary review session. I made it my mission to discharge as many as possible if there was nothing we could do and sometimes managed half in a session. It meant a lot of letters to their doctors but I felt it was my way of preserving the Health Service.

MISSION ACCOMPLISHED

Lumbar pain at that time was the responsibility of orthopaedic surgeons, something which was eventually corrected and passed to rheumatologists or dedicated back specialists. Genuine prolapsed intervertebral discs were operated on, with great success as I remembered it by the orthopaedic surgeons and that has now passed to neurosurgeons. The treatment for many cases of back pain was the plaster jacket which would immobilise the patient for six weeks. The current method is to do exactly the opposite and get the patient moving! However, it seemed to work possibly by scaring the patient into denying continued pain. If he confessed to further pain it would condemn him to another six weeks in the jacket. I had nothing to do with the decision to plaster jacket the patients but I was responsible for taking the jackets off. I noticed that they all seemed to have lost weight even though they had been less mobile. I began to weigh them before and after and noticed that their initial weight was the same as their combined weight, patient plus jacket, at the end. Thus when they finally shed the dreaded jacket they had lost six to seven pounds, the exact weight of the jacket. It occurred to me that our bodies may have an inbuilt idea of what weight we should be and made sure it was constant. The appliance of an extra seven pounds persuaded the brain that we had put on weight and lost it accordingly. I think there is a lot to this. Sitting down convinces the brain that we are lighter that it thinks we should be and so we put on weight. Reading the Sunday paper today I read that 'sitting is the new smoking!' An exaggeration maybe, but the modern life sitting in front of the computer is exactly the wrong thing!

The modern doctor will have training in breaking bad news and bereavement. He will have been told to ask the poor person, shortly to find out that they are bereaved, what they think has happened and what they expect. He may repeat to them the last three words they have just said and then pause. It is a simple technique to draw people out. I had experienced bereavement when my mother died when I was eleven and I had received a medical education in Yorkshire and deep down I knew that you can analyse the hell out of bad news and it is still just as bad. Breaking bad news in Casualty was all too frequent and in one forty-eight-hour spell I had to do it five times. I had to say it how it was and I hope they could see I understood how they felt.

One day, my consultant announced, "My old friend, Ian Limbery, is retiring, and they will need a replacement. You should apply!" I had not thought about general practice and did not even want it, but this was a command and, clearly, my application was not optional. As I said earlier I had had an attachment with a GP in Leeds, and brilliant though he was, I saw him as a workaholic and it had frightened me greatly. Moreover, I was leaning towards surgery and orthopaedics and Casualty in particular even though there was no career path in Casualty and the surgical route was a hard one. But it was a command! I duly attended the interview in Clayford with Ian and Jock. It was pleasant but pointless – they wanted an older man, and I did not want the job! Looking back it was an extraordinary interview, almost surreal. We exchanged pleasantries because neither side wanted the other so there was nothing to conflict. But it was pleasant. I had done as instructed and all was well and temporarily forgotten. I had no idea or care that this strange meeting would change my life forever.

Another chance occurrence which changed and enriched my life happened shortly after I started. The local Speedway team, the famous Poole Pirates, required a doctor present on Wednesday evenings throughout the summer and the casualty officers had been in the habit of supplying the Track Doctor. Indeed, the races could not be held without a doctor at the track. Thus for £3 each Wednesday I attended and enjoyed a completely new speciality. Speedway is an extraordinary sport with the bike being the most powerful motor pound for pound. They go from 0-60mph in under three seconds with no brakes and one gear. It is the only motorcycle sport where the wheels are not in line. The rider leans to the left and turns the front wheel to the right so it slides round driven by the powerful rear wheel. The best riders will slide both wheels. The noise, the smell of the burning oil, the riders, mostly small men, the leathers, became part of my life from 1970 to 1990. Ironically The Pirates won the league in 1969 and 1991 but never when I was there. The first thing I noticed was that they all limped. With the left foot. This is because they put a plate on the sole of the left boot to press into the dirt as they circuit the track. The only way of stopping quickly is to lay the bike down which all riders were adept at. The leathers saved them from abrasions. The leathers were a major problem because the zip at the rear was short and meant the rider had to ooze into his outfit. Getting an injured rider out of it was a problem depending on the injury. The leathers were brilliantly handmade and very expensive so they were only cut in an emergency. Leg and foot injuries were common and taking the foot out of the boot was another challenge. All the straps on the boot had to be released before the foot could be moved backwards out of it. All this often had to be performed in the red wet dirt of the track. Like the surgeons of old I never wore good clothes to Speedway!

There were some tragic moments, the worst being when a young rider, recently having joined Poole, the club he had always wanted, fell on the first bend and ruptured his aorta. There was nothing anyone could have done. His father by my side was the bravest man I have ever known. Some of the events were thankfully comical. One night our number one rider Christer Lovquist fell and had clearly fractured his nose. A spike of bone was poking out and blood was evident. When a nose is smacked flat the best thing to do instantly is to take the tip of the nose and pull. All the bits just slip back into place, bleeding stops and pain goes and the need for later corrective surgery is prevented. I grabbed Lovquist's nose between finger and thumb and pulled. As I pulled away he came with me. The stadium was treated to their number one rider being pulled around by the nose by the young doctor. One of his assistants came up to me, "what are you doing?" I explained. "But his nose is always like that!" In fact his nose had had multiple fractures and had a spike of bone thinly covered with skin which had merely broken. He did not have a fractured nose, just an abrasion!

Speedway riders often had a history of fractures particularly the collar bone. Leaping animals do not have an ossified collar bone, they just have a ligament and so should Speedway riders. One Czech rider, Vaclav Verner, much loved at Poole, fell and severely injured his wrist. It was very swollen and I told him to get it X-rayed. He declined. The next day I slipped down to the stadium and encouraged him once more. He declined. I asked him why. "If I have it X-rayed and it is broken it will be 3 weeks and no riding, but if it is not X-rayed it will be a week!" They would ride with dreadful injuries and always return far too early. Also, these were the days of the Cold War and Eastern European riders were watched constantly in case they defected. They either rode or were back home. In the event he did have it X-rayed, it was broken in three places and the next day he was in Czechoslovakia.

Having been a medical student with no money for five years I was very keen to work and earn. The fee at Speedway was £3 which would buy thirty pints of beer at the prices of the day. As inflation raged during the 1970s my fee was the price of thirty pints of beer which all the promoters respected.

Another strange incident occurred when one of our riders came off and immediately walked off the track with one arm on the ground and hopping around like a gibbon. There were language difficulties and it took me a while to work out what was wrong. He unfortunately suffered from recurrent dislocation of one of his shoulders. It had popped out when he fell and because of the tightness of the leathers he had found that if he could get the arm leather to the ground and tread on it he could sometimes apply traction and reduce the dislocation himself. He kept hopping for ages whilst the crowd waited presumably, like me, with fascinated astonishment. This time it would not go back and off he went to casualty. It was painful for him but pain threshold for speedway riders was incredibly high.

A semi-retired GP would come in to A & E to work Friday afternoons. This was Tommy Haw, who had qualified at Leeds thirty years before me. Many of our experiences had been similar. His contemporaries had become our consultants. He had become a GP in Yorkshire and then moved down to Corfe Castle where he had been a legend and still lived. He had done the best possible thing in that beautiful village rapidly becoming a holiday town for rich Londoners. He married a local girl and sired three children. He was always available to his patients and even years after retirement when we spent many an evening in the three pubs in the centre of Corfe, his old patients would come in for his opinion. If they wanted him he would leave the pub, attend a sick child or whatever and return when all was well. He worked hard and people trusted him. Amongst other things Tommy had worked at Leeds Maternity Hospital. As students they had had to deliver one hundred babies in the area north of the hospital using the midder bike as transport. He would recite a poem written by Mr Armitage who had used the style made famous by Stanley Holloway. The poem of Albert and the Lion had been written by Marriott Edgar (1880-1951) and Mr Armitage had invented the prequel of his birth. I don't think anyone but Tommy was aware of it and I am glad I wrote it down.

The Birth of Albert Ramsbottom

There's a famous Hospital called LMH
As is noted for midder and fun
And its there that Mrs Ramsbottom
Went to deliver a son.
A grand little foetus was Albert
All wrapped in his cord, quite a swell
With his cord made of jelly of Wharton
And lashings of vernix as well.
'E didn't think much of the liquor
'is quarters was fiddlin' and small
In fact 'e were damned near drownded
There was nothing to laugh at, at all.
So seeking for further adventure
'e decided his quarters to leave.
So 'e kicked and busted his membranes
And the lot went up Sister's sleeve!
Now Albert had heard about Sisters
'as 'ow they was ferocious and wild
And to see one looking so peaceful
It didn't seem right to the child.
So straight way the brave little fellow
Showing of fear not a speck
Took his cord made of jelly of Wharton
And twisted it three times round his neck!

You could see the Sister didn't like it
She gave him a kind of a roll
And took hold of his head and his shoulders
And delivered the little lad whole.

A nurse who had seen the occurrence
And didn't know what to do next, said
She's torn from twain to Beersheba
And Sister said, "ee I am vexed."
The House Surgeon had to be called for
He took out his bag right away
And said, "some'ats got to be done now
Its no use watching all day."
But mother had got proper angry
When she thought where her fourchette had gone
And said, "some'ats got to be sutured"
So that were decided upon.
So upstairs they went to t'theatre
And called in an Honorary gent
And told him the misdoings of Albert
And proved it by showing the rent.
The Onerary were quite nice about it
He said, "what a nasty mishap"
And looked down at our little Albert and said
"He's really a nice little chap."

The Onerary then gave his opinion that
There really was no-one to blame
And he hoped that Mrs Ramsbottom
Would have further sons to her name.
At that mother got proper blazing
And "Thank you Sir kindly" said she
"Spend my life healing soft parts and so on
To be torn by damned midwives – NOT ME!"

Another Leeds graduate came to work at Poole Hospital and was one of my year. It was Bill of the Uncertain Sphincters. Bill is an extraordinary character and has worked all over Australia with the Royal Flying Doctor Service. He worked all over Australia and also the Solomon Islands. Whilst there they had a sort of civil war and it was decided to kill all white people. Bill went to the headman of a local

MISSION ACCOMPLISHED

village, just as I had done at the Makerere medical school Nairobi, and said, "Yes, but you don't mean me do you?" Unlike my experience, however, they made it quite clear that they did mean him! In this case discretion was the better part of valour and Bill moved to more peaceful climes.

It was at a mess dinner after we had been well fed and watered that I was boasting to anyone who would listen that there was a foolproof way of making money. It was simply to bet anyone that they could not eat five Jacob's cream crackers in five minutes. Many try and the first one goes down easily enough and five minutes seems a long time. Water or any drink is forbidden, of course, and very quickly the saliva dries and the crackers clog. I was fully confident having seen so many failures that this bet was a dead cert. "I'll have a go," said Bill. After my sincere certainty that failure would result the bets came in. As I remember we were betting 20p pieces and remember at that time 20p would buy two pints of beer to put it in a modern context. If only Bill and I had been a double act and the thing a confidence trick. In fact I was quite alarmed at how much Bill stood to lose. He began as all did easily swallowing the first cracker. I was waiting for the second to dry his mouth up completely and terminate the attempt. To my horror Bill then put the other four in his mouth, rolled them into a ball, lubricated them with what saliva he had and swallowed them! Where he got the idea from I do not know and I doubt if anyone else could do it. The money went to Bill. No-one had lost much and we should have left it at that but I foolishly said, "but no-one could do it twice." And no normal human being could but as you have probably realised by now – Bill did. The bets rolled in again, more in fact, with great confidence, until, to my horror Bill did it again in the same unnatural way. My reputation as a reliable person was trashed.

At the end of six months I had decided to go the surgical route and take Primary. To this end I simply changed consultants and kept the same job. This meant we could live in the same flat and give some sort of security. In the end I actually continued for another year. I liked Poole and although the work was busy the life was good. During this time something very important occurred. The jump from medical student to working doctor is a huge leap. Confidence is slow to develop and can only come with experience. The intense work in Accident and Emergency was giving me this. I can remember the moment, one Sunday morning when I was on for the weekend stepping outside Poole A & E and saying, "Dorset, you can throw what you want at me, I'm ready!" From that moment I was confident, not overly so but cautiously confident. I imagine all doctors go through that moment. It is the real moment that you become a doctor.

As the year progressed things changed as they do. To pursue the surgical route I was attending the Primary course at Southampton. After all the Anatomy we had done before 2nd MB I realised that there was a whole universe of anatomy yet to be learned. I stuck at it but did not enjoy it. My wife, a nurse, became pregnant and, thus, would be out of work soon. There was no maternity leave then. When a woman went off to have a baby that was the end of the job. When maternity leave came in it was a wonderful progression but was quickly abused. My job was also coming to an end as it was on a six-month contract. Somewhere to live was always a problem with short term contracts and we had twice been within a day of being homeless. I have never been homeless but the fear of it is quite enough for me. We were living in a flat at the hospital and needed a house. In the winter, there were cheap places to rent in Sandbanks, so we took one, but that winter, there were electricity strikes, and it was not much fun to come back to a place with no electricity after a long day's work. No telly or radio but also no hot drink unless the gas hob worked. It was dark and miserable. On the political scene, Edward Heath and Anthony Barber were flooding the country with money and house prices were rising. If we were both sure to be earning, which we weren't, we could have just about afforded the average house at that time, which was around £6000. As money flooded the market house prices began to rise and word went out that it would be more than prudent to get on the housing ladder. Thus it was one Saturday morning that I joined a queue of men outside Estate agents Fox and Sons Parkstone. There was a new housing development, Conifer Park, Lower Parkstone and I needed to put our name down for a semi. Eventually it was my turn. A man was sitting in front of a map of the estate on which were the match-box houses. We only had half a minute to make a decision. I pointed my finger to an unclaimed semi and gave the man £50 in notes and that was it. A few months later we entered the property, still very much a building site and paid £7,500. Six months later we sold it for £14,750! We were on the housing ladder. Unfortunately, at the time we had no way of paying for it as both of us would be out of work!

I had thought of entering general practice and had applied and been offered jobs in Lancashire, Swindon and Wolverhampton, but my wife did not want to move.

One day, as we sat in that miserable bungalow facing the abyss, the phone rang. It was the Clayford practice asking if I was still interested in the job I applied for the previous year. Was I interested? Was I! When I arrived at the practice, Croft House on Ringwood Road, I heard the sorry tale of what had happened in the past year. They had eventually appointed a doctor of suitable age, but he could not cope with the night calls. This, unfortunately, was not the only issue. He was Jewish. Nothing wrong with that, of course, but he allegedly – I've only heard the rumour – had an improper relationship with a nun from the Holy Cross Abbey up the road! This did not go down well in a small, closed community as Clayford was then. He had to go, and he did. This was their first disaster. They then appointed a doctor in his mid-fifties who they thought would be more suitable to the ambience of the area. He was the second disaster. He had a huge array of qualifications in the medical directory – medical, dental and an MD from Malta – but most of them had been bought. A few months after I started, a lady came to me saying she had been bleeding from her vagina. She had called the doctor at Christmas, who said she should come to the surgery when she had stopped bleeding, and then, he would examine her. She came to see me in May when, by some miracle, she had stopped for a while. I examined her, and there was a huge cavity from cancer of the uterus – appalling negligence! She was treated with radiotherapy and, thankfully, responded very well to it. The patients were afraid of him, and the staff loathed him. Jock and a soon-retiring Ian were overloaded.

And so, just when I was desperate for a job, they were also desperate for a doctor. This was a totally different kind of interview to the one that had occurred a year previously and the complete opposite. We were both desperate! Their two attempts at finding a suitable new doctor had been disastrous. Jock would be left with an expanding list with only 'the disaster' to help him! I could not lose! And so, I started working, but six months later, I had no security. A six-month period of consideration was quite normal and acceptable, but there was still 'the disaster' between Jock and me. So, I wrote down all the reasons Jock should offer me a partnership and recited them over and over again to myself. I then asked to see him alone. I walked in, and just as I was about to make my oration, he said, "Oh, before you start, I've got rid of Dr X (the disaster), and I want you to become a partner." I was speechless. I never did make my speech. I still have it – written but unspoken. Six years later, Jock retired, and I was the senior partner for the next thirty-two years! So it was with much regret I ended my eighteen months at Poole hospital. It had changed the direction of my life geographically and also my career aspirations. We had a house and a son – but no job. At the moment of leaving we had a big mortgage and no job between us! It was possible at that time to do general practice without vocational training which was just starting but many years from being obligatory. Later I became a Trainer myself for over thirty years but at the time I just learnt on the job. Therefore, between ending at Poole and starting at Clayford I fitted in two one-month locums. My first surgery was a locum of the old-fashioned type where the patients just turn up and wait. After an hour of work a young lady came in with a large golden retriever and it was some time before I realised that the dog was the patient and not her. Alas there was a vets next door and she had made a mistake. She had wondered why she was the only person in the waiting room with an animal! It reminds me of one of my old patients, Bert, who was sitting next to a lady who said to him, "I hope the doctor hurries up, I have to go to the vets next." "My God," he said, "whatever is wrong with you? It must be serious!"

MISSION ACCOMPLISHED

Croft House - just before it was demolished

CHAPTER 5
GENERAL PRACTICE

When I wrote my book, *The Life and Decline of the Family Doctor*, it grew partly from the memories of the patients who became part of my life and partly from my knowledge and experience over a long period of General Practice. However, I did not set the scene chronologically because it was not that sort of a book. The theme was the decline of an institution, the family doctor. As a result I never really described the place that I was to settle into and which became a major part of my life.

Clayford was a place one passed through. It was close to three towns, Poole, Bournemouth and Christchurch, and a bit further from three cities, Dorchester, Salisbury and Southampton. It was therefore suitable for people who worked elsewhere. It also had its indigenous population and it was those people I inherited from the outgoing partner Ian Limbery. These settled country people were, I found out over several decades, nearly all related which led to a very fast underground communication. It was confusing when there were so few surnames. One might visit Mrs So and So and then to be called back the same day to apparently the same person only to find it was the lady next door who was the sister or cousin or aunt. The village cum town had one traffic light then and I remember the dismay when the first traffic warden began to patrol in 1975. Many of the roads were unmade and the dwellings unnumbered. One lesson quickly learnt was never to go on a visit without knowing where it was. I have always had a problem with first names but became adept at remembering addresses to the amazement of my trainees.

MISSION ACCOMPLISHED

The Surgery was Croft House, above, and this stylish building was on the main road close to the centre of Clayford. I say the centre because it was basically a crossroads with traffic lights and a few shops. It was run by two wonderful receptionists and a finance lady. They were always kind and helpful. One of them was the wife of the dentist who had taken over the upstairs. The other was a very grand, older lady who could be utterly charming or utterly ruthless. "You can't see the Doctor today, you should have rung earlier!" As a 'dragon' she was entirely natural and self-taught! The building was the property of Ian Limbery who on retirement had had a bungalow built in the garden and who resided there. I would often lunch with him and he would tell me tales of the patients which as time went on I found priceless. My wife and I had jumped on the property ladder so we had a house but it was now seven miles away and I was on-call with the phone coming through to the house. We needed to move locally as soon as possible. It is difficult to remember the details after all this time but I do remember telling Ian that all was set for sale of the old house and purchase of the new but I was struggling with a shortfall of cash for a while. "How much?" he asked. "£5,000", I replied not thinking it was any more than conversation. He went over to the mantelpiece, picked up his cheque book and wrote me a cheque for the amount! Just like that. So generous and so wonderful. A few days later I returned £4,000 and the rest at the end of the month.

Young people today think we had it easy and maybe we did but I don't think so. It was certainly different. Apart from the totally different work culture the finance was all over the shop. In 1972 in East Dorset house prices doubled in six months. Either you had climbed on the housing ladder or you were compromised for years. In 1973 there was the Yom Kippur war where thirteen Arab countries had declared their purpose to 'drive Israel into the sea.' At the end of the war Israel had taken the Golan Heights, invaded Jordan and was over the Suez Canal threatening Cairo. The result was that the Arabs thought that controlling the oil was a better way of doing things than losing wars. OPEC was formed under the guidance of Sheik Yamani. The price of oil went up as the supply went down and we all drove at under 55mph to conserve supplies. Shares dropped by seventy percent. Not a problem for most people but many of our patients survived on dividends from shares. If they had been caught between buying and selling the previous year they were doomed to an old age of penury. Many ended their previously well financed days in a mobile home and on old age pension. Then inflation rose until by 1975 at one point it reached twenty-seven percent.

Even the weather challenged us. Today we have global warming and every event is unprecedented! In 1972 midsummer's day was colder than midwinter's day. The next ice age, it was said, due after 12,000 years of the seventeeth interglacial, was coming. In 1975 we had the hottest summer for thirty-five years. I well remember Ian doing a locum for the practice asking me if Jock would mind him removing his jacket whilst he worked. They had been in practice together for thirty years! After a dry winter we then had the hottest summer recorded, 1976. During the August of that year East Dorset burned. The old people's hospital at St Leonards had to be evacuated and the lucky ones bedded at the Smugglers Haunt, a fine pub. They loved it thanks to the generous landlord, Eddie Burns. Part of a nearby village was evacuated because it was close to an army petrol storage dump surrounded by fire.

My hospital hours had been long and hard but those early years in general practice were only a little better. My remembrance was that instead of having five desperately urgent things to do at once I only had two. Mondays were particularly memorable because having started at eight in the morning I would stagger in at eight in the evening just as *Panorama* started. A weekend on would start on Friday morning and end on Monday evening. The time in between could be good, bad or diabolical. I had Tuesday afternoons off to compensate for the fact that we worked all week plus a full Saturday morning surgery and nights and weekends on a rota. The modern GP has an afternoon or whole day off *without* working nights and weekends and yet the current BMA Chair of Council insists that GPs are working harder. That is definitely what Tom Sawyer would have called 'a stretcher.'

The first thing to do was to get to know my patients. I always thought of them as my patients because I had inherited them from Ian Limbery and they had been his patients. They were mine and neither of us was going away. My lunches with Ian were so valuable and I learnt so much. He had known them for so long and I was so young it bothered me that I would be accepted. There were some who wanted to see the old doctor and not the new young doctor. However, there were some who did not want to see the old doctor and were very pleased to see the new young doctor. The most reassuring thing was one day when an elderly lady who must have been with Ian for at least 40 years said that I was the same age as Ian when he started! We were all young once and relationships take years to nurture.

There were also some strange patients to get to know. There was the man, in his eighties who, according to his wife, kept himself fit by standing on his head for ten minutes each day. There was the lady who could not sleep until she had six pickled onions last thing at night. There was the retired colonel who felt 'bloody.' "I feel bloody, Doctor!" was all I could ever get out of him. He would not respond to closed or open questions. We never got very far.

Another retired military man called me for a home visit. His wife opened the door and a fit looking gentleman came down the stairs with the challenge, "I can't play golf anymore!" When I observed that it was not surprising as he was eighty-two I realise that this was not the right answer! Now at seventy-five myself I can see his point. Why shouldn't he play golf at any age. Nowadays I think ageism should be classified as a hate crime! Apart from that I was not a golfer and although I have many friends who are golfers I would not like my daughter to marry one!

Most confusing of all was the 'relaxed' throat. It was a very common presentation. I was familiar with sore throats, pharyngitis, laryngitis, adenoids, tonsillitis both follicular and membranous, but not with the 'relaxed' throat. No patient could ever explain it and to this day I have no idea what it was. There were no physical signs and no sequelae.

There were also the settled travellers of varying Romany descent. Some of the bungalows were like the inside of the archetypal Romany caravan with dolls and mementos everywhere. They were good people and we got on well with them but needed special handling. On visiting, the dwelling would be full of people, children and dogs. It was usually to visit a sick child and there would be massive concern. The trick was to spot the head woman and address all communication to her. One could nod to the mother, (the men were more or less without a role) but you talked to the head woman. If you had her confidence all would be well. What you had just said to her, she would repeat to the other women as though they were all deaf. The concern of the family for each other was touching and in contrast to the Golf Links road people who would call us to see if their eight-year-old should accompany them on their skiing holiday.

There was a quaintness about the village indicated by the number of garden gnomes. There were an extraordinary number of gnomes and because some gardens had ten or twenty I wondered sometimes whether there were more gnomes than people! In later years when I had trainee GPs from urban areas they gently disparaged the semi-rural apparently well off area. But some were very poor and they became sick like we all do. Disease respects no-one. Tom Shearing was the nearest thing we had to a tramp apart from the fact that he biked rather than tramped. He was one of many characters like the milkman who rode to the pub on his horse to make sure he got home safely. There was the lady whose husband had died for whom I inherited pastoral visits. Her long garden drive was a mass of herbaceous colour like a van Gogh painting, almost too much colour, and she was not lonely because three men had moved into her garden shed and although they sometimes annoyed her she did not want to get rid of them for the company. I never saw them, of course, because it was a fixed but harmless delusion. We had been taught all about schizophrenia but not about those people with fixed delusions and nothing else. I had a few. I could never say they were sad people because they were content, but to me they were.

It was difficult for me to come to terms with how sad people could be. One couple had lost their first child before I knew them but went on to have four more. One day mother brought the eldest son in aged eleven. He looked small and his legs a bit bent. He had renal rickets. When they had been in another practice his refluxing ureters had caused an infection which had not been treated. The infection had crept to his kidneys and he was now in chronic renal failure. A dialysis machine was helicoptered into their garden and he was dialysed three times a week until his kidney transplant. The anti-rejection drug cyclosporin was given by mouth in those days and as the years went by he developed a tongue cancer which was removed. It was difficult for him to talk but even more so when another tongue cancer appeared which was also removed. The kidney eventually failed and he succumbed. Meanwhile the second son developed Type 1 diabetes so he was on daily insulin but continued to smoke. While he was being stabilised mother developed Type 2 diabetes and father, also a smoker acquired COPD. The next child, a lovely girl became schizophrenic at eighteen and required full time care. That left a last son and I prayed he would be alright. Whether it was inevitable under the circumstances or not, he developed chronic anxiety. He was scared to go into shops and interaction generally. Our clinical psychologist worked on him for years with little success. He believed himself to be ugly (he was not) and to make sure he was justified and right he self-harmed his face, grew his hair long and never washed it. Strangely he always held down his job as a factory joiner. And one more thing without being judgemental, his fear of shops and the female gender did not prevent him from purchasing women's clothing.

I began to realise that people's homes were an extension of their personal physical signs. One slim and attractive lady with a croaky voice from her chain smoking had a white house. That is to say it would have been but for the smoking. But the carpet had started out white and the walls and the furniture were also off-white. Her clothes were usually a white track suit. There were few ornaments and they were whitish anyway. But further inspection revealed that her neat garden had no deciduous trees or bushes. There was nothing there which would shed a leaf and thus impinge upon its perfection. Outside her house there was a grass verge, neatly mowed and weeded, the only section like that in the road. Her environs revealed so much about her. She did not like abnormalities and would not tolerate blemishes. She was a lovely woman with a fine husband, no children or pets. Presumably he liked it that way as well. Her real blemish of course was her smoking of which she was in denial! Equally there were dwellings where the garden was a mess the house a mess and dog ends piled on the ash trays. One suspected they would tolerate unwellness and be in denial of their health. Where people lived was also a sad thing because many for a peaceful life would move to the village and find a quiet close and get as near to the end as they could. Nothing happens at the end of closes and they would become more and more lonely. They would lose their friends and life was barely worth living.

CHAPTER 6
MAKING A DIFFERENCE

SO TIMES THEN WERE CHALLENGING to say the least. It never occurred to me to want anything else. On the contrary I looked round to see how I could make a difference. I had inherited 2,400 patients, most of whom had only ever known one doctor. What could I do for them?

The major cause of premature death at that time was heart disease. More than thirty percent of adults smoked at that time and smoking was a curse. It had been encouraged in wartime to assuage appetite. It had also been a way of introduction for people who were otherwise strangers often from abroad. The Americans had occupied the 104th Army Hospital just up the road at St Leonards. Bournemouth was a furlough area for American, Canadian and British officers. Also, the cholesterol argument was formulating. Apart from the major risk factors of smoking, hypertension and diabetes, (much underdiagnosed at that time,) high cholesterol was an important factor. The lipid protein fractions were known to be important from work done in the 1960s and the importance of the high-density fraction and its protective quality was known. Apart from the important genetic factors, HDL was raised (a good thing) by losing weight, low blood pressure, giving up smoking and conversely it was lowered (a bad thing) by smoking, obesity, raised blood pressure and diabetes.

I therefore decided to screen the men in the practice. A few doctors were screening their patients but it was a novel thing and I remember introducing it to a large number of sceptical GPs at a talk at the old Boscombe hospital. What they thought of this precocious young doctor

I do not know but I think it went down well. I chose men because it was considered (erroneously) that heart disease was largely a male problem. I chose age thirty to call them in because I thought they were young enough to make a difference and old enough to be motivated. I thought the 'immortality of youth' might be wearing off! The response was wonderful and the motivation was good. I still have all my records and I am glad to say, still meet some of the high-risk candidates who seem to be still, after all these years, in the best of health. I started the screening in 1973 and finished in1978. By that time the concept of mass screening had taken hold. Like a lot of good GP innovations it was taken over steadily by health authorities and consequently there have been countless patients who did not develop heart disease, diabetes or have strokes. I am sure that there was much undiagnosed diabetes causing premature heart disease and sudden death. Spring was the time I dreaded because the semi-rural East Dorset population would be out in the garden, cutting, lopping, digging their vegetable patch – and then keeling over with chest pain. Unfortunately the mass screening of well people had the flip side of creating the bane of the GP's life - 'the worried well!'

As the new drugs, statins appeared, our weapon to lower cholesterol was enhanced. Because most of the evidence measured total cholesterol, the vital protective significance of HDL was forgotten or ignored. A total cholesterol of 6 with an HDL of 2 is preferable to a total cholesterol of 5 and an HDL of 1. I thought I would support this by checking the cholesterols of my oldest patients. Sure enough they had high total cholesterols but HDLs of around 3. They were never going to have a heart attack.

Depression was another area where I thought I could make a difference and started writing down all the different presentations of depression. They were legion and well into my research I thought I would write a paper on it. Alas a doctor from Leicestershire, Watts, had already done it!

The training I had had in Leeds must have been effective to cope with the huge range of challenges I faced. I had never been a fan of paediatrics partly because of not having children of my own (then) and therefore they were an unknown element to me, and partly because the paediatric consultants were amongst the least likeable in the medical school and that was saying something if one thought of the obstetricians apart from the one I worked for. Nevertheless I quickly learnt how to manage sick children remembering that we rarely sent patients to hospital. The threshold for hospital admission was massively lower now than then and yet our outcomes were very good. We learnt to live with uncertainty which has become harder and harder over the years. I learnt to recognise the measles cough. Most parents would let their children cough for a few days before they brought them to us but they brought the measles cough on the first day. There was something harsh and sinister about it. One would tell the parents that in three days the child would get sore eyes and spots in the mouth and then the next day they would come out in a rash. Inevitably they would ring up on the fourth day to say that the child was no better – and now they had come out in a rash! I don't blame them. Measles is a horrible thing, it can be a killer, but thanks to vaccination is largely a memory in the UK. Good riddance.

Another challenge was Roseola. It occurs in very young children who would have a very high temperature but not be particularly unwell. Today they would be admitted for blood cultures and lumbar puncture. Neck stiffness would develop and just when it was becoming really scary, the rash would come out and the child would be completely better. Massive relief. Croup was a common emergency in winter. The parents would have put the child to bed and be watching TV only to be disturbed by that awful crouping cough as the child inhaled through a swollen larynx. It could usually be heard over the phone. I would instruct the parent to wrap the infant in a blanket and walk them round the garden hoping the cool moist air, of which we have an abundance in Britain, would sooth the swelling. Mostly it had gone when I arrived but if it had not or recurred when they went inside it was an ambulance and a night in the croupette. Strangely, of all the nights I sent those worried parents with their offspring round the garden, on only one occasion did it rain.

So I entered general practice, keen to work hard and keen to make a difference. There was much scope then and I found I had the power as an independent practitioner to do things. Today Clinical Governance has crushed this and genuine innovation is almost impossible in general practice. As Jock had got rid of the 'disaster' we were a doctor short and Clayford was expanding. There were acres of land and money was beginning to appear in the economy. Jock and I interviewed about nine would-be candidates and I managed to put them all off because I wanted a colleague from Poole Hospital who duly joined us. In 1974 we moved into a new Health Centre nearby and sadly out of Croft House. Those first days in Croft House were my happiest in general practice and I can visualise them now.

In 1975 I did two things which looking back were incredibly far reaching and life enhancing. The first was to buy added years to my pension. It doesn't sound much but made a huge difference in the end and considering that I was severely short of money and only thirty, a brilliantly far-sighted investment. The second thing was to decide to become a member of the Royal College of General Practitioners. Jock had joined the College right at its onset before it was Royal! Having obtained the Diploma in Obstetrics I wanted a few more letters after my name! In the same spirit of foresight and prudence which made me invest in added pension years I had noted that the fee to take the MRCGP examination was only £28! This was less than £6 a letter. I was miffed to find when the time came that they had put it up to £36. But inflation was in the high twenties! The examination comprised essay questions, a multiple-choice questionnaire and if all was well, an oral examination. I was enjoying general practice and learning avidly so I was confident. The essay questions were about general practice as was the whole examination. The reason I say that is that modern medicine is so bedevilled by irrelevant politically correct modules I fear to think what it is like now.

The multiple-choice section, however, was a challenge for a different reason. The current multiple-choice is sixty questions in five parts which in effect means three hundred different questions. Ours was one hundred in five parts and therefore five hundred questions in the same three hours. It also had the twist in the tail in that there was negative marking! This has now been dropped and you get a point for a correct answer but are not penalised for getting it wrong. We were! It was therefore theoretically possible to get less than zero. Also when the examination came at the College, marking was to be done electronically. By each question were three boxes to say whether the statement was right or wrong or don't know. This was to be shaded in by pencil. It was pointed out that if the pencil went through the paper producing a hole the machine might miss it and thereafter all the answers would be one rectangle early and therefore all wrong. So at the crucial point of preparing to answer these five hundred questions we were not thinking about the answers but desperately blunting our pencils! I went through the paper fairly well and was confident I would achieve about seventy percent. I then remembered the negative marking and confidence drained. Things that a few minutes ago had been certain were now wobbling seriously. Although I hoped for seventy percent I could have nearly a hundred percent or possibly less than fifty and therefore fail. I scoured each question rigorously gently rubbing out and re-shading until I was fairly confident that I would get sixty percent with a range that would guarantee more than fifty percent. It must have worked because a few weeks later came the invitation to attend the College again for the oral examination which invoked memories of those dreaded anatomy vivas which I had endeavoured so hard to bury.

The College building of the Royal College of General Practitioners was then off Hyde Park and had been the American Embassy during World War Two and occupied by Joseph Kennedy, their Anglophobic ambassador. He had placed Indian heads around the fascia making it unmistakeable. The building came to fame later when the SAS used it to relieve the siege of the Iranian Embassy next door. For some reason the College library was flooded in the process. It was to this building that I and a contingent from East Dorset went late on a very hot Saturday afternoon. Most people who accept that 1976 was our hottest year after a very dry winter have forgotten that 1975 was the hottest year for 35 years. Hyde Park was hot, the grass brown and parched and so was I. As I walked in I espied a jug of water and tumblers on a hall table and made for it, or would have, but for a commanding voice indicating that it was for the examiners and NOT the candidates. Clearly the £36 fee did not extend to luxuries such as water!

The questions were straightforward and practical. I only remember one now. Halfway through the morning surgery one had been called out to a man attempting suicide. Then followed the usual format of questioning until one stumbled. If one answered confidently they changed track just in case you were enjoying yourself. To be fair they had two examiners and behind them two more checking the examiners to make sure they were being fair. At least that is what they said they were doing. The interesting thing was what my fellow candidates said when we discussed it later. One friend, a fine doctor had been asked what he would have said over the phone to the would-be suicide. He simply replied that he wasn't very good over the phone! This seemed to impress the examiners who passed him anyway. Interestingly only one of our number when at the end of the interrogation was asked what they would do next, said he would go back and finish the surgery! The consequence of all this was not just that I had five more letters after my name but that the local Associate Advisor in General Practice wanted me to become a GP Trainer. Reluctant at first, it eventually happened and training doctors to become General Practitioners became one of the most fulfilling parts of my life. Apart from the students and later the Second Year Foundation doctors I had thirty full-time trainees each for one year. They were all amazing in different ways and gave me learning and stimulation and a wonderful career.

All that was ahead of me. It was already twelve years since I stood next to that dissection table as an eighteen-year-old, green and bewildered, but determined, student. So much had happened and work was hard but it was exactly what I wanted to do. In many ways it was so much simpler then than now. This was before the days of herpes let alone HIV. The drugs scene had come but hardly impinged on medical experience. Psychiatry dealt with mental illness, not chemical dependency. GP training was beginning and doctors were reflecting on how things could be done differently rather than spending time on the golf course. The big issue was the lack of money. By 1979 you could hardly get a light bulb changed in our local authority owned health centre. The next decade witnessed huge changes as money appeared - we bought our medical centre and council house tenants bought their houses. Many of my contemporaries were very clever people and their cleverness was facilitated by the lack of central control. Postgraduate education was virtually voluntary so those who used it were the zealots; clever and fun to learn with. In 1990 we had a new contract and the government flexed its muscles under the guise of getting value for money. Conversely the more government has controlled GPs the less it has squeezed out of them.

All this was to come ...

During the 38 years in this Practice I could not have managed without our Practice Sister, Jenny (Matron) and my four secretaries, Jan, Sandy, Jackie and for 22 years Janice.

L to R The author, Jan, Sandy and Jenny (Matron.)

Jackie and Matron

The incomparable Janice

LIFE AND DECLINE OF THE FAMILY DOCTOR

MISSION ACCOMPLISHED BOOK 3
BY DR CHARLES REES

INTRODUCTION

In 1954, I was taken to the East Cliff at Bournemouth, where I was born and had lived, to see the Battleship Vanguard. It was our last battleship, and the potential power of its 15" guns was colossal. Had it wanted to, it could have destroyed Bournemouth, Poole, Christchurch and possibly, most of Southampton too without shifting position. I was fascinated by the 20th century Royal Naval history, and the advent of the dreadnought and the subsequent dreadnoughts were very much a part of this. I did not realise at that moment that I was looking at the last of our dreadnoughts. The age of the dreadnought battleship had come and gone in the space of fifty years, two generations, and made obsolete by advances in warfare. When I eventually settled for a career as a family doctor in the National Health Service (NHS), I had no idea that the concept of a family doctor in a group practice would also become obsolete ten years after I retired. The general practitioner (GP) survives, granted, but it is very different from the creature of my day. I realised that there would never be a family doctor who held a personal list of 2000 to 2500 patients for thirty-eight years as I had. There may have been a few but not anymore. I had kept meticulous records of events – always analysing, reflecting and looking for ways to do things differently. I still have the yearbooks – thirty-eight of them – with records of every home visit. I still have a DDA record with every event worthy of requiring strong drugs and the reason thereby. It has a detailed report on the changes in that period. It recorded the epidemics, whooping cough in 1977, Type A influenza in December 1989 and others. I realise that this may be a unique record from the days of family doctors because since my retirement nearly ten years ago from the Practice, much has changed.

After retiring from the Practice, I worked as a locum in six Practices for over seven years. It was a wonderful experience because I was able to work just for pleasure without any responsibilities. However, I did not realise that during that time, the age of the full-time family doctor was fading, and the age of the 'portfolio' doctor was ascending. These doctors, of both genders, worked for just a few sessions a week in GP and supplemented their work with something else. With time on their hands, they were able to become dominant in these areas. There is much to be said for this, but there is the issue that they ended up doing very little general practice and doing much of jobs they were not trained for. A GP is a 'jack of all trades and master of none.' No problem there. In fact, medicine needs at least one generalist. But unfortunately, the best way to learn as much as possible from the huge gamut of medical presentations is to see more patients. The new GPs see fewer patients and, exhausted by the plethora of presentations, decide that the solution would be to drop a session. The correct solution would have been to see more patients, not fewer. Of course, family doctors still exist, but they are aware that they are a dying breed. They carry on with a pervading air of despair. This book is not alluding to a golden age because there never was one. The world was very different then, and I would like to record it and the fascinating patients who affected my life. The generation of doctors I had worked with had gone through WW2. They worked hard throughout the day but often played golf in the afternoon. They largely did not reflect on things but did it because that was the way they were done. In the spectrum of being good and being nice, they tended to be good. It is of merit to be both, of course, but the modern doctor has to be nice rather than good. The weight of persistently being nice to all, however odious, rude or downright aggressive they might be, is very wearisome. There is no outlet. And though being good is virtuous, it is no longer enough. It is now more important to follow guidelines however wrong they may seem. But one size never fits all. The guidelines are very useful to young doctors, especially if they have little experience, but they are framed by people who have read medical papers and not by doctors who have seen patients. So, while the old doctors wanted to be good, though they weren't always nice, the new doctors are nice and follow guidelines.

MISSION ACCOMPLISHED

So, what is the difference between a GP and a family doctor? General practitioners came into existence with the NHS Act of 1947 and started working in 1948. Strictly speaking, a GP is a self-employed doctor who is sub-contracting mainly, but not entirely, to the NHS. This gives the GP some special privileges concerning pensions in particular. Their duty was to fulfil the terms and conditions of service, and naturally, there were always some right at the beginning who simply did this and no more. But most followed the tradition of being constant and loyal to their patients, which meant going beyond the terms and conditions when appropriate. In my lifetime, there were some outstanding role models, such as John Frye from Beckenham in Kent. He started his practice in 1943 and, believing there were few effective treatments, jotted down something about every patient he saw. Nowadays, almost all the existing diseases and conditions have been altered by treatment, and so, the natural history of common illnesses is not known. But thanks to John Frye, it was. He liked to quote WHO's definition of good health – "Health is a state of complete physical, mental and social well-being." He would add with a twinkle in his eye that the only time anyone felt like that was during the act of sexual intercourse! To start with our Terms and Conditions of Service were short enough to be read, and they were negotiated between the NHS and the profession. As time went on, the Government realised that it was the more powerful partner in the arrangement and could change things at will. In 1990, a new set of Terms and Conditions appeared and the writing was on the wall. The Government wanted a population-based approach, which I will explain later, and from that moment, doctors worked for the Government and not their patients. When I retired from my practice, I joined the local Probus. I met men who had held important jobs all over the world. Their knowledge of the world and its working was vast, but their knowledge of the human condition was not. They had been looking through a telescope of world experiences whereas I had been looking down a microscope. When I talk to them and think of my thirty-eight years in Clayford in East Dorset, I marvel at my limited ambition and horizons. And yet, at the time, it did not seem like that. Each year and each day brought forth new challenges to drive me on. The job was never done. It was like building sandcastles on the beach – every wash of the waves undid the previous build. For every condition that was cured or alleviated, the patient brought forth new problems that came with age. I still drink at the local British Legion with some old patients, mostly bricklayers. How I envied them! They could go back ten to thirty years later and still see a wall they had built. So, do I regret it?

The simple way to answer is to relate it to a story. Many years ago, I was pursuing my post-graduate education at Bath. At breakfast, I was sitting next to an interesting Doctor who worked at the Rheumatology centre there. Without prompting, he suddenly dived into a recitation on his glittering career. He had done this and that, received many awards, held a professorship in California and was now a consultant at Bath. People had stopped talking, and there was a listening silence. The room went quiet. And then, for some reason, I started with my response. When I was eleven, I said, my mother died, and in the years that followed, I decided I hated illness and death. I wanted to do something about it and by fifteen, I had made up my mind to be a doctor. I went to medical school at eighteen and was qualified at twenty-three. When I entered general practice, all I wanted to do was to be a family doctor. I wanted to bring people into this world and ease them out of it when the time came. I wanted to diagnose measles, mumps, chickenpox and all the usual illnesses that plague peoples' lives and help them to cope with them. That is what I have done, and it has been a privilege. There was an even heavier silence in the room. I had never meant to put my consultant friend down, but he most certainly had been. Most of the doctors there were just like me with similar stories. There were doctors for whom family medicine was a passion and a privilege and not just an academic exercise. I think that answers the question. That answer and the truth behind it kept me going for forty-eight years and offering help to 300,000 patients in the NHS!

A FAMILY DOCTOR

I HAVE ALLUDED TO THE DIFFERENCES between a GP who fulfils their Terms and Conditions of service and a family doctor. I could explain this in detail by offering a huge number of examples, but here are a few.

I was very lucky because the doctor I replaced had been in Clayford for about forty years, except for six years at the war. Thus, there were a large number of middle-aged to elderly patients who had only ever known two doctors – Ian and myself. He told me many tales that proved to be invaluable as time went on. One of the older characters was Bert. He was a pointer by trade, which was a well-paid but boring occupation. Bert used to talk as a coping strategy. He could keep talking and would always be interesting. He claimed he had never had a day off in his life, which was probably true, in one respect, matched by the fact that he had never done a full day's work in his life! One day, after he had genuinely retired, he had come to me looking unusually glum. I asked him what the problem was, and he mentioned the name of one of his daughters. She had been diagnosed with Huntington's! Huntington's chorea is caused by an autosomal dominant gene; it appears in middle age and results in premature dementia and death. It is awful and could affect fifty percent of any offspring. Bert was upset and wondered how his family of six children would take the news. Thanks to those chats with Ian, I found a way out. "Yes, but Bert, she isn't yours anyway." This information would not help the unfortunate lady, but it meant there were no implications for the rest of the family as Bert had six children but only one of them was his. I wondered if Bert knew how I knew this, but he never asked. He just looked relieved as though he had forgotten about his unfaithful wife's high sex drive and loose morals. I think the modern portfolio doctor only looks at the tip of the iceberg when they see a patient. Knowing them and their families for over decades makes such a difference. I remember another incident involving two sisters who were very close. The elder had carcinoma in situ of the cervix, which, in those days, was treated with a cone biopsy. This was very different from the modern practice of minimal invasiveness, but it did end the issue. The younger sister had regular smears but somehow slipped through the net and went on to have invasive cancer. The progress of the disease was inexorable and awful as those who know will understand. I was involved very closely with the family– her husband and two children – throughout. When she became terminal, she and the family wanted her to be at home. One of the ideas my senior partner, Jock, had impressed on me at the outset of my work was that we need not be confined to our official hours. Visiting at night or on weekends, whenever appropriate, was alright. I knew many family doctors who visited on Sundays, almost pastorally, even when they were not on call because it was quiet. This family who had stuck together through this ordeal realised that their loved one might die in the middle of the night and have the death certified by a stranger, who would mutter condolences but who would not have known the young mother at all. When asked, I willingly gave my home phone number as it was a privilege to be asked to attend. It duly happened at about two in the morning. We chatted as I certified, and it helped them. Clinic doctors don't have this bond that, thirty years later, still exists.

Margaret was a solicitor's secretary and was about the same age as me. She was single with a son whom she brought up alone. I really knew nothing else about her background. She didn't seem to have any other family or support. She had a chronic indigestion problem and, from time to time, had gastroscopies and appropriate treatments. When she returned once with a new case of indigestion, I organised another gastroscopy. But this time, cancer of the stomach was found. She had undergone all the current treatments but with diminishing success. The time eventually came for her to be admitted to our local MacMillan unit for the last time and it was organised for midday. After the morning surgery had been completed, I felt I could not let the moment go. So, knowing she was not to be admitted until lunchtime, I dropped in to visit her. She was pleased to see me and said she would be out and back home soon. I knew it was not to be, but I didn't know if she did. What was I to say? Anything I could have said would have been complete flannel. She was going to die. How do you talk about that without being sanctimonious or lying? I had had a heck of a morning in surgery. Each patient had been an absolute so-and-so, to use our everso-British vernacular. Just then, I had a brainwave – I would not talk about her; I would talk about me. I told her about the morning I had had. I regaled stories of awkward patients with their petty complaints, funny beliefs and chaotic lives. We both began to laugh more with each story until I noticed her discomfort. Her abdomen was full of fluid, ascites, due to cancer, and laughing was making her uncomfortable. I stopped and became serious again. For ten minutes, I had taken her mind off herself. Patients can be very funny; they are people with all sorts of stories, and she had enjoyed listening to them. She too calmed down and then looked at me and said, "my son and I were so lucky to have you as our doctor." That is why being a family doctor is so special. I never saw her again.

Mary was a lovely woman of about sixty, who was well-spoken and well educated. She was fairly plump and, it gives me no pleasure to say this, outwardly quite unattractive. But her personality was warm and lovely, and she was clever. So, I had often wondered why she had married that overweight, coarse, bully of a husband. He was ignorant and odious. She also had very severe psoriasis at a time when treatments for it were limited. Every now and again, it would flare up dreadfully. I sought help from my predecessor, who was like a great oracle. He knew all about it; his depth of knowledge about the patients always astonished me. One often hears people saying on the radio or television that their doctors don't know things because they never inform them. But the truth is they tell us everything, and we don't always want to remember them! Ian recited the whole sad tale. For reasons unknown, this cultured lady had married this uneducated brute who bullied her as and when he wanted sex, to use Ian's exact words, "he trussed her up like a chicken and buggered her." He usually repeated this. She did not like it and became more stressed, which made her psoriasis worse. Psoriasis has a genetic basis but, like a lot of skin conditions, is made worse by stress. At least I now knew what triggered it, though I was unable to do anything about it. However, one day, the hubby, who was a binman, lifted one bin too many and slipped a disc. In those days, many back conditions were treated by immobilisation in a plaster jacket. They weighed about half a stone, circumnavigated the body, and, most importantly, made sex impossible! Mary's psoriasis cleared – a miracle. We continued to talk but never about her sex life. Whatever abilities Ian had to get information out of distressed ladies was not yet available to me. However, she did reveal what a bully her husband was and how he would wait for her to come home with her pension to snatch it from her. I gave her my usual counselling concerning bullies. Most ladies, not surprisingly, are afraid of what might happen if they stand up for themselves, but most bullies are frightened of losing control over their victims and not over themselves. One day, she came in with a smidgeon of triumph on her face. She had confronted hubby and told him that from now on, she was her own woman and would take no more. "What did he say?" I asked with admiration. "He took it," she began, "but," she stretched out the word, "he doesn't like Dr Rees!" Well, so be it. I could take that if it meant the restoration of her self-respect. About a year later, I received a call on a Monday night, it being my night on duty. It was Mary. She said she thought her hubby had died in his chair. I shot around, and indeed, he had. We sat and talked, and I asked what had happened. He was not a healthy man with heart disease and diabetes and was well overweight. "I made him dumplings for his dinner," she said, "and he had two, which was quite enough, but he said, 'give me two more." I told him Dr Rees would not like it! He then said, "give me the dumplings; you can sod Dr Rees." "He ate them and then, he died!" I was not sure whether having my name cursed in a dying breath was a good thing. One thing I did know was that she was genuinely upset at his passing. Despite everything, she had sincerely loved him. But the fact that you could cure a lady's psoriasis by putting the husband in a plaster jacket was another thing they had not told me at medical school!

Charles and his wife were in their sixties, and one winter's night, they had decided to do some late-night shopping. They got into their car and had set off onto Wimborne Road but had rammed straight into a parked car. At the moment of contact, the owner was filling his car up with petrol. He was squashed like a fly on a window. The previous evening, he had run out of petrol but had just managed to roll his car down the incline to rest it outside a local garage. He had walked home and was not able to return until the following evening when he had filled a can from the garage and had proceeded to fill the tank. At that moment Charles and his wife were on their way to do some late-night shopping. Charles was interviewed extensively by the police. He hadn't been under the influence of alcohol, his vision was good, and he was fully conscious with no known medical conditions. Moreover, he had never been in any accidents. He simply didn't see the man or the car. The man could have come and gone at any time in the past twenty four hours – it was just one of those frightful things. Life went on, but two weeks later, something got into my head, and I knew I had to ring Charles up. I asked him if he was alright and he said he was. "You haven't been out for two weeks, have you?" I asked pointedly. He said he hadn't. I knew it somehow and understood it too, but this could not go on forever. So, I tried to counsel him. Did you mean to kill the man – of course not; what did you mean to do – late night shopping. Could the night have happened differently – of course it could have if they had started earlier or later or not have happened at all or if the man had not run out of petrol or come and gone at any other time. Thus, we went through the entire scenario. Someone else could indeed have resuscitated Charles's confidence (not his wife, who was equally traumatised) but surely, it was right and proper that the family doctor do it pro-actively.

A family doctor was also the advocate for the family at times when there seemed to be none. In this country, the final arbiter of the management of a child is the court and not the parents, which is not so in most European countries. Though the family has no rights at all, they may have strong opinions. A common example is when a young girl is pregnant with an unwanted baby. Through social services, the baby is put up for adoption. Though the parents of the girl may not want their grandchild adopted, who is their flesh and blood – their daughter's child – they have no rights. Fortunately, I had been involved in several cases where the grandparents had adopted the child as their own and all ended well. And as a family doctor, I was glad to play my part.

Though I have tried to explain the differences between being a family doctor and a GP, there is no more poignant explanation than that given by Don Berwick in his John Hunt lecture, and I make no apology for quoting it because he puts it across far more articulately than I could. He describes his father, who was a family doctor in a small rural town in Connecticut. "He was a person of privilege. His privilege was to enter the dark and tender places of people's lives – our people. He knew secrets. He knew – we didn't – that Mary, browsing the market shelves next to us for her cereal, had miscarried again; that Nicholas, who sold us shoes, was struggling with alcohol; that Maureen, our Club Scout leader was quietly beside herself because Jonas was depressed and using drugs. He knew that Mrs Krazinski, who taught fifth grade, had lung cancer and was going to die from it, even though she did not know because they hadn't told her yet." Those dark and tender parts of people's lives were what we had to live with. It was a privilege, but it took its toll.

HOW DID IT ALL START?

When I was ten, the family had moved to Southport in Lancashire. My mother, who was said to have developed asthma when she was nineteen, had become ill during the second winter, presumably with a chest infection. We all took turns to be with her; there was no TV then, we just had to sit by an electric fire. Eventually, she grew worse and was admitted to a hospital. I went to stay with a saint of a lady, Mrs Murgatroyd. She was totally selfless and lived for her family, friends and anyone in need. She was an extraordinary woman. She had two sons but had had a third child, a daughter, and the girl was severely handicapped. She was told to take the baby home and turn her every two hours and she would live for a fortnight. Mrs Murgatroyd took her baby home and turned her every two hours for eighteen months before she died. She would bring me bars of white chocolate and assorted books. One book I loved was a series about a doctor who went to Tanganyika, as it then was. Occasionally, as the weeks passed, I was able to visit my mother from the garden of the hospital. Children were dirty things and not to be allowed in as they might bring infection. I stood in the garden and talked to her as she leant out of the window. The visits became fewer, and when the phone rang, Mrs Murgatroyd would answer it after closing the door. One Monday evening, my father arrived and told me that my sisters and I were going to the hospital and Mummy was going to die. We trailed in to see her in an oxygen tent. She did not see us. The next morning, my father arrived and said she had died at 4 am that Tuesday morning. The years that followed were difficult for the family as my sisters left home and my father remarried. His new wife had been a nurse in the Queen Alexandra's Royal Army Nursing Corps and had received the Burma Star during WW2. You had to be within a certain distance of enemy lines for two years to get it. According to her mother, she had never had any childhood infections or any of the infectious diseases she nursed, which was just about everything except Typhus. She was a frequent smoker but gave my father at least fifteen years of a quality life after his stroke. I always say it's the smoking that got her because she died when she was 97 in comparison to her mother who did not smoke and died at 101. However, the point is that, by the time I was fifteen, I had decided I did not like illness in general and death in particular. I was determined I would do something about it; I would become a doctor. And whatever one might think about that sort of vocational slush, it made me a doctor at twenty-three and work for forty-eight years. One of my daughters had obtained a degree in Maths and had a good job in London. But she had decided it was not going to fulfil her and she changed course, gave it all up and was lucky enough to get into Hull and York Medical School. She found she had qualified on exactly the same day of the week and date of the year that my mother had died and which had made me resolute in my career. Coincidence? Probably. Spooky? Definitely.

WHY CLAYFORD?

I DID NOT WANT TO BE a GP. At medical school at Leeds, we had spent a week in general practice, and although I had not known it at the time, I had spent mine with a legend – Barry Colville. I have never seen anyone work so hard. We started at eight in the morning with surgery and visits and arrived at his house at 1 pm, ate for twenty minutes, and then we were on our way for more visits and the evening surgery, which ended at about 7 pm. I jotted down something about each patient. I found it amazing as one patient after another, who were known to him, came in with clear trust in him. My head reeled. It was stimulating, impressive and exhausting but, to a fifth-year medical student, it seemed too much like hard work! I really wanted to be a surgeon, particularly, an accident surgeon. I loved the emergency and trauma side of orthopaedics. At that time, there was no career path in accident and emergency, which posed a problem. Also, to be a surgeon, one had to start by passing the primary FRCS examination, which was not only hard in those days but had a 95% failure rate! It was a time consuming and expensive feat. But things are easier and certainly more different now. One day, the orthopaedic surgeon I was working for announced, "My old friend, Ian Limbery, is retiring, and they will need a replacement. You should apply!" I had not thought about general practice and did not even want it, but this was a command and, clearly, my application was not optional. I duly attended the interview in Clayford with Ian and Jock. It was pleasant but pointless – they wanted an older man, and I did not want the job! But it was pleasant. I had done as instructed and all was well and temporarily forgotten. A year later, things had changed as they do. My wife, a nurse, became pregnant and, thus, would be out of work soon. There was no maternity leave then. My job was also coming to an end as it was on a six-month contract. We lived in a Hospital flat and needed a new dwelling. In the winter, there were cheap places to rent in Sandbanks, but that winter, there were electricity strikes, and it was not much fun to come back to a place with no electricity after a long day's work. On the political scene, Edward Heath and Anthony Barber were flooding the country with money and house prices were rising. If we were both sure to be earning, which we weren't, we could have just about afforded the average house at that time, which was around £6000. I had thought of entering general practice and had applied and been offered jobs in Lancashire, Swindon and Wolverhampton, but my wife did not want to move. One day, as we sat in that miserable bungalow facing the abyss, the phone rang. It was the Clayford practice asking if I was still interested in the job I had applied for the previous year. Was I interested! When I arrived at the practice, I heard the sorry tale of what had happened in the past year. They had eventually appointed a doctor of suitable age, but he could not cope with the night calls. This, unfortunately, was not the only issue. He was Jewish. Nothing wrong with that, of course, but he allegedly – I've only heard the rumour – had an improper relationship with a nun from the Holy Cross Abbey up the road! This did not go down well in a small, closed community as Clayford was then. He had to go, and he did. This was their first disaster. They then appointed a doctor in his mid-fifties who they thought would be more suitable to the ambience of the area. He was a disaster. He had a huge array of qualifications in the medical directory – medical, dental and an MD from Malta – but most of them had been bought. A few months after I started, a lady came to me saying she had been bleeding from her vagina. She had called the doctor at Christmas, who said she should come to the surgery when she had stopped bleeding, and then, he would examine her. She came to see me in May when, by some miracle, she had stopped for a while. I examined her, and there was a huge cavity from cancer in the uterus – appalling negligence! She was treated with radiotherapy and, thankfully, responded very well to it. The patients were afraid of him, and the staff loathed him. Jock and a soon-retiring Ian were overloaded. And so, just when I was desperate for a job, they were also desperate for a doctor. Their two attempts at finding a suitable new doctor had been disastrous. Jock would be left with an expanding list with only 'the disaster' to help him! I could not lose! And so, I started working, but six months later, I had no security. A six-month period of consideration was quite normal and acceptable, but there was still 'the disaster' between Jock and me. So, I wrote down all the reasons Jock should offer me a partnership and recited them over and over again to myself. I then asked to see him alone. I walked in, and just as I was about to make my oration, he said, "Oh, before you start, I've got rid of Dr xxx (the disaster), and I want you to become a partner." I was speechless. I never did make my speech. I still have it – written but unspoken. Six years later, Jock retired, and I was the senior partner for the next thirty-two years!

Jock's retirement was a huge event for the practice. When I had started, the practice was run by two receptionists and a finance lady, Miss MacDonald. By the time Jock retired, the practice and our staff had more than doubled. We decided to throw a big event with a presentation and speeches, where Jock would retire and the new partner would be welcomed. Ian Limbery, who had retired when I had joined, arrived with Miss MacDonald in a car. I never knew her as anything else but Miss MacDonald. She was single and ageless. Ian Limbery had been very fit in his day but had osteoarthritis in both hips and a very early hip replacement, the Jouet. It was what is known as reverse geometry, but the problem was the metals used. They formed an electric cell and disintegrated. He would not have a revision, and so, he hobbled around on two sticks in a fair amount of pain. The patients who called out to him felt mortified when they realised that he was in a worse condition than they were. He hobbled out of his car with a cry, "A glass of water for Miss MacDonald," and hobbled back in. A secretary rushed out with the water to find Miss MacDonald dead in the car. Was it Ian's driving? His car had so many dents that you would avoid parking next to him. Or was it Miss MacDonald's sense of timing? Maybe if she could not work for Jock, she would work for no one! We did not know the reason, but thirty-eight years later when I retired, some clearly remembered this incident and waited expectantly for something to happen.

Jock enjoyed his retirement until he was eighty. One Easter weekend, he was admitted to hospital with a chest infection. They told him he had pulmonary fibrosis; he said he did not. They showed him his respiratory function tests; he disputed them. He died the next day. One of his many sayings was, "Charles, you must be 100%. It doesn't matter if you are 100% right or 100% wrong; you must be 100%." He believed in the placebo effect due to much experience. Unfortunately, in his last case, he was 100% wrong! I missed him terribly and still do.

FIRST DAY

M<small>Y FIRST DAY AS A</small> GP in Clayford was on April 4, 1972. The senior partner, Thomas Cecil McDougall-Morrison, asked me to see a few patients and do some visits afterwards. He was known to his friends as Jock, and after about a year, he asked me to call him Jock. I loved that man, and it was easily the happiest time of my career. Jock said many memorable things and one of them was "Charles, the first twenty-five years are the worst!" It was a bit of a joke, but as the decades went on, I realised how right he was. Looking back, the world seemed so primitive. There was only one traffic light in Clayford. Only 40% of the homes had telephones. The first traffic warden did not appear until 1975. And that year inflation reached 27%. Many of the roads had not been constructed, and travellers often stayed in the woods or common land, of which there was a great deal. The first visit of that morning was a few miles away where two children were unwell. Their mother was young, attractive and very pleasant. Over the following weeks, she came to see me, and we built a rapport. She struggled with headaches. I analysed her carefully eventually told her that I believed she was experiencing migraines but had a background of tension headaches. Tension headaches are said to be caused by muscular tension (never proved, I think) which can be due to physical or stress-related issues. I told her I could treat the migraines, and then, we could review the situation. When she returned the next time, she informed that the migraines had gone; she still had other headaches, but she was content to leave things as they were. A few weeks later, I received a message asking me to drop in if I was in the area. On one hand, I was always in the area because we did a lot of home visiting; on the other, I was aware that she was an attractive young woman who was around my age, and this was something to be cautious about. In those days, the remotest liaisons with patients were hanging offences! I decided to call in anyway and sat down as she brought a cup of tea. Then, she started talking. "When I was seventeen," she began, "I was courted by a man twice my age. He was very worldly, as I was not, and courteous and polite. He was the same to my parents, who liked him and were reassured by his business and money. We eventually got married, and after the wedding, on the first night, he took my clothes and underwear off and put them on himself. I was horrified. That is why I get headaches." I reflected later that they never taught us this in medical school! "But you had two children," I said. She admitted that she was floundering and confused, and then, her mother fell ill, so she just went along with it. She had two lovely children and, apart from the cross-dressing incidents, the marriage was a good one. But she did not like it. She then offered to show me the drawer where he kept his other underwear. I declined! I met her again, and we had several counselling sessions. I suggested she confront him. Bullies (I was not convinced he was a real bully albeit he had groomed her) hate being challenged. He was not a violent man, and so when she challenged him, he was horrified. The cross-dressing in her presence stopped and so did her headaches. I knew him socially and he was always good company. He was a builder. He smoked and drank heavily, and at age fifty-two, he had a heart attack and died. His wife and I always had an understanding. I was the only person who knew her secret and that was enough. Years later, I bumped into her while she was crossing the main road with a new husband. We looked at each other, and she was clearly very happy. As I said, they don't tell you all the causes of tension headaches in medical school!

Sometimes, the bond between a patient and their doctor is priceless. David was a tall, strong young man with whom I played football. I had joined the local football team, which brought along many long-lasting friends. David developed a non-Hodgkin lymphoma and was treated accordingly. When remission did not last, they realised it had been staged wrongly in the first place. Sadly, he died aged thirty-five. David's mother (I never knew his father, but I believe he was a good man) was a hard woman. She looked and talked hard and had difficulty

MISSION ACCOMPLISHED

in expressing her emotions. That was probably why she had few friends, and as the years went by, they passed on as well. But she had her family doctor, who knew her son when he was in his prime. Sometimes, she would come in just to talk about David. Sometimes, she would come in just to be there. I knew that, however superficially, I was a link to her lost son, and I was happy to just sit and be.

WORST MOMENT

U NDOUBTEDLY, THE WORST EXPERIENCE IN my medical journey was in 1986. A young man was brought to me by his family. He was a very pleasant person, but his mind was a bit mixed up after travelling to Hong Kong and beyond and taking all sorts of drugs. This was a new era of drugs, one which neither I nor the psychiatric department was prepared for. Drug abuse had occupied a very small part in my work life; there were plenty of other things to attend to. I had attended a post-graduate meeting on chemical dependency at that time, and the psychiatrist had explained how it was overwhelming their psychiatric work. Mental illness outside drug and alcohol abuse was peripheral, and doctors could help by referring as few patients as possible. The NHS was overwhelmed with work, but some occasions were worse than others. However, a psychiatrist and I managed this man with some success over a couple of months. His parents had lived in Hong Kong and were lovely people. His father had ankylosing spondylitis and, around this time, had eventually succumbed to it. His mother was a lovely smiling lady who coped with it all and the father had asked me to look after her when he had gone. Mondays were always bad and felt like stepping onto a rather fast treadmill. Just after lunch, I received a call that there were two visits with patients who had hypomania and were at opposite ends of the practice. Knowing that there would also be a full afternoon of surgery of goodness knows what, my heart sank; I always liked to be running at the same speed as the treadmill. The days were always at least ten hours long, and after thirty to forty patients with two, maybe three, problems each, my mind was tired and befuddled. Nevertheless, I sped off to the first patient, whom I did not know very well. He was not taking his medication but did not seem too bad. I retraced my steps and crossed the practice to our young man. When I arrived at the house and looked through the window, I saw him climbing over the wall at the end of the garden into the woods by the river. What was I to do? Should I have chased him? And if I caught him, what was I to do with him? I talked to his mother. She was confident he would return but had called because she thought he was deteriorating. I returned to the practice and called up the psychiatrist to ask for a domiciliary visit, which was the accepted way to deal with these situations. One psychiatrist for the whole of East Dorset was clearly not enough. The Mental Health Team have taken over this now. However, the psychiatrist was not eager to come that day. I remembered the education session previously where the psychiatrist had urged us not to press for responses; so, I just informed the psychiatrist that I needed a domiciliary visit for two patients – one who would not take his medication but I was not worried about and the other who I was worried about but would take his medication. I later rang up the mother, who confirmed that her son had returned home and taken his medication. I was always on-call on Monday nights, so I thought that if there was a problem, I would be there to deal with it. At about 7 pm that night, the young man hallucinated that his mother was a witch and suffocated her with a pillow. The incident was not discovered until Tuesday afternoon, which was my afternoon off, so I only learned of the tragedy on Wednesday morning. As my partner who had been called on Tuesday recounted the event, he also told of his irritation at being disturbed during the surgery! It was almost surreal to listen to this horrific story from my partner who was completely oblivious to the horror of it. Could I have done things differently? Churchill had reassuringly said, "let those people who have been in that position be the judges." Looking back through the retrospectoscope, one can always find an alternative. But, what about in reality? I think I made a written statement but was never asked to attend the inquest. Maybe doing so and making a verbal statement would have helped me, but life went on, barely missing a step. The family was very understanding. The young man was admitted to a mental hospital and, for all I know, may still be there. Normally, one would want a person to be cured and their mind restored but, in this case, to what reality would he be restored? This is what haunts me – his reality is that he had murdered his mother.

MENTAL ILLNESS

ONE OF THE MOST DIFFICULT, time-consuming and unrewarding tasks in the early days was obtaining a certification of mental illness. Now, one has to only make a phone call to Social Services or the Mental Health Team to deal with this onerous and unpleasant job. But in those days, the whole responsibility fell to the GP. First, the psychiatrist would have to be called, who may inform that sectioning under the Mental Health Act was required. Sometimes, one would have to arrange the psychiatrist as well as social workers, an ambulance and, often, the police, all at the same time. Getting these four agencies plus oneself and, of course, the patient all together at the same time was a tricky juggling act. They all had other jobs to do and were often reluctant, and you would always have another surgery waiting. And unlike delivering babies, there was never a happy ending. It was made more difficult by the fact that my senior partner, Jock, would have nothing to do with sectioning. Years ago, he had sectioned a lady when she was psychotic. Subsequently, she had recovered, and when she was better, she sued him in the courts. It must have been a very unpleasant experience as it went to the Winchester Crown Court. Anyway, he would not do it anymore, and so, more fell to the rest of us. It was the only task he was unhelpful with though as one of his favourite sayings was "if everyone does a bit, then nobody does too much." He was against doctors who cherry-picked, but not in this case. Rarely did everything go to plan, but in one case, it went right off the rails. One Wednesday morning, one of my partners asked me if I could certify one of his patients. He had been trying to do it all week but one agency or another, including the patient, had always been absent. The psychiatrist had signed his part of the certificate, and he just needed the social workers to apprehend the patient with the help of the

GP. Since Social Services knew all about it, he said it was just a formality. At lunchtime, I received a phone call from Ted Balls, an elderly social worker I had worked with before. He was highly competent, and I had a lot of time for him. I was relieved. The patient in question, a woman, lived in a flat above the shops on Ringwood Road. She had just gone out and was probably on the way to the Post Office around the corner in New Road. My time was precious as I had a huge antenatal clinic to do. So, I suggested that I drive around, park on the wide pavement in front of what is now the Chianti Italian restaurant, and wait for them to bring her to my car. Since it was a Wednesday afternoon, shops were closing early, traffic was light on the roads and there were few people about. I parked and waited, watching through the rearview mirror. I saw a lady appear; two men closed in on her and ushered her to my waiting car. She was naturally in a state. As Ted pushed her in my car, the lady remonstrated. Then, Ted asked me, "Do you know this lady?" Of course I did not! It was my partner's case! You could have heard a pin drop. "Neither do I," said Ted, "The case was handed to me an hour ago." There was an icy silence as the two social workers and I realised that no one present knew the lady we were trying to section! We had apprehended the wrong lady! We had lifted a blameless human being from the roads of Clayford. And now, she was in my car. I was an accessory to kidnap! Thankfully, she was a sport. Apologies and weak explanations were repeated, and she took it all in good faith. Ruffled but relieved, she got out and walked away. Thank heavens we had never heard of her after that. Did she relate the story to her friends? Was she famous for a while? Luckily, there were probably no witnesses to the scene. All credit to Ted and his co-workers who had multiplied to four by now, also not cognisant of the lady in question. They were not fazed by the occasional unexpected kidnap; they wanted the job done. So, they went back around the corner and returned with another lady, angrier and feistier than the last. They dragged her into my car. "Call the police," she kept shouting. I needed no prompting. I sped off the pavement onto the road, shot across to the police station a few hundred yards down and deposited them all there before wishing a rapid farewell and making a speedy return to the antenatal clinic. That was enough excitement for one afternoon. Amazingly, I never heard any more about the incident.

EPIDEMICS

As I write, the world is in the grip of the COVID-19 infection. Such a pestilence had been forecast for ages because the vast population and extensive travelling was bound to rapidly spread disease. In 2015, Bill Gates suggested we prepare for a pandemic instead of war. When HIV arrived in the 1980s, it fooled everyone because it was nothing like any known viral infection. However, it stimulated progress in the knowledge of viral infections and encouraged reflection. It alarmed the Society of Actuaries because it introduced mortality in a younger age group, which seriously upset their Life Assurance predictions. In the 1990s, they produced a paper offering five scenarios that may or may not occur. In the end, none of them came true because of the clean needle campaign. The lesson we should learn here is that even the cleverest brains can make wrong predictions because of an unknown factor. I became interested in type A influenza and the epidemic of 1918–19. It is now known as the seasonal flu, probably because every generation has to take ownership by renaming everything to the confusion of historians. Those experts who refer to the seasonal flu, however, are probably unaware that the seasonal element is in the very name. Type A influenza has the intriguing property of spreading at an inversely proportional rate to ultraviolet radiation. It occurs during winter in the Northern and Southern hemispheres. It follows a cold snap; hence, it was named *influenza di fredo* – the influence of cold. So, don't go out without your coat! In the 1990s, it occurred to me that many patients in their nineties would remember the 1918 'flu and be able to tell me about it. How I wish I had recorded these interactions, but all that is left are a few stories in my head. I managed to get about a dozen candidates. Strangely, half of them remembered nothing of this terrible epidemic – nothing at all. Among the other six, four remembered it but could add little new information. One woman, Queenie, had been at school in Bournemouth and remembered that they had all been sent home, but they were not anxious because they knew they would not get it. They believed it would affect young adults but not children. Trestles and tables were taken from the school to accommodate the bodies of the victims. Maurice had been eight or nine at the time and remembered it clearly. He was aware that people had been used to death as news of it came regularly from abroad during the Great War, but they were not used to funerals. The bodies of the soldiers were the property of the War Office and were eventually buried by the Commonwealth War Graves Commission near the place where they had fallen or the hospital where they had died. Suddenly, with the 'flu epidemic, funerals were frequent happenings, and he clearly remembered the fine black horses with their black tassels pulling shiny black hearses. A prominent memory was that a horse had once knocked over his bike and buckled the wheel. The incident was compounded by the fact that the bike was not his!

The absence of bodies of the soldiers who had fallen in battle meant that the grieving families had nowhere to go to pay their respects. This led to the advent of cenotaphs, of which there are 33,000 in Britain.

In my early years, when immunisation was much less comprehensive than it is now, childhood diseases were rampant. I well remember the dreadful cough that heralded measles. It was the kind of cough that made the parents bring their child in on the day it started. Then a rash appeared on the fourth day. But in 1977, a different type of cough appeared which I had never heard before – whooping cough. The campaign against the whooping cough vaccine, later to be discredited completely, led to a population that lost its herd immunity. Later studies showed that the long-term consequences of whooping cough were not as bad as it was feared, but at the time, it was grim. A child would start coughing; after two weeks, the glue-like sputum would cause the child with a brisk cough reflex to cough until it resulted in a desperate, inhalatory whooping cough. Vomiting was part of this infection, and it would go on for another four weeks before tailing off two weeks later – two months of hell! I found that Mucodyne (Carbocysteine, given to thin down the secretions in people with cystic fibrosis) would relieve the whoop and the vomiting in a day, but three days after stopping it, the cough would return. However, some relief was better than nothing. The effect of whooping cough, because of its prolonged presence, was brought home to me in stark fashion. Our house was situated in front of a forest, and one day, we had decided to take the children out there for a walk. As I opened the back gate, a lady walked by. She stopped abruptly and stared at me intently, which is when I recognised that she was our old neighbour, Mrs Tucker. I had not seen her for probably thirty years. "You're Charles, aren't you?" she said suddenly. I replied that I was. "You gave our Heather whooping cough when you were six months!" she said and then she walked on. I never saw her again. The time her daughter had caught the whooping cough was vivid in her memory; a thirty-year gap had not lessened the resentment. One of my daughters had caught whooping cough at six months, and during the two months of the cough, she had vomited over every visitor and piece of furniture we had. Infectious diseases were part of being a family doctor and seemed to strengthen our immunity and prevent illnesses. Decades of being coughed on, sneezed on, vomited on – not to mention the diarrhoea – must have done some good. I have to say that the patients were terribly thoughtful in that it had never occurred to them that they might give us something! In December 1989, we had a real flu epidemic, and I remember it well, although sometimes, I wonder if anyone else does. I was doing, as my diaries record, about fifteen visits a day. Hardly anyone came to the surgery, so the workload was about the same. The new hospital at Bournemouth had just opened, and it bore the brunt just as the older hospital at Poole had done in East Dorset for the past many years. Two wards were closed at Poole, and a host of nurses were off duty due to illness. The tragic part I remember is that because of a patient overload, those with illnesses other than the flu were neglected, and everyone was treated as though they had the flu. Thus, we lost a man to acute pancreatitis and a lady with inappropriate antidiuretic hormone secretion, both of which were eminently treatable. In 2009, we were warned of the advent of the swine flu, and this introduced a situation I found to be quite sinister. I believed that we were witnessing a precursor of the shutdown of our economy and the limitation of our freedom as we know it today. Instead of doctors ministering to their patients, the central government controlled everything. First, we were told that each practice had to draft an action plan. This stimulated reflection, but just as we put our reflection and local knowledge into words, a template appeared to do the job for us. It was presumably thought up by some manager who was responsible for drawing up meaningless templates. It commanded that we appoint a lead. It is one thing to appoint a leader for, say, diabetes or mental health, but quite another for an epidemic. What would happen if the lead was ill? There was no advice in the template. Surely the obvious thing to do would be for all the partners and leaders in the practice to meet at 8.30 am each day and plan the fight. If one was ill, no matter – the rest would continue. The question of what we would do if the lead was ill and the suggested solution drew no response. Central control was paramount. The possibility that the key workers might fall ill had not occurred to them. One such section of key workers that I worried would be affected was the tanker drivers. A few years ago, we had endured a tanker drivers' strike and, very quickly, the petrol stations had closed. What if the tanker drivers caught the flu? How would we visit the sick? But being a family doctor had its advantages. The manageress of my nearest petrol station and her family were my patients. While chatting with her, I found that to avoid contamination in the petrol, they close the pumps when they are still one-third full. In fact, they have plenty of petrol. Thus, I was able to continue home visits during the strike with no trouble. Was the health authority aware of this? How would doctors visit without petrol? But they were not interested; they had total control. Our phones were to deliver a message to all incoming calls, warning them of the possibility of flu and informing them whether or not they should have Tamiflu. What was Tamiflu? I had never heard of it and nor had anyone else to start with. There was an anti-viral drug, Relenza but this was now ignored in favour of Tamiflu. Both were neuraminidase inhibitors. Years later, its use was discredited, and its enormous cost was revealed. But for every patient who rang in during the summer of 2009, the only question to be considered was whether they should take Tamiflu. One such call came through to me one Wednesday afternoon. It was the husband of a woman whom I had attended her home delivery twenty-five years previously. He asked if she should have Tamiflu, and I asked about the symptoms. At this point, it would have been easier to say yea or nay and put the phone down. But I listened and the whole thing sounded strange and unlike the flu. I asked her to come down. On listening to her and examining her, it was clear she was ill, but I was not exactly sure why. She hadn't passed much urine, but if she was ill, she might not have been drinking much fluid. I took her blood and said I would call the next day. The results came back; she had acute renal failure. She was admitted immediately, dialysed and went on to have a kidney transplant. The controlling nature of and over-reaction by the authorities led to the mildest but (at that time) most expensive epidemic in the history of the human race. COVID-19 may not be as mild, but it will be infinitely more expensive. Also, the control which was exhibited in 2009 has become intolerable in 2020. Social distancing is being observed at large but the police have been admonishing ordinary, solitary people who are exercising. While cycling in the New Forest, we saw a policeman; I had never seen a policeman in the forest before, placing stickers on solitary cars. Had all crime been suspended? A few weeks previously, the police said they were so busy that they could only deal with serious crime! House sales have frozen, but the Land Registry Office telephone informed us that we cannot contact them due to increased workload because of the virus. They have no workload! It is all very strange to me when I hear of doctors isolating themselves because of some minor association with the disease. For forty-eight years, I was face to face with patients who coughed, sneezed, vomited and dribbled over me. And don't forget the sputum and diarrhoea! Was it nerve-wracking and uncomfortable? Yes, it was! But we never cut and ran. In the 19th century, without knowing what a virus was and with precious little information on bacteria, diseases were controlled with sanitation and quarantine. We now have physical distancing and hand washing as preventive measures; so, did we need a lockdown? What we did need to do was quarantine the people who came into the country and trace their contacts. What we should not have done was send the elderly COVID-19 cases back to ill-equipped care homes. If we had been at war, this would have been called a war crime! We should not have admitted patients with infectious diseases to the general hospitals. They should never have got past A&E. We probably do not have infectious diseases' hospitals now, but we could have made isolation units. Typically, science hides behind the R number – the number of cases one infected person infects. It is a surrogate marker beloved by doctors and scientists. It makes them sound as though they understand it all. It makes a killer disease the property of the leadership rather than the other way round. It is easier to talk about the surrogate marker than the individuals who suffered and died. Who is in charge? Are they ever brought to justice? Yes, I do know the answer to that! Many years ago, I had two elderly ladies as patients who were admitted for minor procedures. But they acquired Norovirus in the hospital, and because they thrashed around with violent diarrhoea and vomiting, they sustained abrasions that were then infected with MRSA. Finally, they both died of MRSA septicaemia. They had entered the hospital thinking it would be a place of safety and found it to be a source of infection which then killed them. This was all because someone thought that hospital cleanliness contracts should be given to the lowest bidder! Hospital cleanliness should surely go to the organisation that will best be able to sanitise it. The monetary burden of reversing Norovirus and MRSA was colossal; the human cost, pitiful. One extraordinary finding is that every medical mishap in this epidemic has been blamed on the government. Where was NHS England during this and the £28 billion they consumed which never comes out? Our NHS is appallingly centrist and controlling. As I write today on April 24, 2020, of the 100,000 beds in the NHS, 45,500 are unoccupied! And yet, a few months ago, the NHS was said to be overloaded with work. All the staff work "long hours." They are all heroes. The greatest myth of all is that they work harder than their predecessors did. That is a barefaced lie but is used as a lever to get more pay from the government. When I first started in 1970, I knew that no one in their right mind would work for the NHS, and yet, I did for forty-eight years. The NHS is a sacred cow, and I did not ever think that this sacred cow could trash our economy. Our PM, Boris Johnson, who I admire, chose "Save the NHS" as his slogan. But hang on, shouldn't the NHS be saving us? He wrote a wonderful book, the Churchill Factor. I hope his epitaph will not be 'never in the history of freedom was so much taken from so many by so few!'

STRANGE INFECTIONS

ONE DAY, A LADY HAD come in with a lump in her groin. It was an enlarged lymph gland that was only slightly tender. Painless, enlarged lymph glands are worrying, but tenderness suggests infection somewhere in the region the gland drains. There was no sign of infection, but as the days went by, it got bigger and bigger. Routine blood tests were conducted, but eventually, it threatened to burst, and I referred her to a hospital where a biopsy was done. The verdict was cat scratch fever. At that time, the causative organism, a bacterium named Bartonella, had not yet been identified or named. I had not asked her if she had a cat because it had never occurred to me. Doctors are not keen on home visits, and yet, if I had done one, I would have seen that she lived with twenty-four cats! That's a bit of a clue there. The New Forest Wildlife Centre informs that the disease is still about and had killed a veterinary nurse last year.

George was our goalie and a very good one. One day, his wife had rung me up to say that he had a temperature. Indeed, he did – 103°F on the old thermometers. He was sweating profusely but, otherwise, showed no other physical signs of illness, and so, I said I would review him in a few days. On the next visit, he was the same and not otherwise ill. We rarely admitted anyone to the hospital then, so I offered to review him once more. Also, one simply did not admit a case with an infectious disease at a general hospital, as was done during this COVID-19 epidemic. The next visit found him still pyrexial at 103°F; so, I took his blood for serology. The result came back stating that he had Q fever. Q fever is a rickettsial disorder like Typhus. Although a bacterium, rickettsia-like viruses can only survive in living tissues. It can be acquired from cattle, sheep and goats, but George had had nothing to do with any of those. He had worked in a rural village, but the closest thing he had come into contact with were some horses, which he had kept away from. It was a mystery but one that had given him a temperature of 103°F for ten days.

People could be extraordinarily forgetful about what they had done. Once, a man had come in with a huge viral-looking wart on the back of his hand. I asked him whether he had come in contact with any animals even though I was unaware of any connection, and he denied it. A few weeks later, I saw his sister and asked her whether her brother was alright and whether he had contact with animals. She revealed that the lambing was just over, and her brother often had to feed them by hand! Mystery solved! He had Orf! On a different note, I had once been approached by a headmaster with a bowel problem; so, I mentioned the colonoscopy he had had the previous November. He denied any such procedure. We discussed it at length but he was in full denial. It is easy to forget all sorts of things, I would allow, but a six-foot tube up your backside! I think the procedure had been so unpleasant that his mind had wiped the slate clean.

FUNNY MOMENTS

Most doctors share a love–hate relationship with home visits, but one thing on the good side is being able to look at the old photos. When you grow old, you may look older, but in your head, you are the same as you ever used to be. You know it, but the other person may not. When you look at old snaps on a patient's mantelpiece, you get a real idea of who you are dealing with. Often, there were photos of men in uniform or marriage photos. I found it fascinating to know about their military background. For example, Mr Lewis had been in the second Chindits. I doubt if this information would mean anything to doctors now, but I was familiar with the Burma campaign. I had another patient who had been with Orde Wingate's first Chindits. He was thin and wiry and looked just like those men in the old wartime films on their campaign. On the other hand, Mr Lewis did not look thin or wiry and had seen a fair bit of action. He was over ninety and had heart troubles due to which twenty stents had been inserted. Despite everything, he was symptomless, and his wife, a stoical and pragmatic woman of ninety, confided in me that she thought he was a hypochondriac. I thought that a man who had lived so long and seen so much should be given the benefit of the doubt. One day, the practice received a notification from Poole A&E that Mr Lewis had been taken in as an emergency case but had died on arrival. The next day, I rang up his wife to express my commiserations and ask how she was coping and whether she needed any help. She was as stoical and pragmatic as ever, and we had a nice chat, but she said there was nothing she needed me to do. A few weeks later, I felt I should check on her again. I called her and again, we had a pleasant chat about her and her late husband. She remained stoical and there seemed nothing for me to do. A few weeks after that, I was in the treatment room, pottering about as usual, when Mr Lewis and his wife stepped out of one of the cubicles. For an instant, I froze. He was dead. The walking dead! He walked past me as he never said much, but his wife and I exchanged pleasantries. I had had two bereavement phone calls with her! Whatever must she have been thinking? Did she just think I was stupid and was too polite to say the truth? I was too embarrassed to follow it up. We then rang up Poole A&E, who checked and then said it had been a mistake – no explanation, no apology, just a mistake.

Travellers were always fun, and we always got along well with them, partly as they hadn't settled next door! One day, I saw that John was next on the list. I went out to call him and returned to my room. There was no response, so I called out again. "I'm just waiting for the wife," he said with pride in a distinctly Irish accent. He was eighteen, and behind him was a very attractive young girl of about sixteen. He introduced me to her. On conducting the examination, I found he had a raging follicular tonsillitis, and I took a swab and prescribed penicillin. A week later, an older man came in, also accompanied by an attractive young girl. "I want another prescription for my painkillers." I asked him why he needed them, expecting him to describe some painful problem. "My son got married last week." "Ah," said I, "that wasn't John by any chance?" He confirmed it was. The boy I had met the previous week was his son. There had been a wedding, which had gone on for two days, after which they had started fighting, which was when he had lost his prescription. It was all said as though it was the most natural thing in the world to begin fighting after two days and lose a prescription as a normal consequence. "But why do you need the painkillers?" I asked. "My toe," he replied and revealed a gangrenous big toe. The young girl now intervened. "Why does it smell like that," she demanded. It did smell pretty rank. I explained that was what dead and rotting toes smelt like. "There you are," said the man turning on her, "I told you they were meant to smell like that!" He was triumphant, and she was suppressed. I enquired why the toe was gangrenous at all, and he explained that he had been a heavy smoker, his arteries had been blocked and he had required urgent surgery. At this point, he opened his shirt and revealed a vertical abdominal scar from his sternum down to his pubis with another horizontal scar right across his belly. Someone had performed heroic surgery, presumably for what is known as a saddle thrombosis, one which involves the aorta and both iliac arteries, thus cutting off the supply to both legs. His legs had been saved for the loss of just one big toe, which was now gangrenous and ready to fall off someday. I was mesmerised by the stoical way in which he had taken all this, and at the moment, all I could offer was, "Well, at least you don't smoke now." I mumbled this despite the distinct smell of tobacco. "No, no," he replied, and then, as though he knew what I could smell, he added, "but the wife does, twenty-five a day; I send her out to the shed!"

WIMBORNE ROAD

"Old Vidler needs a home visit; he can't get his boots on!" announced my secretary at the end of morning surgery one day. I did not know Old Vidler, and I was surprised any of the staff did because when his Lloyd George envelope was brought in, it was practically empty except for his date of birth, which revealed he was ninety-four! It seemed as though he had gone through ninety-four years of his life without any medical interventions. All the medical notes are computerised now, but back then, they were stored (or not stored) in a beige envelope dating back to the advent of medical care, which was devised by Lloyd George. If maintained carefully, they were surprisingly efficient. On the outside, the envelope held an extraordinary amount of information. Apart from the written notes by the doctors, which were used as an aide memoir, there was a pink sheet for problems to be recorded and a blue sheet for drugs. The name of the drug and its starting and ending dates could be written where appropriate. Thus, at a glance, the drugs a patient was on was clear as was the drugs they had been on and, where appropriate, why they had been stopped. The problem card was also clear, and the doctor could write about not only illnesses and diseases but also major life events, such as births, bereavements, divorce, etc. This gave a real picture of the patient at a glance. Major conditions, such as diabetes and hypertension were represented by a sticker on the outside of the notes. Letters were folded and placed inside the envelope. This was quickly filled without careful culling. Thus, repeat appointment letters, letters without a date, letters in which the name of the patient was wrong or unclear, were all shredded. The current computers, thanks to their ability to do so and to the medical defence unions, scan and record everything. And I mean everything.

The result is a virtually unreadable record of irrelevant information. Every piece of information, however irrelevant, is retained, and the result is a huge barrier of digital rubbish between the doctor and the patient. How many times have patients rightfully bleated "all they did was look at the screen"? As time went on and with an ageing population and co-morbidities, some practices went back to folders. A few years ago, I spent a year culling about 800 such folders and computerising their notes. All the letters and paperwork were filed in the newly available space. Thus, all the documents culled in the Lloyd George envelopes were filed to make a thick, unreadable tome. The tone for the computerised age was set: throw your brains and common sense out of the window but never throw away a medical document! No such barrier existed in the case of Old Vidler; the only obstacle was that there wasn't much to proceed with in the notes. When I visited him, I saw a very old but still feisty gentleman with swollen ankles that prevented him from putting his boots on. He had been widowed nineteen years previously and had lived alone ever since. He held an acre of ground on which he grew anything he could; I could see broad beans, runner beans, fruit trees, cabbages and lettuce all in neat patches with barely any fallow ground left. After ninety-four years of toiling and good health, he had gone into heart failure, and his ankles had swollen with oedema, which prevented the boots from going on. After a long chat, during which all I really learnt about him was his resilient nature, I treated him with a water tablet and, possibly, digoxin for his heart, and over the next week, his condition improved, and he managed to get his boots on. The onset of heart failure in a ninety-four-year-old is pretty terminal, and he only lasted a year or two. The point was that old Vidler was not alone. As time passed by, I discovered more of such characters down Wimborne Road, who had lived long lives and had unblemished medical histories, (and empty envelopes). It reached a stage where I honestly believed that if one wanted a long – and probably uneventful – life, one should live down Wimborne Road. Of course, they have all gone now, but I wonder why they were so healthy in an age of rarely effective medical interventions. It was apparent to me in the 70s that when a man over seventy was ill, it was his last illness. Within a few decades, you could not even say that in the late 80s because, although they lived longer, it was not always in good health. These old, rural characters lived long and had good health. But I often think, are there Wimborne Roads all over the country? Probably.

I discovered such people from time to time, but I once made an interesting but slightly different discovery down Wimborne Road. One morning, ambulance control said they had been called to an elderly lady and asked if I could visit. She lived less than a mile from the centre of Clayford, alone in a bungalow on ten acres of land. Land and buildings in Clayford were at a premium, so how this large area had survived was intriguing. As I entered the property, I could smell the dankness and lifelessness of old neglected buildings. There were also very large cobwebs, which, to me, meant very large spiders! The lady in question was seated in a chair, and it was not clear what the problem was or why the ambulance had been called. There was no sign of an active kitchen, so how she managed to look so well-nourished was another conundrum, followed by why she was unknown to the practice. She began to tell an interesting story, and the photographs on the wall confirmed it. During WW2, some of Dorset was requisitioned by the war department for tank and artillery use before the D-Day landings. One such place was a village called Tyneham in Worbarrow Bay. In 1943, the whole village had been moved out, with only a month's notice, after each household had been sent a letter. The villagers, 225 of them, were heartbroken and pinned a notice on the church saying they would return one day. Alas, the War Department made the decision permanent in 1948, and the villagers never reoccupied their homes. However, the village has now been fairly restored, and not only the church, but the school is also in good condition, and access is granted at prescribed times. In the school, there are two photographs of classes of children. One has the names of all the children but the other does not. On the far left of that one sat a little girl, who looked very much like the lady seated in front of me. I only ever knew her as Miss Bristowe. She had lived in Tyneham until 1943 when the village was cleared. She had an uncle, who sounded pretty well off and had property in Clayford. He moved her there, and there she had stayed. As her health declined, the lady across the road brought food in for her. Fish and chips seemed to be responsible for her good nourishment. So, was she the little girl in the picture? I believe she was, but there was no mention of anyone called Bristowe in the school or village. However, there are many photographs in Tyneham Farm next door which show that the family had a young girl companion named Bristowe. I hope I am not doing her a disservice by saying that she was probably not the brightest girl, but in that old village, she at least had a place. She lived many years in a home in Clayford, and I regret I never talked to her again about her intriguing origins. Thousands of people visit Tyneham each year and hear the sad story of the 225 villagers who were displaced, but they probably never think of what became of those people. Was my old lady one of them? Was she the young girl in the picture? If ever you visit Tynham, walk down to Worbarrow bay and you will realise why you would never want to live anywhere but Dorset!

LAKE WOBEGON?

You may be familiar with those wonderful radio recitals by Garrison Keeler on the tales of Lake Wobegon. It was a place in Minnesota where everyone was ordinary apart from the children, who were all above average. People who showed themselves up were looked down on, and the main virtue in life was to last. In fact, if one died prematurely, which meant at less than seventy years, it was almost as though one had let the side down. There were times when I thought Clayford was like that. The people were happiest when nothing happened and, like Lake Wobegon, when it did, they were either in denial or diverted the event to something banal. My sister, who lived in Clayford for most of her life, was very much like that. She insisted that nothing happened down her road, oblivious to the young couple opposite to her who both died of different cancers or the lady a little further up with schizophrenia or the man trading drugs along the road. Nothing ever happened in Clayford, and she would have been horrified if anything did. Once, a patient of mine went to visit his estranged wife and two children, but she did not let him in further than the doorstep. When the visit was over, he went to his car, parked on the road, filled it with petrol and set it alight. There was a big explosion, and his wife and, probably his children too, came out to see the huge fire that just about destroyed the car as well as the man. It was awful. How do you get over that? But a few weeks later, I overheard two ladies discussing it, and through their voices, I could hear Garrison Keeler droning on in his soft Minnesotan accent, "the Council will never get that black mark off the pavement." This was the place I spent my career!

MINOR ILLNESS

There is much minor illness in General Practice. One of the roles of a GP is to identify minor illnesses and deal with them. That is why it is fundamental that a GP is able to recognise what is and is not within the realms of normality. Recognising what is normal sounds terribly simple, but as any budding young doctor can tell you, it is not. Likewise, nurses with limited, albeit good, medical training face difficulties when presented with challenges outside their speciality. Babies who always lie on one side temporarily develop misshapen heads, but when faced with such a head and an anxious mother, one's confidence drains. When a fourteen-year-old boy comes in with his Dad due to unilateral gynaecomastia, the condition is not an issue, but the anxiety is. When a girl of similar age comes with her mother due to unilateral gynaecomastia and requests its removal, it's a medical disaster. The number of people who discover their inions (the pointy bit at the back of the skull) or their Xiphisternum (which sometimes protrudes at the base of the breastbone) in their middle age is surprising! All these are within the realms of normality, and when the old family doctor said it was normal, it usually was. But if the modern doctor, who is unfamiliar to the patient, says so, there will be pressure for a referral – an unnecessary, time consuming and expensive referral. Providing reassurance was one of the roles taken up by the family doctor, but the modern patient is reluctant to be reassured. This adds to the doctor's frustration, but that is one of the prices to be paid while being a portfolio doctor. Three very common benign conditions that spring to the mind are sebaceous cysts (more accurately called inclusion dermoids), lipomas and fibroids. Sebaceous cysts grow from the grease glands that grease the hairs and are full of rank smelling white stuff.

Lipomas are bodies of fat in a sac that lies in subcutaneous fat. Fibroids are fibre and muscle ball-like bodies in the wombs of older ladies. They are all very common and benign (though fibroids can cause pain and bleeding). But over the years, I have seen a sebaceous cyst become a squamous cell carcinoma (very nasty), a lipoma become a reticulum cell sarcoma (nastier) and a fibroid also become a reticulum cell sarcoma. This encapsulates the conundrum of general practice; most things are benign or self-limiting, but every now and again, lightning strikes. If you work in a specialist department, the incidence of serious issues will be high and so will the index of suspicion. In general practice, the index of suspicion has to be low, otherwise, the referral rate would be sky high and the anxiety engendered by the doctor to the patient would also be high. But if you haven't had enough experience to confidently offer reassurance, how do you reassure someone? In this scenario, the comfort of reassurance, not to mention the placebo effect of the doctor, is lost. One relatively minor complaint is the BCC – the basal cell carcinoma. It is the least malignant of the skin cancers and, fortunately, does not metastasise – seed to other sites. It also has another name – the rodent ulcer! As the name suggests, it can eat away the skin like a gnawing rat. Unfortunately, they appear in two varieties: the nodular, which can be removed easily and completely, and another variety with roots. Like the Japanese knotweed, removing the top is purely temporary as it comes back more extensively later, although, in the case of the BCC, this may take twenty to thirty years. Thus, I always reassure the patients with the first signs that "we have time on our side." 'Snobby' Rose had developed such a BCC when a young man. Snobby, I was told, was a local Dorset word for a cobbler, but I don't have confirmation of this information. The internet says it is a naval term and stands for number one boot specialist, which shows the connection to cobbling. Snobby had had a BCC on his face for years, and whether the treatment had been delayed or unsuccessful, I never knew. As time went on, it eroded one ear, his face and then the orbit; so one of his eyes had to go. This resulted in a huge cavity (I advise the reader to read my words but not to imagine what it looked like). To make Snobby presentable in public, a prosthetic half-face had been fashioned. It was not terribly good but better than the alternative. This needed cleaning out frequently by the district nurse, who observed one day that, when he blew his nose, pus shot out of one ear! To clean everything out, she had to remove the prosthesis, of course, and clean it separately. Snobby had got used to it and did not give it a second thought. One day in the middle of the procedure, which took place at his home, the postman arrived with a parcel and knocked on the door. Snobby got up and answered it! The DN was phlegmatic: "Another patient, a vomiting collapsing postman – all in a day's work."

ON-CALL

When I had started, we were on-call an awful lot during nights and weekends. We had a rota, of course, but time flew quickly and one's turn came round much too soon. When I had started, a weekend on duty began on Friday morning and went on to the following Monday evening. When my daughter started as a doctor and had her first weekend on duty with two other doctors for 500 patients in a hospital in London, I asked if she had reached the stage of never wanting to see another patient again. She said no, but I reassured her that she would one day. It had happened only five times in forty-eight years, but I remember those moments well. It occurred once on a Monday night after a weekend. I should add that the calls came through to our landline at home day and night, so there was no escape. And when I was out, my wife was the doctor! Therefore, early on, I had decided to do an experiment. For one weekend, I had decided to be as nice and helpful as possible, to make follow-up phone calls where appropriate and, in general, be all things to all people. The next weekend that I was on, I did the exact opposite. I did as little as possible, whilst still being good, and operated in a professional but surly way. In the end, I reflected as objectively as possible, whilst acknowledging that true objectivity was impossible. The helpful doctor was exhausted, but the grumpy doctor was still energetic and ready for more. It taught me a good lesson: You always have to be good, but do you always have to be nice? Now, doctors have to be nice all the time, even to the time-wasters, the downright rude and the odious. They have to be nice to those who are outright hostile too. No wonder they suffer from burn out and exhaustion and have to go on resilience courses. It may be of great merit to be all things to all people, but believe me, you won't last! We always had a rota, but as time went on, it became more benign. After six years, I was the senior partner and was able to choose Monday as my weeknight on duty. I well remember those Monday nights. One of the perverse issues with being on-call was the love–hate relationship with it. We did not look forward to it, especially going to bed knowing that any phone call would almost certainly pitch you out of bed for an hour and a half at the minimum. It was not very good for our sleep patterns. But the next day, the doings of those calls would be all you wanted to talk about. And here I am, thirty to forty years later, reciting them again!

Lilah and her husband were as close to Hyacinth Bucket as one could get. She was large, loquacious and snobbish, and he was quiet, loyal and attentive. He had been a harbour master at Ostend during WW2, but that must have been easy compared to looking after Lilah. She was, it has to be said, a wonderful lady but always full on. In fact, many, if not most, of my patients liked talking at me and listening came a poor second. One evening at about 6 pm, her hubby had rung me to say that Lilah had not been eating much and to enquire whether he should give her insulin. She had had type 2 diabetes for years and was now maintained on insulin. As it was the end of a long day, I may not have taken it all in, so I had told him to go ahead, knowing that I would be on call that evening, and if anything went wrong, I would have to take care of it. At 7 pm, the phone rang at home. "I think Lilah may be dead." One thing I learned early on from being on-call was that when the caller says that the patient "cannot breathe at all", they were probably breathing well, but when they say the patient "is only breathing very little", they have probably been dead for hours. However, I knew that Lilah may have had gone hypoglycaemic due to the insulin, which was why she looked like she was lifeless. I was around in minutes and administered intravenous Dextrose 50%, as we did in those days. It had a dramatic effect and did not disappoint us. From being completely moribund, the corpse sat up and gushed, *"Oh, Dr Rees, I'm so glad you're here. Don't send me to the hospital; I don't want to go to the hospital. I hate that new Bournemouth hospital; the bannisters are all painted a dreadful colour of red, and I hate that colour, and the last time I was in, the nurses spent all their time talking at their station and not bothering about me, and it was all because they had examinations the next day, and how they were going to get on....*" Try being unconscious one second and then, in a heartbeat, saying all that in one breath. She could talk for England. On several occasions she called at the end of morning Surgery. I would start listening and without even making listening noises, sign all my prescriptions and take messages and when finished pick up the phone again to hear her still talking! I had seen a whole generation of people like her. I thought they were funny at the time, but when they passed on, I experienced a real sense of bereavement.

Another Monday night regular was Franksy. He was a young man, under thirty, who had issues with drugs – not a huge problem at that time – and alcohol. He also had mental health issues, and they aggravated each other. People who drink a lot become resistant to alcohol. Unfortunately, at the same time, it makes them resistant to antidepressants. Every now and again, his mental health issues, drug abuse and alcohol consumption would come to a head. Then, a doctor would be called, and although all my partners were involved, Monday nights seemed to be his favourite time to go off. He lived with his mother, an attractive but somewhat aloof and uncooperative woman. She behaved more like an annoyed landlady than a mother and cohabited with a man who, I believe, owned the rather nice-looking bungalow they lived in. Having Franksy lumber around the place like a bull in a china shop must have tried his equilibrium. As an aside, no-one grew tomatoes like him. On the occasions where a doctor was called, Franksy would be out of his mind and, apparently, crashing around the house. But an examination of the patient includes their environment, and I noticed that the ornaments were never smashed, and a fine model of a large boat, which would have taken months to build, was never in danger. There was a good deal of manipulation in his behaviour, and deep down, he knew what he was doing. On this particular occasion, the situation was utterly out of hand, and I arranged his admission to a mental hospital. It was never easy to do this, but it was especially difficult when they knew it was Franksy. On this particular night, he had, on top of everything else, swigged a litre of red wine and vomited most of it down his front. Eventually, when an ambulance arrived, there stood Franksy, suddenly quite calm, and his front covered in vomit, dribble and wine. He turned to me suddenly and said "Thank you so much, Doctor, for being so helpful". And then, he gave me a big hug, leaving the wine, slaver and vomit down my front. Thank you, Franksy!

One of the joys of being called up while on duty was the complete uncertainty of what would greet you. One evening, I had received a call from a shaky sounding old lady. "Can you come and see Dennis; he's having one of his turns." Being new to the practice, I knew nothing of Dennis or his turns and made inquiries on whether he was epileptic, had any heart troubles, and the like. All the questions produced vague answers, so off I went. We always tried some rearguard action in the hope we might avoid a home visit but never with much hope. When I arrived, I was greeted by the old lady and a huge man and lady who, it turned out, were the siblings of the patient in question. "What is the problem?" I inquired. They clearly expected me to know all about Dennis and were amazed that I didn't. "So, you don't remember the last time Dennis had a turn?" I knew nothing. "The last time when the old doctor came out and we had to call the police (my attention was seized at the mention of the police) and he put three of them in the hospital." They had my complete attention at this point. He had had a turn and put three policemen in the hospital! I quietly asked what was expected of me. "Maybe you can talk to him," they replied. But about what! With the kind of bravado and foolishness that had caused me a lot of trouble over the years, I asked to be shown to him. They walked me to a bedroom. They were clearly a big-boned family, but I will never forget the tingling I felt as I walked through the door to see the end of a bed with two feet sticking out at least a foot beyond the end! As I bid farewell to my life, a quiet voice said, "Hello, Doctor," in an East Dorset accent. "Hello, Dennis," I replied with some relief. We talked. It was not clear what was wrong but talking was better than being put in hospital. Dennis had had a pituitary tumour years ago, and although surgery had removed the tumour, it had left him blind. He lived with his mother and fine-tuned radios that the local people brought to him. Still, with the thoughts of the hospitalised police in my mind, I suggested giving him something to calm him down. He concurred. He was definitely big, so I drew up Diazepam 20mg and injected it into his elbow vein very slowly. "There," I said, "you will be fine now. You will fall asleep and, tomorrow, all will be well." Relieved and triumphant, I went out and reported the same to the mother and siblings. As I glowed reflecting on a job well done, a gentle voice came from the bedroom. "Doctor." What! He was awake? "Er, yes Dennis, what is it?" "Can I go to the toilet?" I mumbled in the affirmative and, to my amazement and horror, Dennis got up, walked to the toilet and walked back again. The intravenous Diazepam had apparently had no effect on him whatsoever! He did sleep eventually, and he was fine the next day. In the years that followed, I had met and visited him many times, and we had had a good relationship. Strangely and mercifully, he had never had another 'turn' again.

One Monday morning in June at about 5 am, a man had called asking for a visit for his daughter. He was unclear about the problem. There may have been pain; there may have been bleeding – he was uncertain. Eventually, I told him that I did not want to get out of bed for a girl with period problems. He replied that he had been instructed by his wife to get the doctor and that was that. Indeed, it was. Losing all hope of completing a night's sleep and knowing that, whatever it was, I had another day's work to follow, I got dressed and drove off. It was a glorious, sunny June morning. When I arrived, the mother showed me upstairs with a similar lack of explanation. I had no idea what to expect, but as I walked through the bedroom door, I froze. This thirteen-year old girl was not only pregnant, she was about to deliver the baby! "Phone for an ambulance!" I cried, but at that time, only 40% of homes had a phone, and this was not one of them. I don't think I have ever moved faster as I shot out to a phone box which was, fortunately, twenty yards away and begged for help. We used to carry all sorts of equipment, but a delivery pack was not one of them. The ambulance arrived and took the young girl away. The mother, for some reason, did not go with her and so, we stood and talked. "I don't know what I am going to say to her father. We've been apart for the last four years, and he only came back last Friday." I pondered for an answer and said, "Tell him it was his fault!"

A few houses away was another young girl who was pregnant. I used to visit them a lot because the mother had asthma. I was taken by the rough holes in the lower parts of all their doors. It was where their father kicked them, which, evidently, he did regularly. The mother and daughter were scared of him and even more so when the daughter became pregnant at fourteen. It is amazing how young girls, with their abdominal muscle tone, can hide the pregnancy. This girl added to the camouflage by wearing a baggy coat. She wore it throughout the pregnancy, summer as well as winter. Her father never noticed.

One call that senior partner, Jock, attended to is worth relating. I mention it because he greeted me on a Wednesday morning with the opening gambit "Charles, you should have been on call last night." Even now, I don't understand why he said that. When Jock had been on call the previous night, he had received a call from Golf Links Road – "Can you come around, Doctor? My husband has cut himself in the bathroom." No further information was given, and Jock was not a person to waste time on pleasantries. One of my friends went to see him. He said he had walked through the door and said he had a cough; Jock had him take his shirt off before he could even sit down. Good GPs survive by making an art form of taking short cuts. In this case, Jock shot around, and the lady pointed him to the bathroom. Her husband greeted him, and he held out a polythene bag containing his bloody testicles. He had castrated himself! Blood was pouring down both legs from his perineum. I believe he was schizophrenic, but what that explains, I am not sure. I saw him years later. The surgeon had done a very good job.

Not all my tales give me a feel-good factor. During general practice training, we are taught to ask ourselves if we could have done things differently. In this following case, I could have. Trickett lived in a corner house on a council estate. He was a settled traveller whose family had seen better days. He carried a picture of his father, a big man in a waistcoat and a bowler hat, looking very pleased with himself, who evidently bought and sold horses. Trickett was a poor man but had a lovely personality. Unfortunately, he had married a schizophrenic wife and had a drug addict son. His son was frankly a toerag, and he had shacked up with a really weird woman. Nevertheless, Trickett embraced and cared for them all without judgement. That winter, two of my colleagues had been called out to see his wife in the evening, as always – they never called in the daytime – but they made no urgent request for follow up. As I parked the car and approached the house, I could see it was pitch black. It turned out they had not paid their electricity bills. I knocked on the door and was welcomed into the living room. The room was full of rubbish, so it was not possible to move around. The sight that caught my attention was a huge, fiercely burning fire in the fireplace and, almost on top of it, a woman sitting in an armchair, She was so close it threatened to add her to the rest of the contents in the fireplace. Also, the rubbish in the room was mainly newspapers, boxes and generally flammable material. There was no other light source other than the fire, so seeing anything as one's pupils kept dilating and constricting was very difficult. I thought the woman may have looked pale and noted a rapid pulse, but there were no other signs of illness, and she was unhelpful. An added distraction was that my doctor's case was made of black plastic. It was normally very robust, but I had put a previous one too close to an electric fire once, and it had begun to melt. I did not want it to happen again, and I could feel the heat was only just bearable. I told Trickett that I would check her blood the next day, and he was content with this. I suspected she was anaemic but not critically so. The district nurse went to take her blood the next day and found the lady dead. In the post-mortem report, her haemoglobin level was 2 g per decilitre; the normal range was 12 to 15.5. I was mortified. She had what is known as cold agglutinins, which caused her to bleed, usually while passing urine, over a long period when cold. Trickett knew that she hated the cold, and hence, built a huge fire, which inadvertently acted as a deterrent to a proper examination. No-one suggested that I should have admitted her and, sadly, she was unmourned by her family.

HOME DELIVERIES

Having completed six months of intensive obstetrics at Leeds Maternity Hospital, it seemed reasonable to continue home maternity in general practice. Clayford was expanding at that time, and babies were arriving thick and fast. I had a large antenatal clinic each week, and there were frequent deliveries. Many of them were at the Firs, a Maternity Hospital in Bournemouth; it was a lovely place, and the mums loved it. They were waited on hand and foot and would often stay for ten days. This was a luxury, and I sometimes wondered if ladies would become pregnant just for this ten-day holiday, as they used to refer to it. Now, mums are in and out in hours. Although the procedure at Firs would not be considered as a good medical practice now, the modern brevity in stay time is driven by finance and not good medical practice; so is much of our health service. If a lady decided to deliver at home, I would always want to be there regardless of whether I was on call or not. That was part of being a family doctor more than just a GP. It was a privilege. Eventually, in 1998, I gave it up, but not because it was unsafe. A big problem with home delivery was that it was attracting the wrong kinds of mothers to-be. Home delivery is ideal for a second, third or fourth pregnancy with an unblemished record. As far as I am aware, it is safe and does not attract dangerous hospital infections. Unfortunately, the ladies who demanded home delivery were often preparing for their first babies because they had been seduced by organisations that supported natural childbirth. They were primips – 'the untried vessels'. Due to the risks, the other doctors who usually did home deliveries refused to do them and I was increasingly asked to. Instead of one out-of-hours delivery every few months, it threatened to be as frequent as once a week on top of the usual on call. Clearly, the situation has changed now. The mothers are heavier and the babies, bigger. The likelihood of problems is greater. The use of the caesarean section increased five-fold during the 90s despite its four-fold increase in maternal mortality and the likelihood of kidney damage due to blood loss. The art of delivery, which was so brilliantly taught by my mentor at Leeds, John Philips, has been lost. He was Welsh and lived for deliveries. There were many difficult births at LMH as they were the only ones they took. John would stalk the wards late at night looking for those poor women with long labours. He would sit with them and talk in his soft Welsh voice until, despite the pain and exhaustion, they were calm again. Then, he would gently apply forceps or a ventouse and manage the delivery. Thus, calm would prevail where there was panic and hopelessness. He did this most nights. He would appear like a ghost when things were at their worst. When all was done, he nearly always turned to the new mum and mischievously said, "You will not realise the full significance of this for another eighteen years." How true. Some of John's calming effects must have rubbed off on me. One Saturday afternoon, I was at a grand fiftieth birthday garden party at the same place as the North American Bison (see later!). Suddenly a lady came up to me and said, "Hello, Doctor! It's me, July; do you remember me?" I did not at first. After twenty five years we had both aged! Then, it slowly dawned with some apprehension. It was twenty-five years ago. She was one of my home deliveries. I had been playing tennis one Saturday afternoon, but when I got home, the phone rang to say that all was well, July had delivered, but the placenta, the afterbirth, could not be removed. I shot round in seven minutes. Our super midwife and July were talking, and the baby was happy, and as she had said, all was well, but the wretched placenta was stuck! I gave it a pull but no luck. I examined to see how much was adhered to her and what the situation was. The patient, July, and the midwife chatted away nonstop and my examination seemed to give her no distress, so I carried on and began separating the placenta from the uterus slowly but surely. It seemed painfully slow at the time, but once I had started, I could see no reason to stop. It finally came away completely and that was that. In retrospect, the thought of manual removal of the placenta outside a hospital with no blood available makes me cringe, but it seemed fine at the time. July was saved a trip to the hospital. The home delivery had been otherwise uneventful, and now, twenty-five years later, there she was and all was well. There is one amusing sequel to this story. July and her mother, to earn a little money, had decided to set up a home help service, which they named Amy's home services after the above-mentioned baby. It, unfortunately, attracted the wrong sort of customer who was not looking for sweeping and polishing. One man, clearly not a gentleman, was delighted to be told that he could have both the mother and daughter for only £6 an hour!

One day, a new midwife, Philomena, had arrived. She was rotund, small, feisty and Irish. Above all, she hated home deliveries. Therefore, it was such a pity that she was forced to attend the most eventful home delivery of all time! It was on a Monday morning during one of our usual meetings that she appeared and began her tale of woe. She had been on call for the weekend and was called out to a delivery in the country. She was unfamiliar with the lady and circumstances and so, was walking into the unknown. It was a farm-like place, and the door was answered by the husband. He asked her to come upstairs, but instead of being shown into the bedroom, she was shown into the bathroom! The lady was to have a water birth, the husband explained. As much as Philomena did not like home births, she hated water births. Moreover, the bathroom was overcrowded: the patient was in the bath, moaning away, the husband was there, and so were two children from a previous marriage. For good measure, a neighbour, who was good at photography, was there to record the event. To add to the atmosphere, a cow was mooing outside in co-ordination with the mother-to-be. It was in this situation that Philomena completed the delivery of a boy. She vividly described the baby floating to the top of the bathwater mixed with blood and meconium, producing a macabre soup. The baby was retrieved, placed in a blanket and passed to the husband after it had cried. At last, Phil could reach into the bathtub and pull the plug out. But a hand reached down beside her and put the plug back in – not yet! A bewildered Phil was taken downstairs to where a large saucepan-cum-cauldron was bubbling away full of foliage, branches, flowers and other stuff one would normally put in a compost heap. It was explained that since the baby and fluids – the fruits of nature – had left the mother, it had to be put back in! The cauldron was then taken to the bathroom and the contents poured in with the bloody, mucky bathwater. "It was disgusting," said our new midwife. We agreed but believed she had stretched credulity. It was at this moment that she reached into her pocket and pulled out some photographs. "They gave me these this morning when I went round." Yes, credulity had been stretched, but truth beats fiction every time. She reassured us that the mother, baby and cow were doing fine.

MEDIEVAL MEDICINE

When I look back to the medicine of the 1970s, I tremble at the paucity of effective medical interventions that were available to us. The great scourge of the time, for me, was rheumatoid and other forms of arthritis. It was crippling, unrelenting and, above all, painful. The suffering of our arthritic patients was awful and constant. The only treatments were aspirin and steroids. Steroids were usually given in doses that were far too high and produced as many problems as they alleviated. Some managed on very small doses of steroids and, years later, found that they had suffered very little long-term damage. But this information was not known at the time. I once had a woman on 16 x 300 mg aspirin a day. How her stomach endured it, I do not know, but she lived and functioned. Also, it was not known then that rheumatoid makes one predisposed heart disease with the inflammatory process probably affecting the coronary arteries and others. One of my patients used to build swimming pools. One day, he announced that he had a new-fangled device called a jacuzzi. He said it 'offers a sense of well-being and cures all ailments,' and he marketed it as one would market snake oil off the back of a wagon in the old wild west. I discussed it with a patient, she was fifty-two and crippled with rheumatoid, and we decided to give it a go. I called for her, and it was a challenge to get her into my car and then out to where the jacuzzi stood in a large garage. Climbing up the steps and into the thing was another mission, but we did it and sat there for an hour, bubbling away. When it was time to get out, she was able to stand. She walked to the car, and on the way back, I asked her what she was going to do next. "I am going to comb my hair," she said as she raised her right arm above her head. "I haven't been able to do that in years!"

The attitude to illness was also sometimes medieval. The idea that people were ill because of something they had done wrong was common, and it still exists. People with duodenal ulcers were admonished mercilessly for their lifestyle until it was found that the bacteria in their stomach, which was known about and discarded for eighty years, was, in fact, the cause of all their ills. It could be abolished with a cocktail of drugs and antibiotics in a couple of weeks. All that brilliant and developing surgery was unnecessary. The idea that people are ill because of their own shortcomings still lurks in the minds of those whose default attitude is to scold. Shortly after I had retired, the wife of a friend had attended the surgery because she felt she was short of breath. She saw one of the practice nurses who immediately divined that it was because she smoked and was overweight. In fact, if she had known the family as I did, she would have known that this woman's lifestyle was exactly the same as that of her wonderful mother, Fluffy, who lived until she was ninety-three. She also had three dogs, which she exercised every day. She was then referred to a GP, who came to the same conclusion and referred her to a cardiologist. She then had a coronary angiogram, which turned out to be normal. It was only at this stage that a doctor listened to her and examined her. Again, if they had known her as a family doctor did, they would have known that she had no children and had never been on the combined contraceptive pill. A childless, middle-aged woman putting on weight, under those circumstances, should have rung alarm bells. The abdominal swelling was noticed, an abdominal ultrasound was performed, and eventually, the diagnosis of cancer of the ovary was made but too late. Clinical governance compounds this medieval view that illness is the patient's fault. If you don't conform to the surrogate markers it is your fault. By designing a series of guidelines, it suggests that if one does not keep to those guidelines, then they are responsible for the consequences. The alcohol guidelines are particularly severe and, according to Professor Humphries of Stamford University in his paper on alcohol guidelines, uniquely so in the UK in the whole world! These have now been swallowed – no pun intended – by a generation of doctors who have never lived! Young doctors ask you about your drinking habits as though they are talking about crack cocaine!

DARK AND TENDER SECRETS

I DON'T THINK THE INDIGENOUS POPULATION of Clayford had any secrets. Information was transmitted by bush telegraph at high speed, aided by the fact that they all seemed to be related to one another. The secrets that existed among them were probably little secrets like who their real father was. I am still being made aware of family connections. For the affluent and arrogant, their secrets were of a different level. Their relationship with us was different because, as we were not specialists, we were at the level of tradesmen. That was no problem to us, but their dark and tender secrets residing in the hands of tradesmen certainly was to them. Nearly all of them were golfers and, other than Jock, my old senior partner, none of my current partners were golfers. But life is a great equaliser. None of us is immune to events. I found the ex-military and RAF patients in particular to be the most arrogant. One, in particular, continually admonished me, and even when I had saved his wife's life by preventing her from going on a six-week cruise instead of having her bowel removed, he insisted that I had "told her in the wrong way." I think that, no matter what he knew about aeroplanes, he knew nothing of the human condition. His wife was a lovely lady, and as they could not have children, they adopted a girl. She grew into a stunningly attractive young woman. But although physically attractive, she was difficult to deal with and not to be crossed. I kept away from her, which, fortunately, was not difficult because she spent most of her time in Australia. Her adoptive parents were concerned when she had an affair with a man old enough to be her father and more concerned when they had their own child. The father was an Australian surgeon, and the relationship was tempestuous. They reported her tempers and violence, which her lover seemed to aggravate. Her personality edged on psychopathic. Eventually, and painfully, they came in one day and revealed the awful truth. Their daughter's partner and lover – and the father of her child – was not only old enough to be her father, but he was her father! The liaison was not accidental, which would have been unfortunate but innocent. The whole thing had been engineered by the doctor, who had deliberately seduced his own daughter. The dark and tender secret my patient had to live with at the golf club was that their daughter was a psychopath in an incestuous relationship. After that incident, the air vice-marshal was less contemptuous though still arrogant.

Another golfer, who was not only Scottish but living down a road named after a famous golf course, was of a similar mould as the AVM. His wife, on the other hand, was a lovely, mild and pleasant lady; these qualities had no doubt helped her relationship with her golfer husband. They had two children of their own, both grown up. One day, he brought her in for help. She was in a state of anxiety and depression. I listened. A week previously, a man in his forties arrived at their house. He told them that he believed he was her son. Thus, the story came out. Before she had met her husband, she had been in a relationship with someone – probably an American like hundreds of thousands of girls did – become pregnant, and delivered a baby that had then been given up for adoption. Clearly, the trauma to all – her, her husband, her children and her newly found child and his family – was immense. But as the months passed by, they all began to live with it, and the Scottish golfer settled back into his golfing life. He came to terms with it, and I applaud him for it. A year later, they were back again. Unbelievably, another young man had turned up claiming to be her child. He was also adopted as the first one was. Of course, this was not funny in the least, but I could not help being reminded of the line in 'The Importance of Being Ernest' – "to lose one parent is unfortunate but to lose two sounds like carelessness." Lightening does not often strike twice. This time, the counselling was on another level. The stainless bride he had fallen in love with all those years ago had omitted to tell him that she had already had two children by two different men, their whereabouts unknown. There is only so much one can stomach. The Scottish golfer now had severe indigestion, but difficult or not, it was a dark and tender secret he had to take around the course.

One of the strangest secrets involved Jock, my senior partner. One day, I was called to visit a gorilla of a man. He lived in a very smart bungalow in an adjoining village with his slim and attractive wife who drove a pale blue Mercedes convertible. When I arrived, he was stripped to the waist and addressed me as "mush". It is not an uncommon form of address around here and comes from the Romany, meaning man. However, it was a bit unusual for me as a doctor to be a "mush." I spoke, as I often did, to Ian Limbery about this rough but pleasant character. Ian told me that many years previously, his wife had given birth to a daughter with spina bifida and, presumably, meningo-myelocoele and thus, paraplegia. She was apparently fairly damaged, and Jock told them she would not live and advised them to leave her in a home. Thereafter, they had nothing to do with her. However, his brother and wife, who were lovely, gentle people, brought her up. She lived, thrived, and one day, I saw her in a wheelchair. She was a highly capable and attractive young lady. The real parents remained in complete denial of her, and she expressed no desire to have anything to do with them. And as for Jock, according to Ian Limbery, he never knew that she had survived and grown into the wonderful person she was. Jock made a huge mistake but never knew.

PTSD

IN 1984, SOMETHING HAPPENED THAT had never happened before. It was the fortieth anniversary of D Day. Now, there is some sort of event of remembrance every year, especially as the veterans are dying out, and we all see the pictures on TV. In 1984, the thing that was different was that they were on TV for the first time. Every news channel said something about it, and the events of that momentous invasion were in every sitting room. This was new. Following this, several older men came to see me, clearly depressed. One of my trainee doctors had suggested that it might be post-traumatic stress disorder. I confess I had never heard of it, but as I listened to the tales these men narrated, I believe she was spot on. One was a lovely man called Philip who had been a chemical engineer. He had been in the army and had been told that the Germans were moving large quantities of chemicals into numerous sites. He was to go in with the frontline forces and find out what they were doing. Presumably, it was some secret chemical weapon. Thus, on April 15, 1945, he and the accompanying troops walked straight into Bergen Belsen. No warning. No preparation. No inkling. He had suppressed this memory for forty years. But the pictures on the news had plunged him into an awful state of depression and nightmares as his memories had been released.

Another man had been thirty-nine on D Day and so was seventynine when he came in. He had been a British quartermaster attached to American units. They annoyed him because they always wanted a gross of everything, never just a few. They did not understand the shortages in wartime Britain. He was dropped in the water at Omaha Beach on D plus 3. Bodies floated all around him. He swam ashore and endured continuous action for ten days with gunfire, explosions and fire while surviving on little food and drink and being sleep deprived, after which he was relieved. That was his war. Ten days of hell. He too had suppressed it for forty years. It is often said that veterans don't talk about their experiences, but many of them said that when they had tried, they got no response. I think it was because the listeners had no idea how to respond. As a result, the vets thought that they weren't interested and buried it. But only for so long. One man, who, it turned out, was beginning to dement and thus had less control over his mind, was haunted by an incident when he was in Burma. His unit was making progress but behind him was an injured Japanese soldier in a cave. The captain ordered him to go back and finish the soldier off, which he did. But all these years later, he was haunted by the thought that he had committed murder. Almost at the end of the war, a member of his squad had trodden on a mine and he was the only one of five to survive, albeit injured. He was captured by the Japanese and thrown in a hospital bed with five others, all dead. On the way, they had passed two men who were crucified upside-down. He was soon rescued, but fate had another unfortunate experience that came back to haunt him. He was in the second Chindits and, eventually, evacuated by submarine. The submarine was attacked by one of our own, a destroyer from the Indian navy. For eighteen hours, they lay on the seabed as the engines went back and forth overhead with the occasional depth charge. A year later, when he went to a hotel in Torquay with a small room at the end of a long corridor and without, according to him, a window, the memories flooded back, and he went mad with acute anxiety. And so, the stories poured in. These were the stories of peaceful men, taken from peaceful occupations, who had to endure a living nightmare. Their colleagues were the same, and they had put it behind them and got on with life until it was there, unasked for, in their living rooms on the fortieth anniversary of D Day. Great fun and pride for us, but for them, it was wakeup call for their nightmares. I remember six men who had been so affected, and they were all dead from cancer within a few years. Strangely enough, after forty-eight years, when I finally retired from all the clinical work, I became quite depressed, and I wondered if it was a sort of PTSD. Forty-eight years of fighting in the National Health Service! No, I don't think so. There is a sort of – I am finding it very difficult to find the right words – comfort in caring for others. However, you may be feeling, when you get to work and sit down in front of the first patient for the day, you will quickly find someone worse off than yourself. Very quickly, you forget yourself and get on with the day. I wonder if that was the case and, maybe, I had suppressed so much over the years that was now emerging. These were not memories of the horrors of war, but these memories had plenty of disease, death, death sentences and the smells of the living, the dying and the dead which I have only hinted at here. Getting back on the job is said to be the treatment of PTSD, but that is not always possible. Another solution is to write it all down. So, I am!

MOST DIFFICULT TIME

ONE MIGHT THINK THE MOST difficult time a doctor would have to face would be caused by overload, the seriousness of a problem or the complexity of a challenge, but the most difficult time I went through was concerned with just one family. Charlie was an old soldier in his seventies. He had been in the Eighth Army and was exactly how one would imagine a soldier to be. He was small to average, fit, wiry and, when he first came in, fun. Unfortunately, that was the problem because his fun was due to hypomania. Manic depressive psychosis causes a person to alternate over weeks, months or even years between being high or low and depressed, The modern term is bipolar, but it has been adopted by people who are just fed up every now and again and who never go through the high phase. When Charlie was presented in a high mood, it was the first time I had seen him; so, I was unaware of his history. He had been sent in by his wife and this was part of the problem. Mrs Charlie did not like Charlie having fun! It became clear as time passed by that she much preferred him in his depressed state when she could control him. But now, he was fun. He had the usual forced speech and flight of ideas, but he was not all that bad. He would go to the bars around town, chat up ladies and spend money on them. He did not spend much, but it was not his usual habit. Mrs Charlie did not like Charlie spending anything and began pressuring me to have Charlie sectioned under the Mental Health Act. Frankly, he was a long way from that, but then, the son weighed in. The son was described by the private psychiatrist, who saw him regularly, to be Schizoid, whatever that was. I received long, hand-written letters after each consultation. Nothing ever changed, and I hadn't seen him until much later. He was definitely his mother's son. It was quite clear that the wife and son regarded Charlie's money as their money, and they were not going to allow any of it to slip away. They appeared regularly to tell me how I should manage Charlie. They threatened and cajoled in the surgery by phone and by letter. However, Charlie was my patient, and his well-being was my responsibility. I spoke to his accountant with his permission, who confirmed that Charlie was spending more than usual, but it was not outrageous, and he was a wealthy man anyway and could afford it. I encouraged Charlie to see a psychiatrist and accept treatment, but he was reluctant. People with hypomania are usually happy with their lot. They know that the dip into depression is likely and associate treatment with the onset of this miserable depression. Furthermore, Charlie found he could stand up to his wife and son when he was high. "I fought a dictator for six years, and I am not being defeated by one now!" was his mantra. So, I was the meat in the sandwich: squashed between my patient and his controllers. It was a surprisingly unpleasant experience, but Charlie eventually succumbed. He accepted treatment, calmed down and lost the will to fight. The last time I saw him, he was subdued and well in the control of his wife and son, who found a different doctor for him.

ASYLUM DUFF

C HARLIE WAS NEVER SO HIGH that he would cause damage to himself or others. When patients become really high, they are termed manic and can be a huge problem. When I worked as a student at High Royds Hospital, Menston, in the admission ward, a man was once brought in for stealing a bus and driving it around Leeds. When he came in, he was as high as a kite and would not listen to, let alone accept any treatment or management. How does one deal with such a problem? This is where experience counts. The charge nurse had dealt with such a situation before. I watched his technique in awe because the man in question was also on the edge of violence. First, he chatted with the patient, and in no time, they were the best of mates. This went on for about an hour until the charge nurse suggested they have something to eat – Asylum Duff! The food was good at High Royds, but the food was traditional English and heavy with old-fashioned puddings like Spotted Dick. A plate-load of a heavy suet pudding was brought in (known in the hospital as Asylum Duff and made for this very purpose), and they ate together. The charge nurse encouraged, and the patient agreed, on seconds, which he devoured. This was followed by thirds! The charge nurse himself, of course, only had a very small portion. He knew that, however manic you are, three large portions of Asylum Duff would calm even the wildest patient. Very soon, treatment was accepted and order restored. Goodness knows what they do now!

CREATURES GREAT AND SMALL

Human beings do not exist in isolation. We are surrounded by flora and fauna, and since we are constantly exposed to animals, a superficial knowledge about them is useful to the family doctor. I would never go to Crickett's Cross without a tick remover, for instance. But sometimes, it is on the edge. One day, only a few years ago, when I was a locum, a lady came in with a highly inflamed gathering on her leg, which looked like a severe reaction to a bite. The worst we were used to seeing was the huge blisters of the Blandford fly, but this was not one of those, and in any case, they were supposed to be wiped out or controlled at least. "I have been bitten by a spider," she said. "A spider!" I responded. I do not like spiders. I've never understood why people are so forgiving of them. Apart from the fact that they scare us rigid, they show no mercy to their prey. They paralyse them, save them for later, eat them in parts and, often, the females devour their mates. Maybe, being a male, I am more sensitive to that bit. And despite their famous fly killing ability, I have never noticed a shortage of flies. "Yes," she said, "it was a false widow spider." I immediately told her that I had never heard of a false widow and wondered how she knew. "It was definitely a false widow," she said, "because I have brought it with me, and here it is!" Thereupon, she took out a small Kilner jar with the angriest spider I had ever seen, and I had seen a few angry spiders in Kenya. It had a large black body, relatively short legs and was very active. I recoiled and questioned the security of the jar but was reassured. The false widow is not poisonous, but some people react badly to it, and she was one. She then explained that they were all over the house, which begged the question of why she did not evict them. The reason, you may have guessed, was that she did not believe in killing spiders! At the other end of the scale was an incident at a local farm. We still had some farms in the area, and one had a manor house and was rather stylish. The whole family were patients of mine and the lady of the house needed a home visit for a chest infection. After attending to her in the upstairs bedroom, my gaze drifted out of the window into the misty fields. I blinked. There were three large brown shapes about fifty yards away in the mist. "For a moment," I said, "I could have sworn there were some bison* in the field." "Yes," said the husband, "there are three." Evidently, there was a herd in Dorset, and because of the foot and mouth disease amongst cattle, some of the local farmers had been trying them. "Terrible job to contain them," said Theo, "they go through anything. And the vet is scared stiff of them. Won't go anywhere near them. By the way, we need to get someone to take blood for brucellosis; you wouldn't care to have a go?" I certainly did not care to have a go! I was not going anywhere near them. In the end, they proved too much for my patients, and they had to be returned to the herd – but not before one of them had had a calf. (*Please don't ask me the difference between a buffalo and a bison. Answer: you can't wash your hands in a buffalo!)

THE PATIENTS

I USED TO ATTEND A HISTORY conference in America every year. One day, I was with some American doctors and told them about my patients. They listened spellbound. Then, one of them said, "my God, who are these people!"

OLD SAM - YOUNG SAM

Old Sam was a small man with a comical round face, except that there was nothing comical about him. He had started seeing me with one problem after another shortly after I had arrived. He was always anxious, a real hypochondriac. He had what is known as essential tremor. It is a coarse shake that tends to run in families and is aggravated by stress and relieved by alcohol, which he did not drink. So, he always presented himself as a shaking, nervous old man with a face full of wrinkles despite his strong-looking frame. Luckily, the retiring partner was still present, whose patients I had taken over, to talk to. Dr Limbery confirmed his hypochondria but whilst Sam came to us, it was just as a backup. His main source of help was from a herbalist who he paid to visit him. We Doctors were free and, thus, not worth much. One day, I challenged him on this. He always complained of indigestion and my remedies never helped. He revealed that the herbalist would prescribe various ingredients that he would put together and give him. I asked to see them and, one day, he produced a folded white paper that contained a white powder – no name, no instructions, just an anonymous white powder. It occurred to me that the powder may have been aspirin, which would explain why Sam gained relief whilst, at the same time, suffered from continuous indigestion. I shared my suspicions with him, but there was not much else to be done, and so, we trundled on together. One day, Sam decided to forestall the grim reaper and take matters into his own hands. He hanged himself from the apple tree in his front garden, which was clearly visible from the main road when I had made the last visit to him. He was in his eighties, but as far as I could see, he had no physical illnesses. Thereafter, when driving past his old place, I always looked at the great apple tree in case he was still there. It was cut down shortly after. When Young Sam walked in months later – a taller man in his sixties but, otherwise, like another pea in the pod – it was quite a déjà vu moment. Character-wise, they were like chalk and cheese. Young Sam was happy and confident and nearly always smiling. Clearly, Old Sam, his father, had only passed on his physical characteristics to his son. I loved chatting with him, and we did it often. It always ended with him telling me that I had the rest of the day to myself. He must have known I had the evening surgery to deal with, but it was his joke. He had been a paratrooper during the war and was dropped as part of the relieving mission at Arnhem. The eleven in his squad crossed a river, but only four made it to the other side. That was the only time I ever saw him sad; it was while telling that story. The rest of the time, there was a huge grin on his face. When he returned from the war, he got married, and he and his wife put all they had on the table; it came up to 9d. After that, he and his wife worked every day, and whenever he could, he bought land. After the war, there was no money, and land was cheap in East Dorset, though it was not very good land. Scrub, pines and travellers mostly. But times changed, and in the late 70s, it was decided that an industrial estate would be built there. Some, by no means all, of Tom's land was compulsorily purchased. In compensation, the council gave him six and a half million pounds. What did he want with money? Nothing really. Years later, they gave him another three and a half million for a bit more. He still had plenty of land and wanted only one thing for it – he wanted it to lie untouched during his lifetime. After our conversations, he often chatted with my amazing secretary, Janice. In his eighties, he confided to her that he had never seen his wife naked. His wife, by that time, was no oil painting and suffered from dementia, so I suppose he never did.

PARKES

A NNIE WAS A WONDERFUL LADY. I think she died when she was ninety-three, but she was full of mischief whenever I spoke to her. She loved relating times of her girlhood in Portsmouth, where she worked cleaning the public toilets. To pass the time, they would wait for a passing tram and, with their long mop handles, knock the bowler hats off the gentlemen's heads, preferably without them knowing why, and watch them look back as they disappeared down the street, confused as to where their hats had gone. She had lost a child when it was just three. I was able to talk to her about grief. Did it fade? Did it get better? No, she said, it never gets any less, but you don't think about it as often. I found it so helpful. In grief, the bereaved, whilst suffering in their own grief terribly, don't want to think that a time may come when their loved ones are forgotten. The pain is just as awful, but you don't think about it so often. One day, she called me to see her husband, whom I had rarely seen. He had a chest infection, and thus, I had to examine his chest. We were alone, but he was reluctant to take his shirt off. I insisted and he slowly unbuttoned his shirt. There, hanging from his chest down to the umbilicus was a sac of something about the size of a baseball. With his permission, I felt it. There were convoluted veins on the outside and inside were what felt like bones and cartilage. I must have been the first person after his mother who had felt this. He was never without a shirt. His wife had never seen him without a shirt. This sac, quite large and difficult to hide, was the remains of a lost twin or what may have been meant to be a twin. I asked him if he would like it removed but he did not. He lived and died with this strange collection through his childhood, adolescence and marriage to an old age. Annie had never questioned it.

THE REVEREND

Possibly the strangest couple I had ever seen was the Reverend Buckfast and his wife. He always wore a dog collar, spoke 'very far back' and had definitely taken holy orders, but to my knowledge, had never been a vicar, pastor or any official in any church – Protestant or Roman Catholic. But he wore a dog collar and looked like a vicar and his loyal and skeletal wife added to the picture of reassurance and piety. He was tall, good-looking and had plenty of dark hair, which my secretaries told me was dyed. Initially, he had a falling out with my receptionist at the time, who, wonderful lady that she was, was the archetypal dragon. In this respect, she was entirely untrained and a natural. The reverend told me later that it was at that moment that he had "decided to love her." Needless to say, this was the last response my receptionist wanted, and it drove her mad. I have no doubt that he used this fine ideal of "loving thine enemy" as a weapon very effectively, albeit harmlessly. Looking honest and reassuring was seen by the reverend as an edge to be used. He came down to the town and used this quality to buy and sell property. Please believe me when I say that he did nothing dishonest ever, but he was able to use his shrewdness to great financial advantage. He would look at a property and target the ones difficult to sell. He would then offer to take it off their hands at a reduced price, say 5–10K lower. Meanwhile, he and his wife, and she was just as sharp, would have divined the reason it was not selling. Often it was very simple: a coat of paint, a new drive, a hedge removed – just minor cosmetics. Then, he would sell it at his leisure for 10–20K more. Everybody was happy. He would always visit the house next door. The neighbours would reveal any shortcomings in the house. It was a short cut survey of his own. His dog collar was able to loosen the tightest tongue!

Another money-spinner was to make icons for the Russian Orthodox church. He would acquire pieces of wood, get pictures of various Saints, glue them, varnish them and sand them until an attractive icon had been made. He would then drive a batch or send a batch to his various contacts abroad. He was always sure to add the name – Reverend Buckfast – to the icons so that they would be reassured that they came from a religious source. Another wheeze was to go to church fairs and buy old books for prices as low as £1. Many books were almost given away. He would then sell them for a few pounds more. Small beer, perhaps, but a profit that is tax-free of 300–500%! And then, when he had accumulated a few thousand pounds, he would give it to a charity of his choice. So, his life went on. He fascinated me because I had never met anyone like him and his wife before and also had never met a person so in command of his life. Alas, nothing goes on forever and nor did they. The terribly thin wife, who had never come to me as a patient, was clearly abnormally thin. She declined investigation, and nothing could be found on examination, apart from her low BMI. But eventually, I persuaded her to have a barium meal, which was the least unpleasant investigation we could do and the only one acceptable to her. The result was extraordinary. The pylorus, the outlet to the stomach, appeared to be a dead end. Nothing went past her stomach! The stomach was absorbing anything she was eating, if indeed she was eating at all. The rest of her gut was redundant. No counselling on my part changed their view that there was nothing to be done, and her condition slowly went downhill, and she died. Why they took this course, I often wonder. Sometimes, you can know people for years only to realise that you didn't know them at all. The reverend, of course, was desolate, and he too declined slowly. Living alone was hard for him, but he had money. He asked me if I could find him a home help of some sort. I knew that there were several needy women in the area and mentioned it to one of them one day. She was delighted. I reassured her that he was a fine, elderly gentleman and would be a good and generous employer. I brought them together and got on with my life and work. A few weeks later, the lady came in angry and hurt. "Did you know what he wanted?" she asked angrily. Apparently, I did not. I had no idea and was embarrassed and mortified when she told me. I had no idea that his slender, wrinkled wife had, for all their married life, masturbated him to an orgasm every morning in bed and the reverend expected his home help to do the same! With the best will in the world, I had put together what I thought was a reasonable and sensible arrangement, only to find that I had been undone by something I could never have imagined. To say I apologised and grovelled might be an understatement. Even now, it bewilders me. After a few years, he moved to a nursing home. He declined seriously with no particular pathology. One day, I wheeled his chair out of his room and went down by the lift until we were outside in the garden. "What can you see up there," I asked. "What is that yellow thing; what is all that blue stuff; what are those yellow flowers with the trumpet petals?" It was, in fact, a glorious day in March, with blue skies and sunshine, and the daffodils were out. To my relief, he got the message and began to live again and did so for many years.

I knew from his comments that he was fairly well off. "Have you made a will," I asked one day. He had not but promised he would when I pointedly asked him if he intended to leave it to the inland revenue! After some encouragement from me, he eventually drafted a will. After he died, I found out, triggered because some relatives, previously unmentioned, came out of the woodwork as they often do, he had made a new will every month for the previous thirteen months! Each month, a new charity was chosen, and the lucky final beneficiary turned out the be the occupational therapy department at a local hospital. I imagine it was swallowed up by the NHS. I never heard of any good coming from his donation after all his hard, if unconventional, work.

THE RAVEN

I'VE BEEN TOLD THAT MORE than 400 people are homeless in Bournemouth. By contrast, when I had lived there as a boy, there was one tramp! When I had practised in East Dorset, I had heard of one named Tom Shearing. Tom did not walk; he had a bike. He was black from head to foot with dirt and grime and cycled all over Dorset, picking things up and placing them in the front basket of his bike. It might be a screw, motor parts, food from the supermarkets, anything. It was said that during the war, he was quite useful as, if one was short of something, Tom might have one. Because he was black and ravens were believed to pinch things (should it have been a jackdaw), he was nicknamed the Raven. He was a patient I had inherited from the outgoing partner. When he came to see me, he was always sent in last because of the smell. He was ammoniacal in the extreme, but there was a powerful musty smell as well. My room was still barely fit to enter in the afternoon if Tom had been there in the morning. Nowadays, all doctors have to recite at their appraisals that they will treat patients with respect. We managed to do it without instruction in those days, and I always treated Tom with respect. On one occasion, after I had carefully treated a skin abscess, he said "You're a gentleman." I glowed. Then, he added, "Not like the old doctor. He lanced my boil with his penknife! Just took it out and cut it." Later, I mentioned it to Jock. "Yes, he probably did, but he did it with his private patients as well!" I suppose now that Tom might have had some sort of autistic spectrum disorder. His talk was forced and verbose. His descriptions of every event were detailed: he would add how the sky looked and the weather at the time. He described Lawrence of Arabia's bike in intense detail from when he had met him in the thirties. I assume they were all accurate. He lived under some corrugated iron down Barrack road. I was never sure how old he was or what family he came from, but he survived, and there was a place for him in the world, unlike those homeless in Bournemouth. One day, he arrived with quite serious leg ulcers. It was clear after a few weeks that no progress was being made, and so, I admitted him to Poole Hospital. He went without persuasion. His own agenda perhaps? A great friend of mine, Ray Matthews, was a charge nurse there, and we talked regularly. It turned out that no matter how many times they bathed and scrubbed Tom, they could never get rid of the whole smell. The ammonia went soon after admission, but the mustiness never left. It was probably just him after all those years. As the weeks passed, they wanted to discharge Tom, but he became reluctant. Tom was a survivor and adaptable. He was always seen in a wheelchair and used it to visit all parts of the hospital. They hid his wheelchair, but Tom found another. Eventually, all the wheelchairs in Poole Hospital were impounded and locked up. The next day, Tom was seen wheeling himself around in a wheelchair! The genius of acquisition which had allowed him to survive a lifetime was still intact. They discharged him in the end to a home in Clayford, where he had lived in comfort until he had died. I am sure he had kept acquiring bits to the end.

A BULL IN A FIELD AND CROSSDRESSING

Stan had lived in the middle of a field with his horses. He had never looked old but neither had he ever looked as though he had been young. He just was – red-faced and smiling. He hated going to the doctor's, so I am not sure how he came to me, but I think it was because he was short of breath. He kept a load of his own horses and kept them for others as well, and he had a stream of young ladies to help him for probably nothing but the enjoyment of being with horses. Girls seem to fall in love with horses in a way that boys never do. Anyway, it all seemed to work out, but as time went on, it was clear that he had experienced a degree of heart failure, and I referred him for further evaluation. To say he was reluctant would be an understatement, but my persuasion of possible benefits eventually worked. We were in an age when medical interventions, especially cardiac, were coming thick and fast and making a huge difference. The cardiologist, who was a friend of mine, said that Stan had walked through the door and announced that he would rather face a bull in a field than be where he was then. The cardiologist suffered from the same problem I had been accused of – being blunt but good! But he listened and realised that Stan was a horseman. He, the cardiologist, had two horses. After that, they got on like a house on fire, and there were many subsequent consultations. Time passed, as it does, and Stan got to the end of the road. I was talking to my buddies in the pub one night and mentioned Stan or vice versa. Did I know he had parties up at his shack with all his girls? I did not. Did I know that they all danced together and Stan wore a dress as well and was one of the girls? Well, I didn't know that either. Being a family doctor means that you get to know your patients in a way that others don't, but like the sermon from Beyond the Fringe about the sardine tin, there is always a bit of sardine you miss!

GONE FISHIN

TOM WAS A CHARACTER. A retired builder, he enjoyed retirement and fishing in particular. He was always jolly and in good health, but his wife had asthma and bronchitis and was frail. I often had to visit and sometimes he was there and other times he was not. One morning, a desperate call was put through to me. Tom said his wife was very breathless, worse than usual, and he asked if I could come around soon. It was only a mile and I did. No one answered the door, so I walked in. His wife was gasping her last breaths. "Where is Tom?" I asked, horrified that he was not there and had apparently left her. She could barely breathe let alone talk, but as I desperately called for the ambulance, I could just hear, "gone fishin." Those were her last words. I asked Tom much later why he had left his wife to go fishing, but he never seemed to understand the question. He lived to be well over a hundred and had several girlfriends.

LEARNING QUICKLY

CORBIN HAD BEEN ONE OF my first patients. He was thin, oldlooking and when he eventually died he was only aged fifty-two. "Those pills you gave me, Doctor, were the best I have ever had. Much better than anything the old doctor gave me." This was his opening gambit. We learned that patients would open their conversation like a chess game, and we analysed it carefully. Never oppose an opening gambit however unacceptable. For instance, "can I have more Thyroxine to lose weight?" or "Can I have some iron tablets to help my depression?" Clearly, there is more to depression than iron tablets, but we now know that low iron, even with a normal blood count, can make people tired; so, maybe there was something to it. However, this opening gambit made me glow. The old doctor was well-respected, and I was a young colt, and here was this man comparing me favourably to the old master. He had widespread osteoarthritis and the tablets, Indomethacin, had freed him up for the first time in ages. I continued to glow until he said, "but I can't take them!" He explained that they had given him indigestion and had to be stopped. I was deflated, but just before I recovered from it, a document was slid in front of me. "Would you sign this, Doctor?" Of course, I would. It was the rescuer in the persecutor-victim-rescuer triangle. Basically, the patient challenges the doctor with something, such as "why am I not better?" The patient is now the persecutor and the doctor the victim. How can the doctor respond? He responds by finding a rescuer, which turns him into the persecutor and the patient the victim. "Have you stopped smoking yet?" Hopefully, the patient has not stopped smoking, and the doctor has been rescued! Corbin was trying this on me having had no training whatsoever. He was a natural. Thus, I found myself signing a document that might entitle him to a free TV licence. I did not mind. I was watching; I was learning, and I kept on learning.

On another occasion, that is what made me do a home visit to adjudicate between rising damp and condensation. The lady in question insisted it was rising damp and, thus, the council's responsibility, and the council said it was condensation and hers. I learnt, read and learnt. The worst opening gambit is the one that shuts all the doors. For instance, hay fever is a seasonal, debilitating problem. The solution is avoidance, antihistamines, eye drops or nasal sprays. So, when the patient presents themself with this opener, "I have hay fever again, Doctor. But I can't avoid it as I live next to a field; antihistamines make me drowsy; eye drops sting and nasal sprays make my nose bleed!", for the doctor, all the doors have been closed, and there is nowhere to go. But I learnt that there are seven possible ways out, the last of which, and I am always tempted by it, is to announce that you have already had a dreadful day and throw a tantrum! This could be the rescuer, but I have never dared to try it. I had experienced failure early on when I was called to an old lady who lived above a wonderful hardware store, which is now no longer there. She, clearly the matriarch, was in bed surrounded by her large middle-aged family. They clearly took themselves very seriously. Her problem was widespread arthritis and she announced that, "pain killers were no good as they made her drowsy and constipated; anti-inflammatories gave her indigestion; all the operations had failed; physiotherapy was too painful," and a load of other things I cannot remember. All the doors were closed, and I had nowhere to go. To be fair, at that stage in my career, I should not have been asked to see her. I inquired what it was she and the family expected me to do. The next day, a load of NHS cards was on the desk from the whole family who wanted to change to someone else. But patients were signing on in droves, and I was learning. Later, I would have handled things differently.

IDLE MEN

Ever since I stopped being a youth, I have been a man and for the first part of my life, was quite happy with this state. But after a decade in practice and learning more about the human state, I began to lose confidence. Men – this is not universal, of course – can be incredibly selfish. Some men can also be incredibly idle. So idle were some that I formulated a league table of idle men. They only existed thanks to some selfless women who, apparently willingly, sacrificed their lives for those men whose only resolution seemed to be idle. At the top of the league was Bert Holberton. He had eventually taken to his bed with no apparent physical or mental reason. His wife had waited on him hand and foot and even a bit more than that! She would wheel a commode into the bedroom so that he did not face the inconvenience of walking to the bathroom. His wife asked me to counsel him on these matters, but he told me that wives were there for what their husbands wanted, and he had no intention of changing. His wife colluded. She was a nurse and had had two fine daughters, a policewoman and another nurse. They did not like the situation, but they also colluded.

Bill was almost in the same mode. I remember visiting him and watching his wife struggle with a huge bucket of coke brought in from the outside. I sympathised that he could not do this as he was ill. I was told that his wife always brought the coke in because that is what wives do. Bill was a barcellarman at the nearby pub and had no problems shifting 18- to 24-gallon casks around.

There are many other examples, but they manifested themselves with the advent of Viagra. There was a time when the only recommendation from a doctor for a man with erectile dysfunction (ED) would be an electric toothbrush and a shoehorn! Without meaningful treatment, there was not much else to offer. When Viagra came on the market, the whole ED issue became frontline medicine and became serious when research showed that after the onset of ED, a cardiac event may occur within three years. In other words, ED was now a prodromal marker for heart disease. But not all men wanted Viagra for complications of their diabetes or prostate problems; they wanted to boost their waning abilities. No problem there. But what if the man's partner had begged you not to prescribe? Divided loyalties required careful management. Especially if the man was known for abusing his position.

There is a twist in the tale with Viagra. Many people think that it increases their libido, but it does not. It maintains an erection by inhibiting the destruction of the hormone that dilates penile vessels. Desire and titillation have to start the process for the Viagra to enhance it. This is where the idleness came in. What occurs in the dinner queue when seventeen does not behave in quite the same way when fiftyseven and so on. But many men behave as though it should and make no dispensation to their age. They will wine and dine with a lady, have three or four pints and a curry or a three-course meal, and thus furnished with food and drink, expect to be able to function as they used to. They then take Viagra and guess what, it doesn't work! Apart from the fact that there is a lot more to foreplay than food and drink, I have to explain basic physiology, which could be explained as basic plumbing. If the average man has seven to eight pints of circulating blood with two to three swishing around the lungs at any given moment to be oxygenated, that leaves five to six pints for the rest of the body. If the man then has a large meal, two pints will be diverted to the splanchnic vessels for digestion, thus leaving three to four pints for the whole of the rest of the body. It is an accepted fact that the average man does not have enough blood to supply both his brain and erect his penis at the same time, which explains, according to women, a lot about male behaviour. But likewise, it is not easy to supply the erect penis, the brain and the gut at the same time. In other words, and I will paraphrase mildly, if you are going to eat, eat, and if you are going to have sex, have sex, but not both at the same time. If you are going to make love to a woman, make that the priority! So, many of the men I referred to decided that the food and drink were the priority and any more was too much trouble!

Please forgive a moment's digression because erectile dysfunctions are not always what one would imagine. Once an old chap had hypertension, and I had given him a long-acting water tablet to be taken in the morning. It is a mild and relatively harmless way of treating mild hypertension. Alas, it must have been a very long action for him because it was still working at night and filling his bladder with the surprise side effect of an unwanted erection! He sat in front of me with that indignant look country folk are good at throwing and berated me, "I wake up and there it is. And at my age, I've no use for it!" On another occasion, at the end of morning surgery, I met an exhausted-looking man called Morgan. During the war, he had been hailed as a hero but quite mistakenly, he explained. When the shells started landing at Alamein, he jumped in his lorry and cleared off as fast as he could. As he drove, he kept on being stopped by injured men, whom he took on board. When he arrived back, he was lauded as the saviour of the injured whereas he was desperately trying to save his own skin. It was he who, tired and drained, was seated in front of me. He had recently been presented with depression with all the classical symptoms and standard sleep disturbances and had warranted an antidepressant. That night, he and his wife had decided to make love. One of the symptoms of depression is supposed to be the loss of libido, which never seemed to be the case in East Dorset. One of the side effects of anti-depressants is delayed ejaculation. Both he and his wife had felt that sex was not complete without male ejaculation, so they had carried on and on until the state of exhaustion had overcome resolution and required an angry consultation the next day!

...AND FRUSTRATED WOMEN

I ALWAYS WENT TO MEET MY patients in the waiting room. My partners preferred to use the tannoy, but I always felt that it discriminated against handicapped people who might not hear properly despite our loop system or because of infirmity or other factors. Also, I liked the exercise, and I liked to know what was going on. One comfortable middle-aged lady took advantage of it. She would jump up and announce to the waiting room that she had a bone to pick with me and, equally suddenly, would come over, declare that she had forgiven me and hug me! I would accept it. What I did not know as the years went on was that that was all the physical contact she had with a man. Her first husband had died, and in widowhood, she had wanted a man. She was married again to a very pleasant, avuncular man but was horrified to find that there would be no physical contact. Not just sex – nothing. No hugs, no touching, nothing. For some people, probably most people, that is a diabolical form of sensory deprivation, and there was nothing she could do about it – apart from taking advantage of me. I found many women frustrated like that. Early on, a lady of fifty-two, would come in and ask for her Mogadon. Mogadon or nitrazepam is a benzodiazepine used to help induce sleep. It would be considered wrong now, but no doubt, many of the things we consider right now will be considered wrong in the future. One might ask why so much is wrong if we have so much right now! Anyway, we did prescribe such drugs but, of course, I asked her why she needed them. She too had a husband who declined physical contact. She confided that each night, she would take her two capsules and grip the sides of the bed until she went to sleep. How awful for her. Was a late-night cuddle too much for her husband? Apparently, it was. He had no impediment, as far as I knew. Decades later, I saw her in a nursing home. She was dementing. I reflected on all those frustrating years she had endured. She didn't deserve it. In this enlightened age of LBGTQ, it is hard to remember that when I had started my practice, homosexuality was a criminal offence. It existed, of course, but closeted. One coping strategy to mask the issue was for the homosexual male to hide behind the cover of marriage. There were several such marriages amongst my patients. Those poor women, unknowing, perhaps, or knowing and believing they could change their man, were then condemned to a sexless, contactless, barren existence. The ones I knew faced such a life for the rest of their marriage. They must have married innocently, looking forward to physicality, children and all that marriage can bring, only to endure physical abnegation for life. My heart bled for them.

NO BLUE LIGHT

English people, in general, and Dorset folk, in particular, are quiet and modest. Being forceful is referred to as "showing yourself up." Often, foreigners, who have always fought for all they have, misinterpret this and take advantage of it. One amusing example of reticence is when Mr Copeland, aged eighty, came in and confided in me that he had a bit of chest pain. There were no physical signs, so I said we would need to take an ECG. A few minutes later, I was explaining to him that he was having a heart attack and needed to go to the hospital immediately. "No blue light," he responded quietly, "I don't want a blue light and people talking." Amazing. He was having a heart attack and knew exactly what that meant but did not want a blue light ambulance! As it happens, this presented a problem for me. When calling for an ambulance, they have their own protocols. If you want an ambulance pronto, it has to be 'blue light.' Anything else takes four hours or, if less of a priority, much longer. The ambulance control can be less than helpful at times. We were all under pressure. The worst experience I had was when I was called to a man who had been seen by two of my colleagues already. As I walked through the bedroom door, I could see the poor chap had a fractured neck of femur and a bladder up to his umbilicus! He had urinary retention, having fallen and broken his hip. I called an ambulance and demanded it to be as quick as possible. Because I had not specifically mentioned the 'blue light,' the jobsworth at the other end put him on a four-hour wait. I complained on behalf of the patient, but health service complaint procedures are designed to make you lose the will to live. Therefore, I was now begging for a blue light ambulance that did not flash its blue lights! When it arrived, I had a quiet word with the ambulance men who smiled and understood. They were also Dorset people.

ALADDIN'S CAVE

Howard Andrews irritated me; there was no doubt about it. It did not matter whether you asked him an open or a closed question, his answer was protracted, flowery, circumlocuitous and went around the houses. In a busy surgery, he was a pain. He had a slight accent, and he revealed that he was, in fact, Polish. I knew all about the role Poles played during WW2 and how they fought well, made great fighter pilots and started the enigma code-cracking. I had a trainee doctor at the time who was the son of such a Polish family and was proud of his background. He was disapproving though of Poles who changed their names. Real Poles, he contended, should have names that read like the bottom line of the optician's eye chart. Howard certainly had physical complaints, with only one kidney, and I was usually busy, but on one particular day, he didn't have much, and I had spare time. I took the opportunity to satiate my curiosity. "Howard, why did you change your name?" He looked at me thoughtfully and, in his soft accent, began, "When I was a boy in Poland, we holidayed in Ukraine." Here we go, I thought, round the houses again or, in this case, around Eastern Europe! He continued with his story and explained that when the war had started, he was only fifteen but still managed to lie about his age and join the army. They were eventually heavily beaten in a three-week campaign in the end. He had managed to survive and, being familiar with Ukraine, decided to go there and pretend to be a Ukrainian peasant boy since he knew the language. As the years went by and he heard of the stand made by Poles in Warsaw, he returned and took up fighting again. They fought in the streets and the sewers, but eventually, seeing the hopelessness of the situation, he got out. He worked his way across Europe and was able to surrender to

American forces who interned him in France. It was there, in France, that he had learnt English. He could speak French, and it was from the French speaking background that he learnt his English. That was why his English was so flowery. I remembered my cycling days when I had read French cycling magazines. They could spend a whole page talking about Jacques Anquetil's legs! He had then been transferred to England, worked where he could, met a girl, got married and the rest, as they say, is history. This tale, of which I have related a small part, was mesmerising. This quiet, modest man was living the history of the Polish struggle and survival. It took me a while to take it in, when suddenly I remembered, "But Howard, the question I asked was why did you change your name?" "Oh," he said, "in view of what had happened, I thought my name was the least of my problems!" It wasn't really an answer, but at least it was brief. Patients and people are like Aladdin's cave. When you say the magic words, jewels are revealed – hidden most of the time but priceless when found.

TRAINING

After about five years in General Practice, I had been approached to start training GPs. I thought it was too soon, but the Associate had seen something in me. I had given a few talks and we had a spare surgery room available for a Trainee GP. He must have really seen something because I went on training without a break for the next thirty years! I was very lucky with my trainees, and training became a major part of my life. I never had any breaks for the first six weeks of the year until the new doctor had become functional and confident in the practice. My first trainee was, in fact, a year older than me and had left paediatrics. It was the blind leading the blind, but it was great fun. I realised that the best way to learn was to teach others, and as medical knowledge was expanding so fast, I always had a head start. My whole year revolved around the advent of the new trainee. The concept of a year's training in GP had just begun, stimulated locally by Dr George Swift. This vocational training was to be based on the apprenticeship system, and although apprenticeship is one of the few validated methods of teaching, there was no assessment. Therefore, it depended on the quality of the trainer, who could transmit their bad habits as well as good. Apprenticeship was ideal for a "jack of all trades," which was what we were. It gave the new doctor confidence and was alright if – and this was the big if – the future job would be the same as the old.

Apart from George Swift, there were many inspiring leaders. John Fry from Beckenham in Kent had written something about every patient he had ever seen from 1943 and had compiled a book on the natural history of common diseases. Today, no disease has not been interfered with by modern medicine, so often their natural history is not known.

The classic example is Prostate cancer. In half the cases the cancer is dangerous and in half it is benign. Which half is the patient in? Thus, millions of men who did not need it were vigorously treated for prostate cancer. Michael Balint made us reflect deeply on the doctor–patient relationship and our power in the healing process. We became aware of the orientation of our work. Disease-orientated medicine focused on the disease rather than the patient. James Willis wrote The Paradox of Progress, which explained that the more we focus on diseases, the more we discard other factors. Our disease-oriented approach facilitates the exclusion of knowledge, and this is the exact opposite of what a 'jack of all trades' needs in the environment he or she works in. We became aware of the technical–healing spectrum; a patient can have technically good treatment but may not feel or get better. I related elsewhere about a man who had a pacemaker put in quickly and efficiently, but he needed his doctor to explain that he would no longer fall and could join the land of the living. We learned of the doctor–patient contract. We knew that the best medicine was holistic, and the only true holistic medicine was our family medicine because it embraced the parameter of time. No other medicine does this; they are clinic medicine. In 1987, Roger Neighbour published The Inner Consultation, which helped us to reflect on and understand the consultation. It became the bible of the trainee but, like all progressions, had an unforeseen casualty. Prior to this, we had used consultation analysis, which did exactly what it said – it analysed the consultation. Consultations have a beginning, a middle and an end. We learned never to reject the opening gambit and we became masters of terminating the consultation, something that young doctors and nurses find the hardest to do. We were also aware of the anatomy of the middle of the consultation and how to use it. The Inner Consultation provided insight, but the mechanics of getting through the consultation tended to be lost. A part of the training was using videos. We saw ourselves for the first time! That was a shock and was only needed once! But we asked ourselves what had gone well and what had gone not so well. We asked ourselves what could be done differently. We discussed if there was a learning need and how it could be addressed. Apprenticeship had no assessment, and this was clearly a problem; so, we began formative assessments. It was a constructive way of learning and assessing learning needs. The trainer and trainee formulated mutual statements of teaching. The next stage was a sort of test, which was called Summative Assessment. It was initially a test to eliminate the 2% of doctors who were a danger to the public and themselves. But it was quickly realised that you could not set a test that 98% of the candidates would pass! So, the test was tightened up and eventually absorbed by the Royal College of GPs. All this sounds like progress, but as G. K. Chesterton observed, not all progress is in the right direction. Apart from the fact that the act of measuring something alters it, there were changes. The first thing to go was the video and, with it, the observation of the doctor examining the patient. This was now left for the trainer to do as the examination was lost as part of the consultation and became an isolated event to be prepared for. To explain in simple terms, while on the video one might observe that the doctor failed to examine the chest of a breathless person properly, that would not be the case if the doctor was instructed to examine a chest while being observed. In 2004, the video was replaced by a 'simulated surgery' or Clinical Skills Assessment. It was considered to be better because it was thought that some trainees might cherry-pick their patients and their conditions, and also, some trainees said they could not make videos. But CSA does not include examination, which is still a flaw for the reason I stated above. The biggest change occurred in the relationship between the trainer and the trainee. The trainer was no longer obliged to teach; the trainee was obliged to pass the test! The obligation was now firmly on the trainee who jumped through the hoops or failed. The tests altered the training and resulted in some doctors wanting to extend their training to learn basic procedures. The video was dropped completely, and a brilliant learning tool was replaced by a grid of boxes to be filled in. The process of assessment took away the power of the video to do things differently and to change ourselves. The habit of the modern doctor in spending the consultation looking into a screen would have been cruelly exposed as he looked at himself! To be fair, bad doctors now had difficulty slipping through the net, and there was quality control. The excellent probably excelled anyway.

The three big changes that altered training was the advent of clinical governance in 1990, NICE guidelines in 2000 and the Quality Outcomes Framework in 2004. I do not wish to examine all these processes, which were very useful to young doctors, but I recommend them to those who suffer from insomnia. However, we came to realise that the word "guideline" in fact meant "written on tablets of stone." They began to shackle the thoughtful GP and were invasively prescriptive. They were unhelpful to the "jack of all trades." QOF, which I mentioned earlier, was target driven, population-based, disease orientated and driven by protocol rather than guidelines. As I hinted at earlier, QOF was good for those included, but not so good for those outside the targets and non-existent for the excluded! It medicalised a vast number of people at a great expense with uncertain outcomes. It exhibited a touching faith in the current guidelines and a blind spot to its shortcomings. In many ways, the NICE guidelines and clinical governance were ways of hiding the downward pressure of prescribing and referral. We began training the new GP with high hopes. We had detached ourselves from the doctor-orientated approach where doctors controlled the consultation; we detached ourselves from disease-orientated medicine driven by specialists. We developed ways to train them for patient-sensitive and patient-orientated care. As the changes developed, we found ourselves going back to the disease-orientated care based on targets, controlled by NICE and QOF. Could that be why doctors spend their time staring at the screen after you waited three weeks to see them? To lighten the mood, I would like to quote W. H. Auden.

> Give me a doctor partridge plump
> short in the leg and broad in the rump
> an endomorph with gentle hands
> who'll never make absurd demands
> that I abandon all my vices
> or pull long faces in a crisis.
> But, with a twinkle in his eye…
> will tell me when I have to die!

MISSION ACCOMPLISHED

Alas, this one by Marie Compton is more appropriate today.
Give me a doctor underweight
computerised and up-to-date
the businessman who understands
accountancy and target bands
who demonstrates sincere devotion
to audit and to health promotion.
But, when my outlook's for the worse...
refer me to the practice nurse!

COMPUTER

WE GOT OUR FIRST COMPUTER in 1982. We were one of the first fifty practices in the country to have one and it was very much our own thing. We had a computer geek named Mike who wrote his own programme. It was presented in MS-DOS, there was no Windows then, and written in a computer language called MUMPS.

MUMPS is described in Wikipedia as follows: MUMPS ("Massachusetts General Hospital Utility Multi-Programming System"), or M, is a general-purpose computer programming language originally designed in 1966 for the healthcare industry. Its differentiating feature is its "built-in" database, enabling high-level access to disk storage using simple symbolic program variables and subscripted arrays; similar to the variables used by most languages to access main memory.[1] It continues to be used today by many large hospitals and banks to provide high-throughput transaction data processing.

Each patient was given a number based on their date of birth just as my bank does today. As the information was entered, a disease code could be ascribed to that patient, e.g., DIA for diabetes, and then, by entering DIA, all the information for all the diabetics would be presented. And it could hunt for free text! Was that brilliant or what? Of course, we could not impede the advent of Windows-based systems, but frankly, they were not as good. The NHS offered financial help, not much, and suggested a 4GB floppy disk as memory. It sounds risible now, but it fact it was risible at the time. They had no idea how much memory healthcare required and even now, because everything is retained, they still don't. The real reason we had to change was not that the new systems were better but because we were unconnected to other systems. Thirty-eight years later, there are still different systems in General Practice. Hospitals are much worse now with one system for basic consultations, another for X-Rays, another for ECGs and another for pathology. Often, the poor doctor can only get into one at a time. No wonder the patients in the emergency department have to wait so long despite all the departments working their best. Hopefully, that will have improved by the time this is published. Progress is painful at times. Recently, while doing GP appraisals, I was shown that the doctors were given laptops to access the patients' notes anywhere. Before I had retired, I used a Blackberry to do that!

It was said in the early days of computerised records that it should be our servant and not our master. As always, it is a bit of both. But one thing that did happen was that it facilitated the control of GP by the government. They were not just our paymasters; they were our masters.

FROM OPPORTUNISTIC TO POPULATION AND THE RISE OF THE WORRIED WELL

IN THE EARLY DAYS, A patient went to the doctor when they were ill. We also took the time opportunistically to review their health in general. If a man came in, say an overweight smoker, whose blood pressure turned out to be high and, perchance, had sugar in his urine, we would pile in our advice and treatment options. In this way, we would provide that man many years of quality life. QALY (quality-adjusted life-years) is a measurement of perfect health and is used to assess the benefit of advice or treatment. The man I just described may gain ten to twenty QALYs as a result of a change of course. This meant a huge difference to the individual. Conversely to the national health statistics, it meant very little. Such interventions would barely show as a hiccup in the larger assessments of health. Statisticians realised that to affect overall health statistics, a population approach was needed. So, a reduction in blood pressure of x in the whole population would mean a reduced rate of stroke in y. So it was with blood sugar, cholesterol, weight and smoking. This was good for statistics but very little good for the life of each patient and dispiriting for doctors. The worst effect was that it turned almost everyone over fifty into a patient. Patients were no longer ill; they suffered from having surrogate markers outside the most favourable ideals. Everyone began to know their total cholesterol. They did not suffer from heart disease; they suffered from cholesterol. I remember an elderly lady proudly declaring that she had cholesterol! I explained that since the cholesterol molecule was a fundamental building block of most of the body's complex molecules, it was not surprising. It is as important as bricks are to houses.

Instead of seeing sick people, the GP was now manipulating these surrogate markers. This job was intended to be the role of nurses or clinics, but it never fully happened, and it was all focused through QOF. The Quality and Outcomes Framework was introduced with yet another new contract in April 2004. GPs were required to achieve hundreds of targets and received money for doing so. This, as I have said, was money taken away from them to pay for it. Year after year, it was adjusted to take in new areas or drop old ones. There are two things I must clarify. First, just in case anyone thinks I could not cope with QOF, our practice gained maximum points for every year that I was there. I take no credit as it was a fastidious partner and our staff who always reached the final few markers. Second, it definitely improved the management of a large number of patients. However, many, if not most, were patients who were not ill and at medium to low risk. It diverted a huge amount of time and effort of the practice and had one gigantic flaw. There were some patients with many morbidities who were almost too complicated to manage. These patients required very special attention and care. Believe it or not, it was possible to exclude them from the QOF. The very patients who needed the most were exempted! Nine categories of patients could be excluded, and each reason sounds perfectly reasonable on its own. But in practice, doctors just took the patients they could not cope with and reported them as an exception. Some doctors were worse than others, but I have never seen an 'exception' being challenged by the health authority. The population approach altered Nation Health Statistics and improved the health of those with moderate or medium risk, but it diverted the GP from opportunistic screening and the seriously ill. Appointments with one's own doctor became more difficult until the concept of "one's own doctor" became a memory. One's own doctor was, in fact, busy fine-tuning the worried well because that was the way he or she earned money. There was no mileage in attending to the acutely sick. At a post-graduate meeting, I remember being told by a cardiologist that we too busy to continually visit patients with heart failure. Heart failure has a prognosis compatible with the major cancers. That is exactly what we should be doing.

There is a lovely cartoon of an old GP sitting behind his desk, pen in hand, writing his notes. A man comes in wielding an axe. He says, "Doctor, I have an uncontrollable urge to chop doctors up with an axe." The old doctor continues writing, does not look up and says, "There's a lot of it about,

bowels alright,

how's the wife?"

It is meant to be a joke, but there is enough truth in it to provoke a chuckle. But if it happened today, a similar doctor, eyes glued to his screen, would reply,

"Did Sister take your BP,

I don't think I have your BMI,

shouldn't you be on a statin?"

Having increased the number of patients by redefining them as having a problem, naturally, people became interested in these imaginary conditions. This led to the rise of the "worried well." The rock-solid common sense of the semi-rural indigenous population was being replaced by the anxieties of the retired elderly, who now began to settle in Clayford. They aged and were reluctant to die, but they had forgotten how to live. Their bible was the Tuesday edition of the Daily Mail, which was carefully crafted to exploit their fears. They would come in clutching the relevant pages with sections marked for my opinion. Many of the articles suggested that their doctor was, in fact, trying to poison them and not help them. Whilst not denying that there might be some truth to this, I can honestly say in my case that it was accidental and not deliberate. What I really wanted was for them to start living again. Atul Gawande defines it clearly in Being Mortal. The concept of people who never die is not new. The bitter satirist, Jonathan Swift, was aware of them in the 19th century and wrote that Gulliver, on hearing of this race who never died but were unhappy, wished to visit them. You can find his visit to Luggnagg to see the Struldbruggs in book three, chapter ten. Unfortunately, although they did not die, they could age. One feature that rings a bell is that the younger generation began to use different words that could not be understood by the older ones. Swift's Struldbruggs were different from mine, but the point was made. Having a long life is not the same as a long experience of living. At this point, it is pertinent to quote Aldous Huxley: "science has made such tremendous progress that there is hardly a healthy human left."

Having redefined what it is to be a patient, an unintended consequence followed: doctors embraced this new 'patient' and concentrated on the surrogate markers, the guidelines and the governance. They forgot that the chief factors for good health are clean water, good food, exercise, warmth, hygiene and yes, genes. I am fortunate to have three friends who are all aged ninety-six (two of them are previous patients). They are all active and in good health. One had survived a plane crash; one had flown Spitfires during WW2, was shot down twice and endured a prison camp from which he escaped; the third is different in that, although he had flown planes, he had never crashed. They had all smoked at some stage of their lives, and they drink; in fact, when the Spitfire man came to brunch recently, he started his full English breakfast with a brandy. None of them went to the gym or ate 'healthy.' Conversely, young and middle-aged people lose their lives for no apparent reason. There is the element of luck in this that confounds the patients and doctors who think that continual fine-tuning of the surrogate markers will lead to a long and healthy life. It merely consumes the life of the patient who has forgotten how to live and the Doctor who is now married to his targets.

EQUIPMENT

THE MOST IMPORTANT PIECES OF equipment for a doctor are indeed their eyes and ears – looking and listening. The sense of touch from one's fingertips and the sense of smell follow closely behind. The sense of taste I would exclude, although I had once tasted a lady's urine because I was so certain that she had taken her specimen from the tap for reasons known only to her! Most people would think of a stethoscope when thinking of medicine. But the otoscope, ophthalmoscope and other such devices are also useful. I have found that one of the most useful pieces of equipment is the scales and was obsessive enough to calibrate mine with a 56 lb wt. It is the simplest and easiest way to monitor fluid retention or loss in heart failure. Apart from obvious cases in thyroid disease, diabetes and cancer, a patient with depression and weight loss is far more concerning than one without. I was very proud of my ear syringe, donated to me by my previous partner. If you could restore a person's sight, it would be classed as a miracle, but for some reason, restoring hearing by the simple act of removing whatever is blocking the ear meatus is not. Also, it is not done now very often. "We don't do it now," is one of the familiar calls of the practice nurse as though that is a reason in itself. One of our local consultants sent around a request to practices asking how many ear syringes they did in a year. It was huge. Then, he asked the ENT casualties how many problems they had each year attributable to ear syringing. The answer was zero. He concluded that ear syringing was safe and effective. Can it ever be classified as an emergency procedure? One patient thought so as he told my secretary, who then fitted him in at the end of surgery. Ear syringing needs no preparation and takes minutes, so I did not mind, but I was intrigued why this was an emergency. So, he told me: one of the managing directors had dropped dead the day before and an interview for a new one was to be held at midday. He wanted the job but knew he was markedly deaf. A quick syringe and all ended happily ever after!

The equipment was mostly kept in the doctor's bag. In the days when we could call consultants out on a domiciliary visit and joke about was what they kept in their bags. It was said that a surgeon would have only one thing – a glove! A neurologist would have a patellar hammer, a psychiatrist's bag would be full of psychotropic drugs, and so on. But our bags held everything! We had pills, injections and all the scopes we could hold. I had three thermometers of the old mercurial kind – oral, rectal and low temperature. But the item we learned very early in our careers to never, ever – and I am tempted to add another ever – be without, was a glove. I always had plenty of gloves in my bag and a full pack in the car. The advent of lady doctors meant that the size of the available gloves changed from large to medium or even small, and if you weren't careful to check, you could reduce the male hand to something small and white with all the blood cut off, which would nullify proper examination.

However, the strangest and possibly most useful piece of equipment I had was a crystal ball! I daresay you may have an odd smirk at this stage because it is not possible to see the future, and there is no such thing as a crystal ball that can. So, let me explain. Imagine you are in the surgery and this patient who is facing you asks,

"Doctor, do you think I should go on holiday next week?"

"Yes, of course, you should."

"But I am afraid of being ill again."

"Well, if you really think you are going to be ill, you should not go."

"But I have been really looking forward to it."

"In that case, you should go."

"But I am really concerned about what might happen."

"In that case, you should not go."

"But I have paid a lot of money for this holiday, and I may not get it back."

"In that case, definitely go."

Trust me, dear reader, this sort of mindless conversation can go on for ages if uninterrupted. One of the things we used to teach was how to regain control of the consultation. There are many ways, but in this case, I would have reached across my desk and brought out my crystal ball. I would then explain that we needed to see into the future, and I would intently gaze into my paperweight with bubbles in. The penny would always drop; the patient would get the message and respond with either a sigh or an apology. I must have saved days of consultation time over the years with this strategy. Another piece of equipment I used, which was unique to me (and the fictional Dr McCoy,) was the cantilever couch. I noticed from watching Star Trek that, while our aged rheumatic patients had to clamber up on the examination couch, Captain Kirk, who was perfectly able to leap up unaided, never did so because of the slick cantilever couch used by Dr McCoy. I decided my patients should be treated with this sort of care. It took a while, but eventually, I found the right couch in three sections and used it thereafter.

PROGRESS

IN 1972, GENERAL PRACTICE WAS run by the Executive Council, one of the three branches of the National Health Service. In Dorset, it was administered by a chief executive, a finance officer and someone else! The practice was paid for the work done, and we also had modest expenses. Therefore, money came in and went out, and what was left was the profit to be divided amongst the partners. The sums were small, and the accounts were simple. 1974 saw the re-organisation of the health service and the EC became the Family Practitioner Committee. It was decided that we would purchase certain aspects of health care and would be reimbursed for them. Money began to pour in but, equally, money poured out. The accounts were not complicated, but the transactions were many, so we thought it best to appoint our own finance officer. We were lucky enough to get a retired chartered accountant, and he became a bit of a legend in the practice for his miserly care of our cash. As things became more complicated, we thought it a good idea to appoint a practice manager to oversee the processes in the practice. We employed our own practice nurse and, shortly afterwards, a secretary for her. Although the sums of money rose five- to six-fold, our profits remained the same! Likewise, the work we did remained mostly the same apart from the increasing list size due to development. The EC, which was run by three people, became the FPC with a huge department. Progress was being made, but it was difficult to see in what direction. The FPC also expanded greatly to bill us and send out corresponding remuneration. Also, the accounting bills went up, and accountants became more important in our planning. Everyone had become much busier, but as doctors, we did the same work and made the same profit! The best appointment I had made was our practice nurse in 1974. Four years later, we rebuilt the health centre, expanded the treatment room and gave her a secretary. She was an expensive item of labour (but worth her weight in gold), and we did not want her to answer the phone and do clerical work. She was super-efficient anyway, and the treatment room became a vital part of the practice where a lot of the action took place. During the 80s, there was more progress. The managerial revolution was summed up to perfection by an article in the BMJ. Slowly, the administrators who had guided the health service through its early decades were retiring and being replaced by managers. It was felt that the old administrators were holding things back due to their experience (in truth their main experience was in running the health service on a shoestring). New people with no experience would be much easier to promote and 'change' was the new watchword – we were all to embrace change. The mantra of the managers was to start with a clean sheet of paper and a level playing field. The current practice was to be discarded and the problems thrown in the air, whereupon the managers would sort them before they landed. Managing was considered to be a generic skill, so it did not matter what speciality they came from; they could be trained. Thus, we had chiropodists managing the physiotherapists, the health visitors managing the district nurses and any combination you could care to think of. I don't think anyone managed the midwives but the midwives themselves. Unfortunately, the administrators had been professionals with professional values, just like the doctors, and this quality was lost. It reminded me of Socrates description of the 'Ship of Fools' where the sailors try to pilot the vessel 'with no knowledge of the year and seasons and sky and stars and winds and whatever else belongs to the pilot's art.' Success on the 'Ship of Fools' is defined not by the skills to navigate but by the ability to persuade others that such skills are not necessary and the job can be done regardless. Change was the watch word and those who embraced it got the jobs and those who counselled hard work were derided. By 1979, the country was in a dire state, and it was difficult to even get a light bulb changed in our health centre, but by the end of the 80s, this had all changed, and in 1990, we had a new contract and were able to re-build our health centre once more. Health promotion was the new mantra, and we were given money to do virtually any sort of health promotion we could think of. Where did this money come from? Why, out of our pockets, of course. It is worth saying a word about GP money because the NHS had now realised it had a wonderful way of controlling a speciality, who were ostensibly self-employed. The terms and conditions of service I had mentioned earlier were readable at first, but the NHS, being more powerful than the profession, realised it could change them at will. A review body worked out the total sum going into general practice and how it was divided was in the terms and conditions of service. Thus, money could be taken out or reduced and then offered back to the doctors if they did the things that the NHS had thought up for them. Like all ideas, this sounded hopeful in the beginning. Before 1990, innovation had emerged from individual doctors and practices, and some of the changes were remarkable. In my practice, the way we developed our treatment room in the 1970s and the advent of our first computer in 1982 were examples. But we were just part of a great innovative surge in general practice. The problem was that this was not universal, giving rise to inequalities. One might say that this was perfectly reasonable in independent businesses. However, it was not acceptable to the government, which felt quite rightly that the taxpaying public (this was the age of Mrs Thatcher who constantly reminded her ministers that there was no such thing as government money, only the taxpayers' money!) were entitled to equality in health care. Unfortunately, the solution was to standardise general practice in every way. Remember the law of unintended consequences? This is an example as it was good to raise the standards of poor practices, but it completely paralysed the innovation of the good practices that had developed. Good doctors stopped thinking. Worse, the doctors coming into general practice became used to this control and, in my opinion, became used to being bullied. Clinical governance became the watchword, and whilst there was much good in this, there was little room for manoeuvring. One size never fits all. There was much downward pressure on prescribing costs, which at first sight sounds perfectly right and proper. But ask yourself this question – would you go to a shop that only sold the cheapest items? The answer is that you would for some things but not for others. A second question – would you prescribe this drug to a member of your family? If you, as a doctor, cannot say that you are treating your patients exactly as you would treat your own family, you are being dishonest and not fit to practice.

COMETH A WHITE KNIGHT

C LAYFORD DID NOT HAVE MUCH to its name. It was a place people passed through. It had three distinct populations. There was the semi-rural, indigenous population, whom I had inherited from Ian Limbery. They were the people who had previously worked on the land. Some were settled itinerants, some settled travellers and some genuine settled gypsies. They seemed to have few surnames, and as time went on, I suspected they were all related to one another in some way. Indeed, through convoluted pathways, I found myself connected to one of the larger families. The second group had the retired army officers, often from the Indian army, brought in by my senior partner, Jock, who had spent his war days travelling around Bombay on an elephant with the governor. The third population was the newcomers. The land was cheap at first and the area nice; hence, new estates grew. It was a handy place being approximately equidistant from three nearby towns and three further away cities. Though it did not have much to recommend it, it had a famous golf course, and associated with it, but not part of it, was a small but attractive hotel, the Dormy, which, in golfing terms, I believe, means you can't lose. After I had been there a few years, the long-standing manager of the Dormy, a real character, retired. He was replaced by a young man who quickly ran away with a barmaid. My remembrance is, I confess, that she was worth running away for. This was followed by another young man, who was stepping onto uncertain ground after years of stability. How would he fare? The answer to that is he fared badly at first. After a few weeks, a man broke into the hotel one evening and badly assaulted the deputy manager. I can't remember if that was before or after a dead body was found floating in the swimming pool. The pool was in the open air in those days, but either way, it set a bad example. I was called one day because a lady had gone mad in one of the rooms and was scaring the guests and staff alike. When I went to report to the new manager, he was sitting slumped behind his desk, accompanied and supported by three staff members who were, no doubt contemplating the trinity of assaults of his deputy, the body in the pool and the psychotic lady. My initial reaction was "This boy won't last!" How wrong I was. To be fair the Hotel was flooded two weeks later and he confided to his wife that maybe the move to Clayford was a mistake. He was wrong too! The new manager, Derek, turned out to be an extraordinary man – ebullient, confident, capable, honest and modest. He was always thinking of new ideas, especially for charities, through his beloved golf. He nurtured contacts, knew everyone and was universally liked. From my point of view and the Practice's, he was also a white knight, although I doubt if – until he read this – he knew how. We had moved into a phase where practices could buy and use medical equipment. To this end, I had started an equipment fund to which grateful patients could contribute, and we had raised about three to four thousand pounds. The Health Authority wanted practices to modernise but effected it by making the practices earn their money by doing, frankly, stupid things. Goodness knows who came up with them. They wasted huge amounts of time, especially in practice strategy meetings. At a BMA conference in Bournemouth, they were openly described as 'destructive innovation'. Derek allowed us to ignore some of these things because we had our own money. He approached me one day and asked if we needed money for equipment. Anything was welcome, I replied. "Would £10,000 do?" My eyes were wide in shock. He had planned to use us as the recipient of the money he had raised at the pro/am golf tournament. He also managed to get the captain to designate us as his charity as well for another £10,000! This was big money then and fairly big now. Thus, we acquired computerised diagnostic ECGs, respiratory function monitors, videos for teaching, relaxation chairs, label printers and anything and everything we wanted without having to jump through hoops for it. He did it again after a few years and on my retirement, which gave us another chance. Since I was retiring, it was up to the remaining partners. But they were not interested. The sum was £60,000! This money gave us independence and control. Priceless.

SLOWLY DE-SKILLED

Not all doctors want to do all things. So, why take away skills from the ones who do and have been for decades?

Minor Ops I and my partners would perform minor operations on most weeks. We reinforced our skills with courses, and the service was cheap and convenient for the patients. The patient would present a lump or mole and, if appropriate, would be put down for the following session. It would be removed and sent to pathology. A week or so later, the patient would return for the doctor to remove the sutures, examine their work and discuss the pathology with the patient. At this point, you, the dear reader, will be wondering where anything could go wrong! Nevertheless, an edict appeared saying that a register must be kept of all the transactions. The doctor, a professionally trained person, was no longer deemed to be responsible enough to keep this register. It had to be kept by a clerk. Next, a paper appeared locally to say that GPs made too many errors, and 40% of biopsies were unsuitable. In what way was not defined. It was outrageous nonsense, but nonetheless, GPs were forbidden from removing anything but the most innocent-looking lesions. Our patients now had to travel seven miles to the Poole dermatology department to be seen by another doctor who would make the same diagnosis. An appointment would then be made for a nurse, who was trained for this purpose, to remove the lesion – another fourteen-mile round trip. Doctors who had been competent for years were now deemed to be incompetent. Soon, the dermatology department was swamped, and the facio-maxillary unit was asked to help out. I think they were swamped as well! A first-class reliable and convenient service had just been wiped out, and for what? In August 2018, a paper was published in the Journal of General Practice. It compiled the results from a whole-Scotland melanoma cohort in primary and secondary care. It compared those patients who had had their first cutaneous surgery done by their GP and those who had gone to a hospital. The results were as follows: "Patients in Scottish rural locations were more likely to have a melanoma excised in primary care. However, those in the rural areas did not have a significantly increased mortality (in fact, they had none at all) from melanoma. Together, these findings suggest that the current UK melanoma management guidelines could be revised to be more realistic by recognising the role of primary care in the prompt diagnosis and treatment of those in rural locations." Too late for GPs and their suffering patients.

IUCD Inserting intrauterine contraceptive devices, also incorrectly but commonly called coils, was something I had always done. Having done an obstetrics job, I believed I knew my way around the uterus. In thirty-eight years, I had never had any trouble and had only used local anaesthetic on two occasions. If it hurt, I did not do it. The fashion of ladies seeing lady doctors was inexorable, so it was inevitable that one day, being a male Doctor – something I never thought I would have to apologise for – I would have to stop, but the pressure for IUCD insertion to be only done in clinics was unnecessary. I had attended many updating sessions over the years, and the questions from the attendees did not reveal the complexity of the procedure, it indicated their lack of experience and vested interest though the experience was very hard to come by. Insertion training of IUCDs had to be done through the Family Planning Association and meant that the doctor had to visit the clinic on around a dozen occasions. Why not let them do it all? As a result, many young doctors do not bother to learn the procedure. As it happened, I was pretty slick at inserting IUCDs, and part of the credit must go to Timothy Spall when he played the part of Albert Pierpoint, the last hangman in a TV play. Anyone who has read George Orwell's A Hanging in Burma will remember his observation that there was no-one present who actually wanted to go through with it. The decision had been judiciously made, and it was the law that the law and the condemned should be executed. It occurred to me that this situation shared similarities with the insertion of the IUCD. The patient and doctor had concluded that it would be a good idea, but when it came to the point of execution, neither party was terribly enthusiastic. Albert Pierpoint, whose father and grandfather had been hangmen, was approached at the end of WW2 because there were a large number of war criminals to be despatched. He did not want to do it but concluded that if he did not do it, someone else would and nothing like as well as he! Therefore, he developed a technique to do the act in as humane a way as possible. The time between him entering the condemned person's cell and that person being dead was as short as possible because preparation had been completed beforehand, and the terrified thoughts in that person's mind would be over as quickly as he could manage. He said his PB (personal best) was seven seconds! I was very impressed with this and decided my technique would be equally quick and terror free. I never used stirrups as I always thought them to be humiliating. Everything was kept ready before the procedure began. There was no unprofessional struggle to open the plastic containers holding the IUCD – all of that would be ready. And by the time the lady asked if it was going well, I would tell her that it was done. I never had the time to measure my PB, but I do know that Albert was quicker!

VARICOSE VEINS

Having been to see Fegan (Fegan developed Fegan's technique of treating varicose veins) twice and being coached by his assistant I thought I would start treating varicose veins. The Health Authority had a love – hate relationship with varicose veins. When they had money they would introduce varicose vein clinics but as soon as fund waned and the clinics became overloaded they would be dropped. The usual NHS mantra is 'we don't do that anymore' as though that is a rational reason. Their argument is that varicose veins are not medically significant. In fact inflammation of the veins, thrombophlebitis is very significant cardiovascularly and neglect of the veins leads to dermatolipodystrophy and leg ulcers. Leg ulcers, apart from their pain to the patient, consumes a huge amount of nursing time. There are many ways of treating varicose veins but none of them is perfect. Even if they are stripped out they will attempt to regrow.

The valves in the deep vein of the leg are desperately important to an upright creature such as ourselves. They are hugely efficient so that the slightest wiggle of a toe will send blood pumping upwards and back to the heart. The outer or superficial veins also have valves and connect with the deep vein through perforating veins which also have a valve. It is damage to this valve in the perforating vein that causes the problem so that instead of blood moving from the outside to inside and the deep vein, blood now is pumped by the deep vein to the outside. Eddys in the flow cause the breakdown of the collagen in the vein and the bulging varicose vein. Fegan's technique was to sclerose these incompetent perforating veins. It was time consuming involving injection, review and then a vigorous walking regime for six weeks by the patient. Results could be good and I videoed the process for review purposes. The worse the veins the more determined and enthusiastic I was ably abetted by our nursing staff.

To facilitate this time and effort I considered the Practice was entitled to a fee. I rang the BMA for their advice. It stumped them but they came back with a derisory figure of £13 per patient. I rang up our local Nuffield to see how much it would cost privately. £900 was their fee! After prolonged wrangling with the Health Authority the conceded £60 a leg which was better than nothing but with the proviso that I was instructed by a doctor with FRCS. There was one in Practice a few miles away and he was appointed. The fact that he had never had anything to do with varicose veins and I had already been instructed by Fegan who had had private clinics in London, Dublin and New York did not persuade them.

I stopped doing varicose veins.

FAMILY DIASPORA

It is not easy to be a real family doctor without families! In the early part of the new millennium, our practice manager had informed us that our list size was falling. The numbers were few, just three to four each quarter, but it was consistent and persistent. We were perplexed. We believed we were good doctors. We knew we ran a top-class practice, and our staff were superb. So, what was happening? I delved into the statistics. They showed that more people stayed than left. Most practices have a turnover of 5–10%, depending on the circumstances, but it was gratifying to note that more were staying than leaving. However, when I looked at the births and deaths, the problem was clear. We had far more deaths than births. The demographics were changing. The families that had moved in during the 1970s and 80s and had four to five persons to a household now had children who had grown up and left. So, these households were down to two persons. Also, the big houses were being replaced by flats for the elderly. And the youngsters could no longer afford to live in the town; they were moving to new towns attached to villages in the county. We were left with fewer families and more elderly folks. There is nothing wrong with this, of course. They all have to be looked after by someone, but the family doctor was no longer necessary or required. The new towns would attract their own family doctors but both the doctors and patients would start from scratch. I was lucky with the patients I had inherited, and if I started again, I would not work in Clayford or the new towns.

CHANGING WORKING PRACTICES

We were the first port of call for virtually any crisis – chest pain, stroke, renal colic, vertigo, whatever. We referred very little. I referred one patient in every twenty-two consultations to a hospital and my partners about one in twenty. When we were called out, we kept most things at home. One marker of what we did was the occasions when we administered a drug that came under the Dangerous Drugs Act, such as morphine or pethidine. These had to be recorded in a book we carried with us, and it acted as a record of some of the serious conditions we dealt with. So, in 1973 I gave, by injection, a DDA on fifteen occasions. In 1977, it was thirty-five occasions. Myocardial infarction was a common reason. This was usually followed by admission but not always. There was very little to be done that would be effective for a heart attack in the 70s. Once, a patient I had referred with unstable angina returned after he consulted with the specialist. "What did he say?" I asked. "He told me to make a will," was the reply. He had a heart attack a few months later and died. Biliary colic was another recurring reason as was abdominal pain and gastroenteritis. A surprising number of cases suffered from migraine, which could be terribly severe without the preventive measures we take today. Renal colic was a reliable one, especially in the dry hot summer of 1976 when you could almost say we had an epidemic of renal colic. The records show that apart from 1983 (goodness knows why), there was a steady decline in calls for such diseases. As time went on, chest pain and stroke cases went straight to the hospital, largely because the new treatments were effective; things could be done that made a difference. Even the diagnostic challenge of abdominal pains, which were so difficult to deal with in general practice, could be solved with a rapid CT scan. We were still busy but not with real emergencies. They began to bypass us, and in 2004, I gave my last injection of DDA drugs. Our ratio of visits to surgery consultations fell from 1:3 to 1:4 and so on until there were days with no visits.

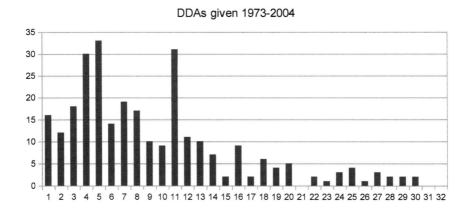

CO-MORBIDITY

Co-morbidity means having more than one condition, which seems a bit unfair to the patient but is increasingly happening as we prolong life with more medical interventions and we alleviate illness without a cure. It is a problem for the specialist as they specialise in one discipline. The more the specialisation, the less they are inclined to stray into another speciality. Willis summed it all up in his book The Paradox of Progress. As the specialist (and this is not only in medicine) focuses more, they can discard information not appertaining to the speciality. Eventually, in this rarefied atmosphere, the specialist feels able to set rules and laws for others to obey. Unfortunately, in the real world, people don't confine themselves to artificial specialities and, thus, don't obey the laws. In the end, they have to fall back on a generalist, and the way things are going, the only generalist is the GP. As medical interventions become more complex, so do management problems. This is not new, and I well remember such a complex problem of co-morbidity. The man in question had moved down here not too long ago and frequently called an ambulance, so I was asked to follow up. His wife, a heavy smoker, and his two adult daughters were unforgiving as I struggled with the problems. In the end, I decided that some sort of counselling was required and asked the three of them to step outside onto the front doorstep out of earshot of the patient. "How many," I asked, "heart transplant patients do you think I have?" There was a silence that became heavier when I asked them how many GPs in the country had patients who had had a heart transplant. I then asked them how many GPs in the country had a patient with a heart transplant which was in the process of rejection. So, I went on with one question after another. He was undergoing heart failure for good measure and was also experiencing kidney failure. By the way, the transplant people had felt there was nothing further they could do, the cardiologists wanted the kidney side sorted before they acted, and the kidney people would not manage someone with heart failure. Additionally, he also had Type I diabetes and, diabolically, he had had shingles with severe post-herpetic neuralgia. It was the severity of the neuralgia that made him call an ambulance. My last question was to ask how many GPs in the country had a patient who had had a heart transplant, which was failing, and was experiencing heart failure and kidney failure and had Type 1 diabetes and uncontrollable neuralgia. I could have added, 'and had been kept at an arm's length by an assortment of specialists.' Clearly, there was only me, but even so, I was expected to pull a medical rabbit out of a hat. There was silence. I don't think our relationship changed, but I hope they had some insight into the challenge I was facing as a generalist. I added that their father was the bravest man I knew, which was a fact. This was an extreme case then, but I doubt if it is now. After retirement from the practice, I was drawn into locuming, at first against my will, but later, I realised that it was work without the responsibility – the icing on the cake. During that time, I worked in 'majors' at the local hospital. The contention was that GPs would, somehow, with their knowledge of the community, be able to prevent admissions. Alas, they were too far gone on arrival for that. Only on two occasions in six months was I able to prevent admission. Both were 'stroke' cases, but one was a total global amnesia case and the other was a Bell's palsy case. A typical problem was as follows: "Can you see a head injury," I was asked. "He has just fallen and bumped his head and may need a stitch." Simple, except it is always a good idea to find out why the person fell. Was it neurological? Was it cardiac? Were they pushed! The man had a large bandage around his head and some blood was coming through. I asked him about the fall. There had been no loss of consciousness. He had not tripped. But then, he suggested it might be because he could not feel his feet. Could not feel his feet? Why? "Oh, because of the neuropathy," he proffered. "What neuropathy?" I asked. "The one secondary to the lymphoma," he replied. So now, he had a head injury, a lymphoma and peripheral neuropathy. "Anything else?" I quavered. "The lymphoma seems to have upset things, and I have had clotting problems, so they put me on Warfarin two days ago." So now, we have a man with a head injury, lymphoma and peripheral neuropathy, who was on blood thinners which was almost certainly not stabilised. And when the bandages came off, the little cut on his head turned out to be a macerated collection of lacerations and abrasions which took two of us two hours to sew up. This is co-morbidity, and it is a nightmare. Medical problems are now so complicated, even the simple ones!

2004

In 2004, something happened which, on the face of it, was a godsend and certainly encouraged me to continue for another six years but also was probably the last nail in the coffin for the family doctor. A new contract was put forward, which offered to release us from our night and weekend responsibility for our patients for £6000 a year. We leapt at it, and the warnings of a few doctors who foresaw the death of our independence were ignored. £6000 sounds like a lot of money, but after tax, NI, superannuation, and the money we were paying deputies to do the 11 pm to 7 am shift, it was almost nothing at all. But having relinquished our 24-hour, 365-day responsibility, we had little power. GPs, having become 'clinic' doctors, steadily grew further away from their patients. Gordon Brown did one more wonderful thing. He increased our pension by 32%. He, in fact, said it would be 40%, and the BMA took him to court over it, won, and we got our 40%. As Aneurin Bevan said in 1947, our mouths were stuffed with gold.

"GPs work very little, are paid too much and have abrogated their responsibilities to secondary care. They get paid enough to work when they feel like it and only have responsibility to themselves." These were the words of a well-respected local consultant. He means them with bitterness, and I have to concur. Many young doctors, male and female, do not want the responsibility of partnership. They are happy to be "hired hands". A BMA paper in 2018 demonstrated that their lifetime earnings would be half of that of a Partner, but this does not influence them. They had enough money and enjoyed their lifestyle. They had no ambition, but also, no yen to change anything. These young professionals are not very professional.

FINAL OBSERVATIONS

IT WOULDN'T BE ANY FUN if, after writing all this stuff, I was not allowed to give my unasked-for opinions about all and sundry. Over the years, I have formed several opinions, which were never repeated by anyone, but which I believe and know will be unrepeated and unsupported elsewhere. I believe, after nearly five decades of observation, that spiteful women get early dementia. It gives me no pleasure to say this, but there is a sort of waspish woman who becomes demented early. I can't prove it, and a longitudinal study would take so long and be so subjective that I doubt it ever will. But it is my opinion. Irritable bowel syndrome (IBS) and inflammatory bowel disease (IBD) can often be confused, especially in the early stages. Tests don't always give an answer, but I have always found my suspicions to be right. How do you tell the difference? Simple. Patients with IBS argue with you! That is why they get IBS. They are always at war with someone or something. IBS occurs in all countries of the world so diet cannot be the prime cause, although it may be an aggravating factor. It is stress related. The question of why things that go on in the head influence what happens in the bowel is an interesting one, but it has something to do with the fact that living organisms had bowels before they had brains, and the brain borrowed some of the neurological pathways.

The more you talk about ethical problems, the more complicated they become. There is no limit as to how complicated human beings can make anything. This can be a problem in a ten-minute consultation! In our current world of drugs, gender dysphoria, diversification, medical advances, genetic manipulation, paedophilia, grooming and the danger of hurting someone's feelings, I accept that ethical problems in medicine are more complicated than they ever were. The most common issue in my day was prescribing a contraceptive pill to underaged girls. Nowadays, it is not a problem, but for a family doctor who had to consider the family as well as the patient, it was. But if a girl was having regular sex with a boy of her own age, she needed contraception. Full stop. It was right to ask what the girl's mother or father might think. They used to have an interest in their children in the good old days! Sometimes, the girls would be adamant that they did not want their parents to know and were dismayed when I told them that all mothers search their daughter's handbags, belongings, secret places, etc. I also told them that if they ever did become pregnant, their mother would always stand by them. Not always the father. But in the end, the mother always did. The thing that is going to get you is something that you never thought of. This is not such a brilliant thing to say because, in many cases, if you had thought about it, you would have avoided it. This was a statement I usually trotted out to hypochondriacs. Genuine hypochondriacs are mercifully few, but we all had some. One unfortunate lady had had just about every part of her body scanned and investigated despite my desperate attempts at being a gatekeeper. She was unfortunate because her mother had died in the passenger seat while she had been driving, so she always wondered whether it was her bad driving that had delivered the final coup. One day, I counselled her as we stumbled towards another investigation, "The thing that is going to get you is something you would not have thought of." "I know," she said, "that is why I think of everything!" Some, you just can't win!

LOOKING BACK

When I started in general practice, our week, included Saturday mornings and nights and weekends on a rota. I did that for nineteen years and then, mercifully, another fifteen without the 11 pm to 7 am shift. Who thought that this was a reasonable way of working? The phone went through to the house and a call in the night nearly always meant getting out of bed, driving to a sick patient and not returning for an hour, often longer. There was always another day to work and no guarantee that there would not be another night call before that day's work began. This was not a good way to induce sleep. I would venture that it was impossible for anyone to look happy all the time under those circumstances. And yet, we did it, mainly because it was considered normal. The modern GP does not work nights and weekends and rarely does a full week's work. We had an afternoon off to balance the night and weekend work. The modern GP does not do nights and weekends but still has an afternoon or a day off or more. So, why are they so unhappy? After seventeen years of appraising doctors and delving into their working practices, I can honestly say that I do not entirely know. There must surely be a host of reasons, including the type of person that becomes a doctor. For the general public, being a doctor is a vocation, but in reality, for many doctors, it is an intellectual exercise and a good way of earning a decent living. There is no vocation and no inspiration. For many lady doctors, it is a good option to get a profession with the flexibility to bring up their children. I understand it, but it will not last a lifetime. Undoubtedly, one stressful factor is the obligation of 'niceness'. Young doctors are now chosen because they are 'nice' people. The culture of niceness continues throughout their career. The target, when I trained, was to be good. If you were nice as well, it was a bonus.

But as Roger Neighbour said, "Nobody dies if their doctor is rude or isn't nice to them. People die if you miss their burst appendix. So, the most important is clinical safety, but beyond that, it's communication." But our clinical governance-based medicine and the threat of vexatious complaints means that while the target was to be good first and nice second, the target now is to be nice always and follow guidelines. Not following guidelines is worse than getting things wrong. Vexatious complaints are one of the most dispiriting things for doctors. Many complaints are entirely justifiable; for instance, if you miss detecting diabetes, having never done a blood test or tested the urine. But a vexatious complaint is one where there is no medical issue. You may have been perceived to have been rude or had not noticed a woman's children or had hurt their feelings. The complainant has no come back on their complaint. They risk nothing. They can accuse the doctor of anything they like, and the doctor will always be on the back foot. NHS England, the GMC, will investigate these complaints as though they are potentially genuinely serious. The defence bodies, who make their livelihood from these issues, insist that everything is reported to them and sent to them, which often gives credence to the most trivial patient dissatisfaction. This also gives credence to the patient who, possibly for the only time in their life, is now in a position of importance. In my many years of appraising GPs, many of these vexatious, trivial and outrageous complaints have amazed me. Yes, they are dispiriting indeed. Our target-based culture has to be blamed. Working to meet targets – government targets and not patient needs – inevitably means failure. It is a huge challenge to achieve all the targets all of the time. Some doctors do feel a sense of worthlessness as a result. There was another change, which may be the same reason that I gave up locuming seven years post retirement from the practice. It was great fun at first, but after a while, it was the patients who changed. In my practice with personal lists for thirty-eight years, there was always the incentive to do one's best for the patient, and they reciprocated this, with their families, by caring for the doctor. There was positive feedback, and this sustained the incentive to do one's best. I locumed in several different areas in the county. In one, a deprived area, people had settled there because of low rents. They did not want to be there once they became aware of the drug and alcohol problems that were rife but had no way of getting out. They were depressed, yes, but it was the sense of hopelessness that was so dispiriting. In another area in the centre of the town, about a third of the people I saw were immigrants, mainly from Southern Europe and the Eurozone. They too did not want to be there. Why would anyone from southern Spain want to work in a Bournemouth Hotel? The answer is unemployment in the home country. The effect of the Euro had produced massive youth unemployment in Southern Europe, which was up to 30–50% in some places. It was a huge betrayal to the generation by the EU, which was made merely bearable by allowing them to do low paid jobs in the UK. The title 'unskilled migrants' is usually quite wrong in my experience. These were skilled migrants doing low paid, unskilled jobs. They too didn't want to be there and were depressed. These were the people I saw also with their own sense of hopelessness. The third group of unfortunates is the people in nursing homes. One imagines that when the time comes, one's loved one, or even oneself, will enter a cosy home to be cared for in the twilight years. There's no doubt this happens, but there is another side to it. Modern medicine can maintain a life beyond what is reasonable, sensible or humane. The state we allow people to reach so that the only thing they are aware of is discomfort and pain is pitiful. All in all, I found diminishing pleasure in caring for these people, and I imagine it is the same for the modern GP. The characters I looked after were, well – as the anecdotes about the patients above demonstrate – characters. However quirky, awkward and annoying they were, they were memorable. They all had a place in society like Tom Shearing, the Raven, who roamed East Dorset on his bike. With many of our patients now, one asks oneself what their place is. I am sure they want one. So, the old family doctor, who was always there, faded away. They faded because the medical practice changed, the doctors wanting a life and variety changed, and the concept of the family changed. I understand all this, and I am not advocating what we had but just commenting on it. Usually, at this stage, someone would call me a dinosaur. Apart from the fact that I embraced every innovation I could, including running the practice website and some that others could not see, I would make this observation. The dinosaurs, with hundreds of species, dominated the world for millions of years and were eventually destroyed by the planet. Homo sapiens, just one species, in a hundred thousand years, is destroying the planet. The world at present is undoubtedly a lot worse than the one I lived in. We all look back to a golden time, but it is mainly because we were young. You can't beat youth. Notwithstanding, I am so glad I am not a GP today. What will they have to look back on?

FINALLY - THE FLIP SIDE

Within our families, we have heartache and tragedy – some families more than others. We bear them, and as long as they are not overwhelming, we cope. In family practice, the heartache and tragedy can be overwhelming. One remembers those who did not die well, those with appalling death sentences, like motor neurone disease, the cot deaths and the sudden deaths. I remember a lovely couple who were at home one evening – he was watching TV and she was doing the ironing – when they heard a thump upstairs and found their twentyone-year-old daughter dead on the floor. There were no explainable factors. Post-mortem explained nothing. Parts of the girl's heart were sent to learned pathologists around the country but no explanation for this dreadful event was ever found. Decades later, I saw this couple walking the streets hand in hand. Their only child was taken for no fathomable reason. As the decades went by, there was no road, lane or street in Clayford that I could not relate to some awful happening. On some roads, it was every house. I pass the place where old Sam hanged himself from the great apple tree. On another road is the drive where the young man, I never knew him, gassed himself in the car from the exhaust. That was bad enough, but the poignant part of the memory is the faithful black Labrador that lay next to him, partners in life and death. And so, it goes on. This is why my trips to the town I worked in for so long are brief and infrequent. Even so, as Don Berwick put it in his John Hunt lecture while talking about the influence of his father, "It is a privilege (for the Family Doctor) to enter the dark and tender places of people's minds."

Printed in Great Britain
by Amazon